THE INSURANCE ACT 2015

A NEW REGIME FOR COMMERCIAL AND MARINE INSURANCE LAW

THE INSURANCE ACT 2015

A NEW REGIME FOR COMMERCIAL AND MARINE INSURANCE LAW

EDITED BY

MALCOLM CLARKE
AND
BARIŞ SOYER

Routledge
Taylor & Francis Group
LONDON AND NEW YORK

First published 2017
by Informa Law from Routledge

2 Park Square, Milton Park, Abingdon, Oxfordshire OX14 4RN
52 Vanderbilt Avenue, New York, NY 10017

Routledge is an imprint of the Taylor & Francis Group, an informa business

First issued in paperback 2019

British Library Cataloguing in Publication Data
A catalogue record for this book is available from the British Library

Library of Congress Cataloging-in-Publication Data
Names: Soyer, Baris, editor. | Clarke, Malcolm A. (Malcolm Alistair), editor.
Title: The Insurance Act 2015: a new regime for commercial and marine insurance law / edited by Baris Soyer and Malcolm Clarke.
Description: New York, NY: Informa Law from Routledge, 2016. | Includes index.
Identifiers: LCCN 2016018096 | ISBN 9781138683303 (hbk) | ISBN 9781315544601 (e-book)
Subjects: LCSH: Great Britain. Insurance Act 2015. | Marine insurance—Law and legislation—Great Britain. | Liability insurance—Great Britain. | Casualty insurance—Law and legislation—Great Britain.
Classification: LCC KD1845.A3282015 I57 2016 | DDC 346.41/086—dc23
LC record available at https://lccn.loc.gov/2016018096

ISBN: 978-1-138-68330-3(hbk)
ISBN: 978-0-367-87803-0 (pbk)

Typeset in Plantin
by Apex CoVantage, LLC

CONTENTS

BIOGRAPHIES

EDITORS

Professor Malcolm CLARKE
Emeritus Professor of Law
University of Cambridge

Professor Clarke is an Emeritus Professor of Commercial Contract Law at Cambridge University and Fellow of St John's College, Cambridge. He is well-known for his contribution to insurance law but his expertise also extends to contract law generally and to transport law: carriage of goods by air, road and rail. He is the author of various books including: *Law of Insurance Contracts* (6th edition); *International Carriage of Goods by Road* (6th edition); *The Law of Liability Insurance*; *Contracts of Carriage by Air* (2nd edition); *International Carriage of Goods by Road: CMR* (5th edition) and *Policies and Perceptions of Insurance in the 21st Century* (2nd edition).

Professor Barış SOYER
Director
Institute of International Shipping and Trade Law, Swansea University

Professor Soyer is head of the Department of Shipping and Trade Law and Director of the Institute of International Shipping and Trade Law at Swansea University; he is also a member of the British Maritime Law Association and British Insurance Law Association. He is the author of *Warranties in Marine Insurance* (2001), *Marine Insurance Fraud* (2014) and many articles published in journals such as the *Cambridge Law Journal*, *Lloyd's Maritime & Commercial Law Quarterly*, the *Journal of Business Law*, the *Torts Law Journal* and the *Journal of Contract Law*. *Warranties in Marine Insurance* won the Cavendish Book Prize 2001, and was awarded the British Insurance Law Association Charitable Trust Book Prize in 2002 for its contribution to insurance literature. *Marine Insurance Fraud* also won the latter prize in 2015. He has also edited large numbers of collections of essays on commercial, maritime and insurance law. In addition, he acts as one of the editors of the *Journal of International Maritime Law* and sits on the editorial boards of *Shipping and Trade Law* and the *Baltic Maritime Law Quarterly*. Professor Soyer currently teaches Admiralty Law, Oil and Gas Law and Marine Insurance on the LLM Programme at Swansea.

CONTRIBUTORS

David HERTZELL

Past Commercial Law Commissioner
Consultant BLM

Mr Hertzell was a partner and managing partner of city law firm Davies Arnold Cooper until 2007 when he was appointed Commercial Law Commissioner, a post he held until 31 December 2014. He was responsible for a number of projects updating consumer law, intellectual property law, reforming insurance law and advising the investment industry on fiduciary duties. In particular he is responsible for parts of the Consumer Rights Act 2015, the Third Party (Rights against Insurers) Act 2010, the Consumer Insurance (Disclosure and Representations) Act 2012 and the Insurance Act 2015.

Mr Hertzell is president of the British Insurance Law Association, a board member of Airmic, Chair of the CII Professional Standards Board and the previous independent member of the Judicial Appointments Commission audit and risk committee. He is a consultant to law firm BLM and insurance governance consultants Mactavish and chairs the government task force on insurance fraud.

Dr George LELOUDAS

Associate Professor
Institute of International Shipping and Trade Law, Swansea University

Dr George Leloudas is a graduate of the National and Kapodistrian University of Athens. He holds LLM degrees in Commercial Law from the University of Bristol (England, 2002) and in Air and Space Law from the Institute of Air and Space Law of McGill University (Montreal, Canada, 2003). He also completed his PhD degree in air law with emphasis on liability and insurance at Trinity Hall, Cambridge University in 2009. Before joining the Institute, Dr Leloudas worked as a Solicitor at Gates and Partners in London for several years where he advised on aerospace liability and airlines' regulatory matters. Dr Leloudas is also an instructor at the Training and Development Institute of the International Air Transport Association (IATA) where he teaches international air law for lawyers and legal professionals, law of aviation insurance and air cargo liability. Dr Leloudas is a contributing editor to *Shawcross and Beaumont on Air Law*. He is an active researcher and has recently authored a book together with Professor Malcolm Clarke of Cambridge University on *Air Cargo Insurance* (Informa law from Routledge), published in June 2016.

Peter MACDONALD EGGERS QC

Barrister
7 King's Bench Walk, London

Peter MacDonald Eggers QC is a barrister specialising in all aspects of commercial law, with a particular emphasis on insurance and reinsurance, shipping, energy, commodities, international trade and international arbitration. Educated at the Universities of Sydney and Cambridge, he practised as a solicitor before being called to the Bar in 1999 and taking silk in 2011. He is the author of *Deceit: The Lie of the Law* (2009) and co-author of *Good Faith and Insurance Contracts* (2010). In addition he is a contributor to numerous other books and contributing editor of *Chitty on Contracts*. He is a Visiting Fellow at the Institute of International Shipping and Trade Law.

Peter MacDonald Eggers is described in the Legal 500 as "an excellent counsel: a pleasure to work with." His major cases include *Rathbone Brothers v Novae Corporate Underwriting*, *Sea Glory Maritime Co v Al Sagr National Insurance Co*, *Golden Ocean Group v Salgaocar Mining Industries*, *Arash Shipping v Groupama*, *Masefield v Amlin*, *Gard v Tunnicliffe*, *Limit v AXA* and *AIG v Faraday*.

Simon RAINEY QC
Barrister
Quadrant Chambers, London

Simon Rainey QC is a barrister at, and former joint head of, Quadrant Chambers. He has been in practice since 1983 and took silk in 2000; he is also a recorder and sits as a deputy High Court judge. In shipping work he is regarded as one of the top leaders, being placed in the first division of shipping silks by both Chambers and the Legal 500. He specialises in all aspects of dry shipping and charterparty disputes, with particular emphasis in recent years on heavy shipbuilding disputes (from oil rigs and dry cargo vessels to car-carriers and superyachts); in addition he has handled complex cases arising out of dangerous cargo incidents and safe port disputes, representing variously owners and charterers. He was counsel for the successful buyer on the high-profile arbitration appeal in *The Union Power* [2013] 1 Lloyd's Rep 325 on the application of the implied warranties to the Norwegian Saleform 1993. As well as this he regularly sits as an arbitrator in LMAA, ICC, LCIA and UNCITRAL arbitrations and is a Fellow of the Chartered Institute of Arbitrators.

Simon Rainey is in addition an author, having written *Tug and Tow and Offshore Contracts* (2011), the leading text on offshore industry contracts. This reflects the fact that he is frequently involved in advisory work and litigation on all aspects of offshore marine and construction and energy and natural resource disputes.

He has been a visiting research fellow at the Institute of International Shipping and Trade Law, University of Swansea since 2010 and was appointed Honorary Professor of Business, Law and Economics, University of Swansea in 2013.

Sir Bernard RIX
Arbitrator and Mediator
20 Essex Street

Bernard Rix is a recently retired Lord Justice of Appeal with twenty years' experience in the Commercial Court and the Court of Appeal, who now accepts appointments as an arbitrator and mediator. He is a member of the HKIAC Panel of Arbitrators, a member of the MOOGAS Panel of International Arbitrators and

Mediators, has been appointed to the Cayman Islands Court of Appeal and is an ADR Group accredited mediator.

His university education was at New College, Oxford and Harvard Law School. He was called to the Bar by the Inner Temple in 1970 and practised in commercial chambers at 3 Essex Court. He was appointed Queen's Counsel in 1981. In 1993 he was appointed to the High Court and sat predominantly in the Commercial Court of which he was judge in charge in 1998–99. In that year he was responsible for introducing to the Commercial Court the Woolf Reforms to civil procedure law (the CPR) and for redrafting the Commercial Court's Guide and Practice Directions. In 2000 he was appointed to the Court of Appeal, from which he retired in May 2013.

At the Bar he specialised in international commercial and arbitral disputes as a barrister and latterly as an arbitrator, and also appeared in the courts of Singapore and Hong Kong. He was counsel in *Mareva Compania Naviera SA v International Bulkcarriers SA* [1975] 2 Lloyd's Rep 509, the eponymous origin of the "Mareva injunction", now called a freezing order; in *I Congreso del Partido* [1983] 1 AC 244 (HL) which introduced the commercial exception to English law's previous absolute doctrine of sovereign immunity; and in *Channel Tunnel Group Ltd v Balfour Beatty Construction Ltd* [1992] 1 QB 656 (CA, affirmed in the House of Lords) concerning the operation of the arbitration clause in the contract for construction of the Channel Tunnel. In the Commercial Court, his judgments include *The Angelic Grace* [1994] 1 Lloyd's Rep 168, upheld by the Court of Appeal [1995] 1 Lloyd's Rep 87, which is the modern origin of the anti-suit injunction for breach of an arbitration clause or an exclusive jurisdiction clause. As a member of the Court of Appeal, he has delivered a wide range of judgments on arbitration, aviation, banking, insurance and reinsurance, private and public international law, oil and gas, sale of goods and shipping disputes. They include significant judgments such as *Dallah v Government of Pakistan* [2010] Bus LR 384 on international enforcement of arbitration awards (upheld by the Supreme Court), *Kuwait Airways v Iraqi Airways (Nos 4 and 5)* [2002] 2 AC 883 (parts 22–35 and 43–54 of the Court of Appeal judgment, upheld by the House of Lords) on international law, *R (Al-Skeini) v Secretary of State for Defence* [2007] QB 140 (upheld by the House of Lords) on the jurisdictional scope of the European Convention of Human Rights and *Yukos v Rosneft (No 2)* [2013] 1 All ER (Comm) 327 on the act of state doctrine.

Professor Andrew TETTENBORN
Professor of Commercial Law
Institute of International Shipping and Trade Law, Swansea University

Professor Tettenborn has been attached to the IISTL at Swansea Law School since 2010. He has also taught at the universities of Cambridge, Exeter and Geneva and held visiting positions in Europe, Australia and the US. Professor Tettenborn is author or co-author of books on torts, damages and maritime law, has written extensively on widespread aspects of private, shipping and commercial law and sits on the editorial board of *Lloyd's Maritime & Commercial Law Quarterly*.

David WALSH
Barrister
Quadrant Chambers, London

David Walsh has a broad commercial practice specialising in insurance and re-insurance, dry shipping, commodities, energy and aviation disputes. He is a popular choice both as sole counsel and as a junior to leaders in heavyweight cases. David has particular experience of heavy and technically complex cases, including a number of disputes involving foreign systems of law. He frequently advises and represents clients at short notice and on an urgent basis, in particular in applications for interim relief in the Commercial Court (freezing orders and anti-suit injunctions).

FOREWORD

Over a century ago, Sir Mackenzie Chalmers drafted the Marine Insurance Act 1906. It was observed at the time in an article in the *Law Quarterly Review* by Sir Arthur Cohen that the provisions codifying the duty of utmost good faith were "on the whole framed with great skill, so as to express through very concise language the principles from which most of the law on the subject may be deduced" (Cohen, 'The Marine Insurance Bill', (1903) 19 LQR 367, 372). This contemporaneous praise proved well-founded, with the 1906 Act standing the test of time for so long. Nonetheless, there has over the past decades been increasing scrutiny in relation to the duty of utmost good faith. It is such scrutiny which has resulted in the Insurance Act 2015, in particular with the provision which it makes for a more proportionate approach in place of the all or nothing, and somewhat inflexible, remedy of avoidance which was embodied in the 1906 Act. It remains to be seen whether the 2015 Act proves to be the success which its illustrious predecessor proved to be. Indeed, with the change which is made concerning the burden of disclosure resting upon the assured, it remains also to be seen whether the 2015 Act will achieve its aim in making the duty of fair presentation less insurer-friendly. These are matters which can only be judged in the future. What can, however, be stated with confidence at this stage is that this is an excellent (and very timely) book, reflecting the very considerable experience and scholarship of each of its authors.

By The Honourable Mr Justice Picken

PREFACE

Most would agree that the Marine Insurance Act (MIA) 1906 – the product of Sir Mackenzie Dalzell Chalmers' desire to codify the fundamental principles of marine insurance law, many of which had been originally formulated by Lord Mansfield in the eighteenth century and thereafter developed by successive generations of commercial lawyers, was a success in terms of providing the market and legal profession with an accessible and comprehensible legal framework. It is also commonly acknowledged that the Act is well structured and drafted. Following its introduction into the legal system, rules and principles encapsulated in the Act found application in other areas of insurance law by analogy. However, it is also an undeniable fact that due to advances in technology and changes to underwriting practices, several principles enshrined in the Act no longer serve the needs of insurance practice.

After a number of unsuccessful attempts, when English and Scottish Law Commissions started their work on insurance law with a scoping exercise in January 2006, very few had the genuine belief that this time a positive outcome would emerge. The First Consultation Paper published in July 2007 helped little to inject optimism to the reform process as far as the law concerning business insurance contracts was concerned. The solutions proposed were deemed to be rather radical, and the common view was that the proposed controls on standard terms would have imposed a serious and somehow unnecessary restriction on the freedom of contract. It is fair to say that the proposals, in particular to the extent that they relate to business insurance contracts, came under intense criticism (see in particular *Reforming Marine and Commercial Insurance Law* (Informa, 2008)) whilst there was widespread support for the reforms proposed for consumer insurance contracts, which later led to the enactment of the Consumer Insurance (Disclosure and Representations) Act 2012.

The Law Commissions responded to these criticisms by making a U-turn on most of their original recommendations. The Third Consultation Paper, published in 2012, was a rather different document from its predecessor, and the reforms advocated there gained the support of a large section of the market in a relatively short period of time. Consequently, the draft Bill put forward by the Law Commissions found its way into the statute book by taking advantage of a special procedure available for non-contentious bills. The Insurance Act 2015 gained the Royal Assent on 12 February 2015 and will enter into force on 12 August 2016.

This Act extensively restates and modifies a number of legal principles applicable both at common law and under the MIA 1906, and it represents the first major reform of English commercial insurance law for a century.

The main objective of this book is not simply to offer the usual commentary on a piece of new legislation. Our aim is to engage in a critical in-depth analysis of the important topics and also to identify grey areas likely to spawn disputes in future. In a nutshell, we see this book as a comprehensive, coherent and practical legal analysis of the changes introduced by the Insurance Act 2015. To this end, contributors have been carefully selected from legal practice and academia; each of them has been tasked to deliberate on an aspect of the reforms imposed by the Insurance Act 2015. There is also a chapter on damages for late payment of insurance claims. Although provisions concerning this issue were removed from the draft Bill at the House of Lords stage as being too controversial, they have been reintroduced as part of the Enterprise Act 2016, and when this Act comes into force on 4 May 2017 it will lead to an amendment in the Insurance Act 2015.

We hope that the manner in which this book is designed will be appealing to a wide audience, ranging from lawyers, brokers and other insurance professionals to academics and students. Any statutory change in law is likely to create a degree of uncertainty until courts are presented with an opportunity to clarify the precise (and intended) meaning of the legislation. This process will inevitably take some time. As Lao Tzu once said, "A journey of a thousand miles begins with a single step." It is our sincere hope that this book will be viewed as the first step, making a small contribution to the understanding and development of the new legal regime in insurance law in the years to come.

M.C. and B.S.
February 2016

TABLE OF CASES

TABLE OF STATUTES

CHAPTER 1

The Insurance Act 2015

Background and philosophy

*David Hertzell**

1.1 Introduction

Over one hundred years after some of the original legislation the UK has concluded a series of insurance law reforms resulting in three new Acts of Parliament. These are based on extensive consultation with the insurance market and policyholders undertaken by the UK law reform bodies – the Law Commissions in England, Wales and Scotland. Amongst other changes the reforms have created a new framework for the provision and transfer of information when insurance is purchased and have provided new remedies for insurers. The concept of proportionality, which is familiar in many other jurisdictions, has been introduced into English insurance law. Due to the large amount of international insurance written in London the reforms are likely to have a considerable effect outside the UK.

1.2 History

Insurance allows businesses and consumers to protect themselves against risks that they could not otherwise afford to cover. It has often been described as the oil in the wheels of capitalism. By laying off unaffordable risks individuals and businesses are able to do things they would otherwise fear to do. The development of insurance in London has underpinned wider economic growth in the UK and subsequently internationally. The Marine Insurance Act (MIA) 1906, on which UK insurance law was based, has been copied widely in other countries linked to the UK.[1] The insurance industry in the UK is the largest in Europe and remains the third largest in the world.[2] Insurance is a crucial UK export. Its importance is recognised in the government's Insurance Growth Action Plan published in December 2013. The size of the UK insurance market has meant that English insurance law has had a worldwide influence.

* Consultant to BLM Law and Mactavish and Former Commissioner for Commercial and Common Law. Visiting fellow of Institute of International Shipping and Trade Law, Swansea University.

1 The Act has formed the basis of marine insurance legislation in New Zealand (1908), Australia (1909), Malaysia (1956), India (1963), Hong Kong (1964), Canada (1993) and Singapore (1993).

2 Association of British Insurers, *UK Insurance and Long-term Savings Key Facts 2015* (2015). Available online at https://www.abi.org.uk/~/media/Files/Documents/Publications/Public/2015/Statistics/Key%20Facts%202015.pdf (accessed 1 February 2016), 2.

Despite this success, the law upon which the industry is based, comprising the rules which regulate insurers' relationship with their policyholders, has been criticised throughout the second half of the twentieth century. UK insurance law has consistently been described as archaic, unclear and unfair. Sometimes this resulted in action. In 1957 the UK Law Reform Committee identified possible reforms.[3] In 1980 The English Law Commission recommended changes.[4] Reform was also urged by a report from the National Consumer Council in 1997.[5] In 2002 an eminent subcommittee of the British Insurance Law Association (BILA) consisting of judges, lawyers, brokers, insurers and loss adjusters declared itself "satisfied that there is a need for reform" and supported review by the Law Commission.[6] In 2006 the Law Commission took up the challenge again and began the third major review of insurance law.

How did this situation arise? To answer, it is necessary to look at the origins of insurance law in the UK. These origins lie with the practices developed by merchants in the City of London which led to the leading case of *Carter v Boehm* in 1776.[7] The case concerned the goods of Roger Carter who was the governor of Fort Marlborough in Sumatra. The goods were lost when the French invaded during the Seven Years War. In a leading judgment Lord Mansfield laid out the principles of an insurance contract and the parties' obligations when insurance was purchased. The principles set out by Lord Mansfield in *Carter v Boehm* were further developed during the course of the nineteenth century. Insurance law in the UK was then codified as part of the great nineteenth century series of codifications. As its title suggests, the MIA 1906 is a piece of commercial legislation largely concerned with shipping. It reflected the time in which it was conceived and the market for which it was drafted. The Act has remained the basis of the law of insurance until the recent changes.

The economic and social context in which Lord Mansfield decided *Carter v Boehm* was very different to that which developed during the second half of the twentieth century and continues to this day. Insurance at the time was essentially a commercial arrangement made between knowledgeable businessmen. The range of products on offer was very limited and the market was dominated by marine insurance. Communications were slow and poor. There was very limited ability to store or process information. Underwriters were vulnerable and needed to be protected by the law. It was legitimate to claim that all the relevant knowledge was held by the insured and that the underwriter could be a passive participant when the insurance contract was agreed.

Today much has changed. Like most western economies the UK is dominated by consumer activity. The concept of the consumer has developed since the Second World War and would have been incomprehensible to eighteenth century merchants or nineteenth century legal draftsmen. Communications across the

3 *Fifth Report of the Law Reform Committee* (1957) Cmnd 62.

4 *Insurance Law: Non-disclosure and Breach of Warranty* (1980) Law Com 104.

5 National Consumer Council, *Insurance Law Reform: The Consumer Case for Review of Insurance Law* (May 1997).

6 BILA, *Insurance Contract Law Reform: Recommendations to the Law Commissions* (2002).

7 (1776) 3 Burr 1905.

globe are now virtually instant. Information is widely available. Insurers, brokers and policyholders have the ability to store, analyse and process data in ways that could not have been foreseen even a few years ago. Improvements in IT have allowed businesses to span the globe and to grow to sizes that would previously have been unimaginable.

Insurance itself has also changed. The range of insurance products available and the risks that are insured are now much wider and more diverse. Insurance is no longer dominated by the needs of the marine industries. Likewise, senior insurance lawyers, including judges, emerged in the later twentieth century with backgrounds and experience which lay outside marine insurance. Uninfluenced by marine insurance preconceptions judges began to express concern about how the law functioned in other contexts.

English law has the ability to keep pace with change by developing new precedents. Court decisions can reflect contemporary social and economic conditions and apply existing legal principles to new facts and situations in a way that produces an acceptable outcome. To an extent, this has occurred with insurance law but the courts have struggled to keep pace with rapid change and have only been able to go so far. The MIA 1906 is drafted in clear, forthright terms that hamper the ability of judges to develop the law. In addition, in recent years, consumer disputes have generally been resolved by the Financial Ombudsman Service (FOS) and many commercial disputes by arbitration. Neither of these mechanisms produces new legal precedents.

Both regulators and insurers recognised these problems. The friction between the principles in the Act and consumer insurance became increasingly intense. As a result, the insurance industry agreed a series of guides and codes to mitigate the problem.[8] The regulators too produced rules that differed from the MIA 1906. In 1981 insurers set up the voluntary Insurance Ombudsman Bureau (IOB).[9] In 2000 the Financial Services and Markets Act replaced the IOB with the FOS. The FOS is not a voluntary scheme and it has statutory powers. The ombudsman is not required to follow the law but can make decisions based on what is fair and reasonable in all the circumstances of the case. Over the years the FOS began to develop a framework to resolve consumer and small business disputes that owed little to the MIA 1906.

Whilst well-intentioned these initiatives had an unfortunate effect. The outcome of a dispute would depend on who decided it and whether the policyholder was classed as a consumer, small business or larger business. The law governing the formation of insurance contracts and disputes differed from the rules that the (then) Financial Services Authority would apply in a regulatory context. This did not reflect well on the governance of the insurance market and created both cost and confusion. It undermined the certainty which English law traditionally provided. Some commentators claimed that the disparity between the various rules undermined trust in insurance particularly for consumers.

8 For example, the Association of British Insurers Code of Practice, *Managing Claims for Individual and Group Life, Critical Illness and Income Protection Insurance Products* (January 2009).

9 The first private sector ombudsman scheme in the UK.

1.3 The Law Commissions' project

At an early stage in the project to reform insurance law the Law Commissions in England, Wales and Scotland concluded that attempts by the market to resolve problems without reforming the MIA 1906 had failed. However, the attempts contained good ideas and confirmed that the market itself had concerns that the status quo could not continue. The solutions on which reform could be based were, therefore, likely to come from the market rather than any particular individual source. Moreover, if reform was to be successful it had to be supported by the majority of those in the insurance market and not regarded as something imposed from outside.

The Law Commissions began an intensive round of consultation which was to last eight years. First, the Commissions published a scoping study that confirmed the areas of law most in need of change. This was followed by a series of individual Issues Papers devoted to particular topics. The Commissions published three formal Consultation Papers developing the Issues Paper themes and the market responses. These were followed by two Final Reports, one dealing exclusively with consumer issues and the other with a range of topics including business insurance.[10] In addition, members of the Commissions attended numerous market and individual meetings and participated in many seminars and other discussions.

As a result of this activity the Law Commissions were able to draw a number of broad conclusions on which the final reform proposals were based:

- The market for consumer insurance had developed in a different way to business insurance. The insurance products were different, they were sold in different ways and by different insurers, social policy was often important and the impact of IT was considerable. The availability of data meant that the perceived asymmetry of information between insurer and insured that had shaped the MIA 1906 was much less relevant. At a practical level, brokers who could provide guidance to consumers were less involved than in the business insurance market. Finally, disputes were generally resolved by the FOS and in effect a separate body of jurisprudence was emerging that was not based on the Act. The Commissions decided that reform of the MIA 1906 should, therefore, have two limbs – one for consumers and one for businesses – but in cases where it was not necessary to draw distinctions, common solutions should be adopted. The market supported this division which reflected its own commercial approach.
- The risk pools for business insurance are generally smaller and potentially more volatile than those for consumer risks. Businesses also cover a much wider range of risk exposures. Insurers are less likely to know the details of business risk than they are consumer risk which by its nature and volume is more predictable.
- The MIA 1906 remained more relevant for business insurance. Some of its principles had stood the test of time even though others clearly had

10 All of these papers can be found on the Law Commission's website – www.lawcom.gov.uk.

not. The Act had given rise to many years of legal precedent and certain expressions had acquired clear and settled meanings. Where possible, valid principles and accepted language should be carried forward into any new legislation.

- The consumer reforms should provide a mandatory regime.
- The reforms applicable to business, on the other hand, should provide a default regime. It would be open to the parties to contract on different terms if they wished to do so. This was particularly important for the London Market[11] in the UK where much commercial insurance is international and the relationship between the insurer and insured might be quite distant. The Commissions also concluded that it would not be possible to produce law that could be tailored to cover every eventuality and every different type of business risk, and that the parties would need to fill in the gaps contractually – as happened with the MIA 1906.
- No proposed reforms should be included in the final legislation unless there was very strong support from all sides of the insurance market.
- The reforms would apply throughout the UK.

1.4 The reforms

The Law Commissions' insurance project resulted in three new pieces of legislation:

- The Third Parties (Rights against Insurers) Act 2010
- The Consumer Insurance (Disclosure and Representations) Act 2012
- The Insurance Act 2015.

All three Acts were enacted following the Law Commissions' procedure for uncontroversial bills.[12] That allows bills which enjoy widespread support to be introduced into the House of Lords and considered by a specially appointed committee. Although the bill is thoroughly reviewed it spends less time on the floor of either the House of Lords or the House of Commons and, therefore, takes up less parliamentary time. The absence of available time has often resulted in the failure of necessary and worthy law reform which, whilst desirable, is not perceived to be a high political priority.

1.4.1 Third Parties (Rights against Insurers) Act 2010

The Third Parties (Rights against Insurers) Act 2010 was based on an earlier consultation and improved the mechanisms by which a party with a claim against an insolvent insured can recover compensation from the relevant insurer. It updates an earlier piece of legislation with the same name dating from 1930. It is not directly concerned with the contractual arrangements agreed between the insured

11 A group of insurance companies and Lloyd's operating from London and specialising in international and commercial insurance.

12 Approved by the House of Lords on 7 October 2010.

and the insurer, although as a general principle the third party will have no better right against the insurer than the insolvent insured would have had.

1.4.2 Consumer Insurance (Representations and Disclosures) Act 2012

The Consumer Insurance (Representations and Disclosures) Act 2012 (CIDRA) covers the placement of consumer insurance and provides for what should happen if the consumer gives incorrect information. CIDRA also deals with group insurance in which the proceeds of the policy may be paid to beneficiaries who are not the insured. An example would be a policy taken out by an employer for the benefit of its employees. CIDRA makes the greatest changes to the MIA 1906.

CIDRA is short and targeted. It applies only to consumer insurance contracts: that is, to insurance bought by individuals for purposes wholly or mainly unrelated to their trade, business or profession. The definition deliberately follows the general approach of European law. The definition of insurance is left to the common law.

CIDRA follows FOS practice in abolishing the consumer's duty to volunteer information – often referred to as the "duty of disclosure" and fundamental to the MIA 1906. Instead, the insurer must ask appropriate questions and the consumer must answer them honestly and carefully. CIDRA imposes on the consumer a duty to take reasonable care not to make a misrepresentation. This also applies when a policy is varied or renewed. The essential question is: did the consumer take reasonable care? The standard applied is an objective one; it is that of the reasonable consumer taking into account all relevant circumstances such as the type of insurance and how it was sold. The particular characteristics of the individual consumer are only relevant if the insurer knew or ought to have known about them.

If the consumer does say something which is not true then CIDRA distinguishes between three types of misrepresentation: those which are "reasonable", those which are "careless" and those which are "deliberate or reckless". Misrepresentations that are careless or deliberate and reckless are described as "qualifying misrepresentations" for which the insurer will be compensated provided it can show that, had it known the true facts, it would have acted in a different way. There is no remedy if the consumer's misrepresentation was reasonable.

For a misrepresentation to be deliberate or reckless the insurer must show that the consumer:

- knew that the statement was untrue or misleading or did not care whether it was or not; and
- knew that the matter was relevant to the insurer or did not care whether it was or not.

Two presumptions assist the insurer. First, the consumer is presumed to have the knowledge of a reasonable consumer; and second, if the insurer asks a clear question then the subject matter of the question is presumed to be relevant.

If the misrepresentation is deliberate or reckless (essentially fraudulent) the insurer may avoid the policy and generally can keep the premium.

If the misrepresentation is careless then the insurer's remedy depends upon what it would have done had proper information been provided:

- if the insurer would have declined the risk altogether then it can avoid the policy, and refuse any claim but should return the premium;
- if the insurer would have written the policy on different terms then those terms apply from inception. This may include different limits or the imposition of an exclusion clause; and/or
- if the insurer would have charged a higher premium, then any claim can be reduced pro rata to the underpayment.

These provisions represent a very considerable change to the MIA 1906 where the only remedy available to insurers is avoidance of the entire policy whatever the circumstances of the misrepresentation.

In addition to these changes CIDRA provides that misrepresentations by a beneficiary under a group scheme will affect that individual but not the other members of the scheme. It abolishes "basis clauses" which turn all representations into insurance warranties. The MIA 1906 provides that breach of a warranty, whether relevant to the risk insured or not, automatically discharges the policy. Finally, CIDRA gives some guidance as to whether an intermediary is acting as the agent of the policyholder or of the insurer when the policy is being agreed.

CIDRA came into force in April 2013. Since then research carried out by the Chartered Insurance Institute[13] and confirmed by discussion with the FOS indicates that consumer disputes involving questions of misrepresentation have become rarer. Instead problems arise over wordings and the extent of cover provided.

1.4.3 The Insurance Act 2015

Three years after CIDRA the Insurance Act 2015 was passed. It comes into force in August 2016, and is concerned with both business insurance and consumer insurance. It covers the following topics:

- The pre-contract duty of disclosure for all non-consumer insureds. It introduces the new duty to make a "fair presentation" of the risk.
- The insurer's remedies for breach of the duty of fair presentation.
- Basis of the contract clauses.
- Remedies for breach of warranty.
- "Irrelevant" risk mitigation clauses.
- The insurer's remedies for fraud.
- Contracting on different terms.

The Insurance Act 2015 retains some of the law from the MIA 1906. It codifies some of the developments that have occurred since its enactment and it introduces some new legal concepts. The topics of most interest are the introduction of the

13 CII New Generation Underwriting Group, *The Impact of the Consumer Insurance (Disclosure and Representations) Act 2012* (2013).

new duty to make a fair presentation and the provisions on warranties and similar terms.

The Law Commissions decided to retain the obligation to volunteer relevant information for all insureds who are not consumers – the so-called duty of disclosure. However, the framework of the duty has been developed. The duty to make a fair presentation of the risk incorporates both the law on non-disclosure and that on representation. It also includes the waiver provisions that are found in the MIA 1906. Additionally, the new duty gives some guidance as to how information should be disclosed and who is obliged to provide it. The new duty recognises that gathering information in large organisations involves many processes and seeks to allow for the impact of IT. The duty deals with both the substance of the presentation and the form.

The insured must:

- disclose all "material circumstances" which it knows or ought to know; or, failing that,
- provide sufficient information to put the underwriter on notice to ask further questions.

The insured cannot comply with its obligation by providing a "data dump" of every possible fact and circumstance. A fair presentation of a complex risk requires adequate signposting to draw the underwriter's attention to the relevant facts.

The Insured knows what its senior management knows and what the people arranging the insurance know and ought to know what would reasonably have been revealed by a reasonable search. "Senior management" is defined as the people who "play significant roles in the making of decisions about how the insured's activities are to be managed or organised". Often senior management will be the board. However, the definition is wider than that and some insureds will not be companies. The individuals arranging the insurance could include, for example, the insured's risk manager or broker – although a broker is not obliged to disclose confidential information obtained through a business relationship unconnected to the relevant contract of insurance.

The MIA 1906 provided some limits on the insured's duty of disclosure and these have been carried forward into the new Act. An insured does not have to disclose information if the insurer knows it, ought to know it or is presumed to know it. The insurer knows what is actually known to its underwriter or their agent. The insurer ought to know what should have been passed on to the underwriter (for example, by a surveyor or the claims department) or what the insurer holds in its systems provided this is "readily available" to the underwriter. The insurer is presumed to know what underwriters writing that class of business should know. The Commissions did not think that the law should protect the naïve or poorly-trained underwriter. Instead the Commissions sought to reinforce good professional standards.

If the insured fails to make a fair presentation, then the insurer always has a remedy provided it can show that had it known the truth it would have done something different. If the insured is deliberate or reckless then the insurer can avoid the policy and keep the premium. If the insurer would not have written the risk, then again it may avoid the policy but must return the premium. For all other breaches of the duty of fair presentation:

- if the insurer would have imposed additional terms or limits then these are imposed from inception; and/or
- if the insurer would have charged a higher premium then the claim is reduced pro rata.

Although the duty of fair presentation is based on the existing law, policyholders and their brokers would be wise to review their existing practices. For example, what is the process for gathering information? Is there a reasonable search and how is this documented? Are there adequate discussions with the board or senior management? Are there proper discussions between the insured and their broker?

Insurers too will have to review their processes. Are underwriters sufficiently well trained and knowledgeable to ask the right questions? They are expected to have a reasonable degree of knowledge about the type of business they are underwriting. Is knowledge properly passed across the organisation? Is communication with an agent or surveyor sufficient? Are communications between claims and underwriting adequate? What information is held in the insurer's systems and can underwriters access what they need? What evidence will there be as to what underwriters might have done if a fair presentation had been made?

The provisions in the Insurance Act 2015 relating to warranties and to fraud apply to both business insureds and to consumers. The new Act follows CIDRA and abolishes basis clauses. Any term which seeks to make the information provided when the policy was purchased into an insurance warranty will have no effect.

The new Act does not define "warranty". Whatever a warranty currently is under the law, so it remains. However, rather than discharging the policy from the date of breach a warranty will become a suspensive condition. Cover is suspended whilst the insured is in breach but will be restored once the breach is remedied. For example, if an insured is obliged to inspect an alarm system but fails to do so, cover is suspended until the inspection is carried out.

Warranties and similar terms which seek to mitigate risk will not be effective if the insured can show that non-compliance "would not have increased the risk of the loss which actually occurred in the circumstance in which it occurred". A risk mitigation term is one that "tends to reduce the risk of" loss of a particular kind, loss at a particular location or loss at a particular time. It is not a term which defines the risk as a whole such as an age requirement in a motor policy. To take a simple example, a sprinkler warranty will apply if there is a fire but not if the property suffers a loss by flood from an adjacent river.

These changes are a departure from the current law in which a warranty discharges the insurer from any liability under the policy from the date of breach regardless of whether there is any connection between the breach of warranty and the loss that occurred.

If the insured makes a fraudulent claim then the Insurance Act 2015 provides a clear set of remedies. The entire claim is forfeit – including any honest part – and the insurer can keep the premium. The insurer will remain liable for any genuine claims before the fraud but has the option to terminate the policy from the date of the fraud.

The Insurance Act 2015 is a default scheme for business and all "non-consumer" insureds. As it is based on best practice and was widely supported by the market it is unlikely that insurers will wish to contract out of it on a regular basis. However, it may be appropriate to do so if the risk insured is very specific or complex. Equally, the new regime is probably not appropriate for many reinsurance contracts. If the insurer wishes to contract on different terms and if the term is "disadvantageous" to the insured the insurer must:

- take sufficient steps to bring the term to the insured's attention; and
- ensure that the term is clear and unambiguous.

This is a deliberately flexible test. What would be sufficient in a sophisticated market with well-informed and -advised parties would not be adequate if the insured was a small business buying cover direct online.

One recommendation from the Law Commissions which was not included in the Insurance Act 2015 related to compensation for late payment of a valid insurance claim. By legal fiction in England and Wales (but not in Scotland)[14] each time an insured loss occurs the insurer is considered to be in breach of contract. Payment of an indemnity under the policy is, therefore, treated as damages for breach of contract and not as a debt. As English law will not award further damages on existing damages the policyholder is unable to claim compensation for any loss caused by the insurer failing to pay their claim.[15] This rule does not apply to life insurance and is not followed by the FOS in consumer cases.

The Law Commissions proposed a new obligation upon insurers to pay claims within a reasonable time. The definition of "reasonable" would take into account the insurer's need to investigate and assess the claim. It would also depend on the circumstances of the loss, the type of policy and delays caused beyond the insurer's control including delay by the policyholder. Clearly it will take longer to deal with a large foreign loss than a small domestic claim. The Commissions recognised that an insurer is custodian of the insurance fund on behalf of all policyholders and should only pay genuine losses.

Whilst the majority of those consulted by the Law Commissions believed the current rule on late payment required reform, those parts of the insurance market who wrote a lot of business from the USA feared the introduction of "bad faith" style litigation.[16] In the circumstances, the House of Lords considered the reform to be too controversial for the Law Commissions' bill procedure. However, it was agreed that the proposal would be reintroduced in a government bill. This occurred in late 2015 as the Law Commissions' reform proposal forms part of the Enterprise Bill, with one amendment to limit the time in which claims for delay can be brought. The Enterprise Bill received Royal Assent and the part on damages for late payment of insurance claims will come into force in May 2017 as an amendment to the Insurance Act 2015.

14 *Strachan v The Scottish Boatowners' Mutual Insurance Association* 2010 SC 367.
15 *Sprung v Royal Insurance (UK) Ltd* [1999] 1 Lloyd's Rep IR 111.
16 In particular Lloyd's and other "London Market" insurers.

1.5 Conclusion

It is not an exaggeration to say that after more than 100 years there has been a thorough overhaul of insurance law in the UK. The new laws command wide support. It is to be hoped that they will provide as firm a foundation for the business of insurance in the twenty-first century as the MIA 1906 provided in the first half of the twentieth century.

CHAPTER 2

The fair presentation of commercial risks under the Insurance Act 2015

*Peter MacDonald Eggers QC**

2.1 Introduction

The Law Commission has long desired to reform the duty of utmost good faith borne by the parties to the contract of insurance. The attempts at law reform began in the 1950s and were followed by a review of the law in the 1980s. However, it was after the courts began in the late 1990s to express hostile views towards the draconian remedy of avoidance available to an insurer who had received less than a fair presentation of the risk that the Law Commission began its most determined effort to change the law. Those efforts were repaid by the passage of the Insurance Act 2015 ("the 2015 Act") in February 2015. As far as the duty of utmost good faith is concerned, the 2015 Act applies to business (or non-consumer) insurance,[1] and entered into force on 12th August 2016, applying to all contracts of insurance concluded on or after that date and to all variations to insurance contracts, where the variation was agreed on or after that date, even if the insurance contract was agreed earlier.[2]

The 2015 Act was passed as a non-controversial bill following consideration by a House of Lords committee and a cursory glance by the House of Commons. The 2015 Act was passed to give effect to many of the recommendations made by the Law Commission in its report of July 2014.[3] Both the Law Commission and Parliament explained[4] that the motivation for the change in the law as it applied to the assured's duty of disclosure (under the broader duty of utmost good faith) was to make the law less insurer-friendly, meaning that the remedies for a breach of the duty should be proportionate to the seriousness of the breach of duty.[5] This was the driver behind the reform of the law. It was also the focus of

* Barrister, 7 King's Bench Walk; Visiting Fellow of the Institute of International Shipping and Trade Law, University of Swansea.

1 The duty of fair presentation of the risk with respect to consumer insurance is now regulated by the Consumer Insurance (Disclosure and Representations) Act 2012, which entered into force on 6th April 2013.

2 Section 22 of the Insurance Act 2015.

3 Law Commission, "Insurance Contract Law: Business Disclosure; Warranties; Insurers' Remedies for Fraudulent Claims; and Late Payment" (Law Com No 353), July 2014. See Parliament's Explanatory Notes, para. 5.

4 Parliament's explanatory notes for the Insurance Act 2015 may be found on Parliament's website: www.legislation.gov.uk/ukpga/2015/4/notes/contents (last accessed 1 July 2016).

5 Law Commission Report No 353, paras. 1.25–1.26; Explanatory Notes, paras. 6–10, 14. At para. 7, the Explanatory Notes state that ss. 17–20 of the Marine Insurance Act 1906 "are now significantly

the courts' criticism: the remedy of avoidance, which was all-or-nothing, was seen to be wholly disproportionate for some – not all – failures on the part of the assured to provide full and accurate disclosure of the risk prior to the conclusion of the insurance contract. The criticism was both understandable and curious. It was understandable in the context of simple non-disclosures, because such non-disclosures could result from forgetfulness as much as carelessness. It was curious in the context of misrepresentations, because the law of misrepresentation which applies to all contracts is that the representee can avoid or rescind the relevant contract if it was induced by the making of a material misrepresentation. The representee's remedies were, and are, subject to the Misrepresentation Act 1967, which has been held to apply to misrepresentations made by the parties to an insurance contract as much as any other contract, but which has also been held to be inapplicable to non-disclosures.[6]

In any case, the Insurance Act 2015 has been passed for the nominal reason that it will make the position of the assured more advantageous and the position of the insurer less advantageous. Notwithstanding the criticisms of the remedy of avoidance, the 2015 Act fails to achieve Parliament's objective with respect to the duty of utmost good faith. While it secures a fundamental change to some aspects of the duty of fair presentation, it leaves the law largely as it was before the entry into force of the 2015 Act. One fundamental change, principally to the knowledge of the assured and the insurer in respect of the assured's duty of disclosure, makes the assured's duty more, not less, burdensome. Moreover, although the 2015 Act modifies the remedies available to the insurer, the modifications may still operate disproportionately in favour of the insurer.

2.2 The duty of utmost good faith before the 2015 Act

2.2.1 Introduction

The duty of utmost good faith was developed in the common law courts in earnest from the eighteenth century. In 1906, the law relating to this duty was codified by the Marine Insurance Act (MIA) 1906, which had been drafted by Sir Mackenzie Chalmers.[7] Sections 17–20 of the MIA 1906 set out a number of principles and rules which apply to the duty of utmost good faith. The law declared by

out of line with best practice in the modern insurance market. The law has also failed to keep pace with developments in other areas of commercial contract and consumer law, and with insurance law in other jurisdictions."

6 *Banque Financière de la Cité v Westgate Insurance Co Ltd* [1989] 2 All ER 952, at 1003–1004. In that case, there was no suggestion that the 1967 Act did not apply to insurance contracts. Nor in *Kumar v AGF Insurance Ltd* [1999] 1 WLR 1747, at 1757 or in *HIH Casualty & General Insurance Ltd v Chase Manhattan Bank* [2001] EWCA Civ 1250; [2001] 2 Lloyd's Rep 483, at [51] and [116].

7 Chalmers reviewed more than 2,000 cases in order to set out the relevant principles of marine insurance law. Chalmers changed the law or filled in the gaps by the draft bill only in a few respects: see P. MacDonald Eggers, "The Marine Insurance Act 1906: judicial attitudes and innovation – time for reform?", published as Chapter 10 in D.R. Thomas (ed.), *Marine Insurance: The Law in Transition*, (Informa, 2006), at para. 10.10.

sections 17–20 have been held to be the law governing both marine and non-marine insurance law.[8]

The general duty of utmost good faith is stated in section 17 of the MIA 1906: "A contract of marine insurance is a contract based upon the utmost good faith, and, if the utmost good faith be not observed by either party, the contract may be avoided by the other party." This simple statement reveals that the duty is reciprocal in that it is owed by the assured to the insurer and by the insurer to the assured. Sections 18–20 set out the assured's duty of full and accurate disclosure in more detail, although make no provision in respect of the insurer's duty owed to the assured. The purpose of the duty of utmost good faith is to prevent fraud and encourage good faith,[9] and to ensure that there is a full exchange of information relating to the risk.[10] Nevertheless, whether it is a non-disclosure or a misrepresentation, the insurer need not prove an intention on the part of the assured or the broker to deceive or mislead the insurer.[11]

The duty of utmost good faith insofar as it arises prior to the conclusion of the insurance contract has two facets. First, under section 18, there is a duty of disclosure upon the assured and, under section 19, there is a duty of disclosure upon the assured's agent to insure, the broker. By section 18, if the assured fails to provide the disclosure required by these provisions, the insurer may avoid the insurance contract insofar as the insurer has been induced to enter into the insurance contract by reason of a material non-disclosure in the sense that the insurer would not have agreed to the insurance contract on the same terms had full disclosure been provided by the assured. In addition, by section 19, the insurer may avoid the insurance contract in the event of a material non-disclosure by the assured's agent to insure. Second, under section 20, the insurer is entitled to avoid the insurance contract if the assured or his agent makes a misrepresentation of fact, expectation or belief where that misrepresentation induced the insurer to enter into the insurance contract. In each case, the duty of disclosure or the duty to abstain from misrepresentation is actionable by the insurer only insofar as the duty is not observed prior to or at the time of the conclusion of the insurance contract. Once the contract is concluded, no further disclosure is required from the assured. However, if the contract is amended or varied, the assured will bear a duty of full and accurate disclosure in respect of the amendment. Similarly, if the assured seeks to rely on a "held covered" clause, which maintains cover notwithstanding a breach of warranty or condition, upon the agreement of an additional premium, the assured will bear a duty of disclosure to allow the insurer to enable the insurer to assess that premium.[12]

In order to be entitled to avoid an insurance contract by reason of non-disclosure, pursuant to section 18 of the 1906 Act, the insurer will have to establish that (a)

8 *Pan Atlantic Insurance Co Ltd v Pine Top Insurance Co Ltd* [1995] 1 AC 501, at 518; *Manifest Shipping Co Ltd v Uni-Polaris Shipping Co Ltd (The Star Sea)* [2001] UKHL 1; [2003] 1 AC 469, at [47].

9 *Carter v Boehm* (1766) 3 Burr 1905, at 1911 and 1918 (Lord Mansfield CJ).

10 *Pan Atlantic Insurance Co Ltd v Pine Top Insurance Co Ltd* [1995] 1 AC 501, at 542.

11 *Whitlam v Hazel* [2004] EWCA Civ 1600; [2005] Lloyd's Rep IR 168.

12 *Liberian Insurance Agency Inc v Mosse* [1977] 2 Lloyd's Rep 560; *K/S Merc-Scandia XXXXII v Lloyd's Underwriters (The Mercandian Continent)* [2001] EWCA Civ 1275; [2001] 2 Lloyd's Rep 563.

there has been a failure to disclose a "circumstance", (b) the circumstance must have been material, (c) the circumstance must have been known to the assured or ought to have been known to the assured in the ordinary course of business, and (d) the non-disclosure must have induced the insurer to enter into the insurance contract on the terms agreed. In addition, the insurer will be entitled to avoid the insurance contract, pursuant to section 19 of the 1906 Act, if the broker has failed to disclose to the insurer (a) every material circumstance which is known to himself, for which purpose the broker is deemed to know every circumstance which in the ordinary course of business ought to be known by, or to have been communicated to, the broker, and (b) every material circumstance which the assured is bound to disclose, unless it come to his knowledge too late to communicate it to the broker.

In order to be entitled to avoid the insurance contract by reason of misrepresentation, pursuant to section 20 of the 1906 Act, the insurer will have to prove that: (a) the assured or his or her agent has made a representation, (b) the representation was one of fact or expectation or belief, (c) the representation was material, (d) the representation was false, and (e) the insurer has been induced by the misrepresentation to enter into the insurance contract on the terms agreed.

2.2.2 The assured's knowledge for the purpose of the duty of disclosure

By section 18(1) of the MIA 1906, the assured is bound to disclose to the insurer a material circumstance if it is "known" to him or her. There are three categories of knowledge which are relevant for consideration in this context.

First, the assured must disclose what is actually known to him or her. This does not mean that the assured must know that the relevant circumstance is material. What the assured actually knows is a subjective question; whether the circumstance is material is determined objectively. Accordingly, the assured must disclose material information known to him or her, whether or not the assured considers it to be material.[13] In order for the assured to know something, it must be present to the assured's mind or must be something which the assured remembers. If the assured once knew the relevant circumstance, but has now forgotten it, that does not mean that the assured actually knows it for the purposes of the duty of disclosure. The assured will be taken to be actually aware of a circumstance, even if the assured does not actually know it, if it can be said that the assured has wilfully shut his or her eyes to the circumstance, suspecting that the relevant circumstance might exist.[14] Where the assured is a corporate entity, whether or not a circumstance is known to the company depends on whether the relevant circumstance is known to a person who might be described as the *alter ego* or the directing mind and will of the company for the relevant purpose.[15]

13 *Joel v Law Union and Crown Insurance Company* [1908] 2 KB 863, at 884–885.

14 *Economides v Commercial Union Assurance Co plc* [1998] QB 587, at 601–602 and 607.

15 *Manifest Shipping Co Ltd v Uni-Polaris Shipping Co Ltd (The Star Sea)* [1997] 1 Lloyd's Rep 360 (Court of Appeal); *Group Josi Reinsurance Co Ltd v Walbrook Insurance Co Ltd* [1996] 1 Lloyd's Rep 345, at 366.

Second, there is knowledge which the assured is deemed to have; in other words, constructive knowledge. Section 18(1) of the 1906 Act provides that "the assured is deemed to know every circumstance which, in the ordinary course of business, ought to be known by him".[16] There is a similar deeming provision as far as the broker is concerned in section 19. This definition of deemed knowledge is framed by reference to the "ordinary course of business", which probably refers to the ordinary course of the assured's business, rather than the ordinary course of business as would be conducted by a reasonable person in the assured's position.[17] This means that if the assured does not know a particular circumstance and would not have known that circumstance in the ordinary course of the assured's own business, but would have known that circumstance had the assured conducted his or her business in the manner favoured by a reasonably efficient person in the assured's position, the assured will not be deemed to have known that circumstance for the purposes of section 18(1).

Third, there is a controversial category of knowledge, namely knowledge held by an assured's agent, which is imputed or attributed to the assured by the principles of the law of agency.[18] However, the relevance of such knowledge to the assured's duty of disclosure has been thrown into doubt by the fact that there is no reference to it in section 18, although provision is made in respect of the knowledge of one particular agent, namely the agent to insure, in section 19 of the 1906 Act. It may be, therefore, that the knowledge of such an agent (other than a broker) will be imputed to the assured, only if the assured ought to have known this information in the ordinary course of business.[19] Agents whose knowledge might be imputed to the assured or deemed to be that of the assured include:[20] (a) the agent to insure, who is subject to an independent duty of disclosure under section 19, provided that such knowledge was acquired in the agent's capacity as the assured's agent, as opposed to the agent's capacity as an agent for another principal,[21] (b) the agent who has knowledge concerning the subject-matter of the insurance, for example, the master of the ship, a cargo superintendent, a port agent, a warehouseman,[22] and (c) the general agent who is thoroughly acquainted

16 *Proudfoot v Montefiore* (1867) LR 2 QB 511; *London General Insurance Company v General Marine Underwriters' Association* [1921] 1 KB 104; *Inversiones Manria SA* v *Sphere Drake Insurance Co plc (The Dora)* [1989] 1 Lloyd's Rep 69, at 95.

17 *Australia & New Zealand Bank v Colonial & Eagle Wharves Ltd* [1960] 2 Lloyd's Rep 241, at 252; *Simner v New India Assurance Co Ltd* [1995] LRLR 240, at 253–255; *ERC Frankona Reinsurance v American National Insurance Co* [2005] EWHC 1381 (Comm); [2006] 1 Lloyd's Rep IR 157, at [173].

18 P. Watts & F.M.B. Reynolds, *Bowstead and Reynolds on Agency* (20th ed.), (Sweet & Maxwell, 2014), art. 95, para. 8–207.

19 *Group Josi Reinsurance Co Ltd v Walbrook Insurance Co Ltd* [1996] 1 Lloyd's Rep 345, at 365–366.

20 *Simner v New India Assurance Co Ltd* [1995] LRLR 240, at 254–255.

21 *Société Anonyme d'Intermediaries Luxembourgeois v Farex Gie* [1995] 2 Lloyd's Rep 116, at 143, 150 and 157; *Group Josi Reinsurance Co Ltd v Walbrook Insurance Co Ltd* [1996] 1 Lloyd's Rep 345, at 361 and 367. See s. 4(4) and (5) of the Insurance Act 2015. Only the broker who deals with the insurer comes within s. 19, not a broker previously employed by the assured (*Blackburn Low & Co v Vigors* (1887) 12 App Cas 531).

22 *Proudfoot v Montefiore* (1867) LR 2 QB 511.

with the assured's affairs, such as a family attorney or a general manager of a business.[23] An agent's knowledge will not be imputed or attributed to the principal, however, where the knowledge concerns the agent's own fraud upon the principal or breach of duty owed towards the principal.[24]

2.2.3 Exceptions to the duty of disclosure

Even if the assured is aware of a material circumstance or ought to be aware of a material circumstance in the ordinary course of business, there are occasions where the assured will be excused from any obligation to disclose the circumstance to the insurer. The standard exceptions are set out in section 18(3) of the MIA 1906 and follow those identified by Lord Mansfield in *Carter v Boehm*.[25] These exceptions excuse disclosure, they do not excuse misrepresentations. Further, the exceptions are applicable only in the absence of any inquiry or question from the insurer. If the insurer asks a question about a material circumstance which falls within the scope of one of these exceptions, the exceptions will not apply.[26]

There are four exceptions. The first exception is unremarkable and is perfectly consistent with the rationale of the duty of disclosure. By section 18(3)(a), the assured need not disclose any material circumstance which diminishes the risk.[27] The fourth exception is that, by section 18(3)(d), the assured need not disclose any circumstance which it is superfluous to disclose by reason of the existence of any promissory warranty in the insurance contract.[28] These two exceptions, the first and the fourth, have seldom been considered by the court.

The other two exceptions in section 18(3), by contrast, have received a great deal of attention in litigation. The second exception is that, by section 18(3)(b), the assured need not disclose any circumstance "which is known or presumed to be known to the insurer. The insurer is presumed to know matters of common notoriety or knowledge, and matters which an insurer in the ordinary course of his business, as such, ought to know." This exception is the analogue to the requirement of knowledge which shapes the scope of the assured's duty of disclosure. Just as the obligation upon the assured is to disclose what he or she knows, there is no obligation upon the assured to disclose to the insurer a circumstance already

23 *Blackburn Low & Co v Vigors* (1887) 12 App Cas 531, at 537–538.

24 *PCW Syndicates v PCW Reinsurers* [1996] 1 Lloyd's Rep 241; *Arab Bank plc v Zurich Insurance Co* [1999] 1 Lloyd's Rep 262, at 281–282. See s. 6(2) of the Insurance Act 2015.

25 (1766) 3 Burr 1905.

26 *Doheny v New India Assurance Co Ltd* [2004] EWCA Civ 1705; [2005] Lloyd's Rep IR 251, at [16].

27 *Carter v Boehm* (1766) 3 Burr 1905, at 1910; *Inversiones Manria SA* v *Sphere Drake Insurance Co plc (The Dora)* [1989] 1 Lloyd's Rep 69, at 89–90.

28 *Cantiere Meccanico Brindisino v Janson* [1912] 3 KB 452, at 462; *Inversiones Manria SA* v *Sphere Drake Insurance Co plc (The Dora)* [1989] 1 Lloyd's Rep 69, at 91–92; *J Kirkaldy & Sons Ltd v Walker* [1999] Lloyd's Rep IR 410, at 423; *O'Kane v Jones (The Martin P)* [2003] EWHC 2158 (Comm); [2004] 1 Lloyd's Rep 389, at [240]; *Garnat Trading & Shipping (Singapore) Pte Ltd v Baominh Insurance Corporation* [2010] EWHC 2578 (Comm); [2011] 1 Lloyd's Rep 589, at [152]-[155]; [2011] EWCA Civ 773; [2011] 2 Lloyd's Rep 492 (CA).

known to the insurer. As with the assured, there are a number of relevant categories of knowledge which are relevant in this context.

First, if the circumstance is actually known to the insurer and present to his or her mind,[29] the exception applies. It does not matter where the information has come from. If, however, the information was once known to the insurer, but has now been forgotten, the exception probably will not apply, unless the insurer is deemed or presumed to know such information under one of the other categories of knowledge. If the insurer is a company, as it often is, the knowledge of the relevant individual, that is the contracting underwriter, will be attributed to the company. Second, the insurer may have imputed knowledge, that is knowledge belonging to an agent.[30] Third, if the circumstance is a matter of "common knowledge", for example, the timing of the hurricane season in the Americas, the occurrence of armed conflict in certain parts of the world or the existence of international economic sanctions, such circumstance need not be disclosed.[31]

Fourth, the insurer will be deemed to know matters which he or she ought to know in the ordinary course of his business. Section 18(3)(b) uses the words "as such", in circumstances where section 18(1) has no like words. Similarly to section 18(1), the insurer will probably be deemed to know only that information which ought to be known to the insurer in the ordinary course of that insurer's business, as opposed to the ordinary course of the insurance industry as a whole. That said, the court has interpreted this provision so that the insurer will be presumed to know certain classes of information associated with the nature of the insurance which is being written. For example, the insurer will be deemed to know the "normal risks" associated with the insured activity, but will not be taken to know any "unusual risks".[32] The insurer will be deemed to know the characteristics and usages of the insured trade, such as the characteristics of a port,[33] normal or usual charterparty clauses,[34] the nature and characteristics of the class or type of vessel insured,[35] the nature and characteristics of the type of cargo insured or being carried[36] and the existence and exercise of the master's discretion at sea.[37]

However, if the knowledge in question is knowledge which the insurer obtained in the past, the insurer will not be deemed to have that knowledge if it was not or could not reasonably be present to his mind at the time of the presentation, even if the information is located in the records of the insurer, unless he or she ought

29 *Bates v Hewitt* (1867) LR 2 QB 595.

30 *Hadenfayre Ltd v British National Insurance Society Ltd* [1984] 2 Lloyd's Rep 393, at 400–402.

31 *Carter v Boehm* (1766) 3 Burr 1905, at 1910.

32 *North British Fishing Boat Insurance Co Ltd v Starr* (1922) 13 Ll L Rep 206, at 210; *Greenhill v Federal Insurance Co Ltd* [1927] 1 KB 65; *Marc Rich & Co AG v Portman* [1996] 1 Lloyd's Rep 430, at 442; affd [1997] 1 Lloyd's Rep 225.

33 Cf. *Fraser Shipping Ltd v Colton (The Shakir III)* [1997] 1 Lloyd's Rep 586, at 595–596; *Marc Rich & Co AG v Portman* [1996] 1 Lloyd's Rep 430, at 442; affd [1997] 1 Lloyd's Rep 225.

34 *The Bedouin* [1894] P 1, at 12.

35 *Cantiere Meccanico Brindisino v Janson* [1912] 3 KB 452; *George Cohen Sons & Co v Standard* (1925) 21 Ll L Rep 30, at 38.

36 *Mann, MacNeal & Steeves Ltd v Capital & Counties Insurance Company Ltd* (1920) 5 Ll L Rep 424.

37 *Middlewood v Blakes* (1797) 7 TR 162, at 167.

to have consulted those records in the ordinary course of business.[38] It may be, although it is by no means certain, that information which is held in public records (e.g. Lloyd's List) might be deemed to be known to the insurer, at least if the underwriter would have consulted such records in the ordinary course of business.[39] More importantly, information held in electronic databases (whether they are public or subscription or internal databases) which are accessible and accessed by underwriters in the ordinary course of business may be deemed to be known to the insurer.[40] This is especially so if the database is regularly accessed by the underwriters in question. However, just because the information is available to the insurer does not mean that the insurer ought to have inquired into the information.[41] Even though the court was sceptical in the past, it is more likely now that the relevant underwriter will be deemed to know information held by other departments within the insurer's organisation, especially if there is a database containing such information accessible to the underwriter in question.[42]

The third exception to the duty of disclosure is that, by section 18(3)(c), the assured need not disclose any circumstance as to which such disclosure is waived by the insurer. This is a provision which has received no universal judicial interpretation. Instead, there are various situations in which the insurer will be treated as having waived disclosure. The waiver of disclosure may be contractual in that the insurance contract provides that no disclosure is required.[43] The waiver need not be contractual. An underwriter may expressly state that no disclosure is required or no disclosure about specific matters is required.[44] The species of waiver which is more commonly encountered in the authorities is that of implied waiver. An underwriter may promise or represent that disclosure is not required, not because of any express statement, but because the underwriter's conduct or comments indicate that no disclosure is required. Where an insurer asks questions to be answered by the assured, for example in a proposal form, the nature and detail of the questions may indicate that the underwriter is interested in certain types of information, but not interested in the information which falls outside the scope of the underwriter's questions.[45] For

38 *Bates v Hewitt* (1867) LR 2 QB 595; *London General Insurance Company v General Marine Underwriters' Association* [1921] 1 KB 104, at 111–112; *Malhi v Abbey Life Assurance Co Ltd* [1996] LRLR 237.

39 *Friere v Woodhouse* (1817) Holt NP 572; *Foley v Tabor* (1861) 2 F&F 663, at 672–673; *General Shipping & Forwarding Co v British General Insurance Co Ltd* (1923) 15 Ll L Rep 175.

40 *Sea Glory Maritime Co v Al Sagr National Insurance Co (The Nancy)* [2013] EWHC 2116 (Comm); [2014] 1 Lloyd's Rep 14, [170]-[178].

41 *Hua Tyan Development Ltd v Zurich Insurance Co Ltd (The Ho Feng 7)* [2013] HKCA 414; [2014] Lloyd's Rep IR 1, para. 16.14 (Hong Kong CA); [2014] HKCFA 72; [2015] Lloyd's Rep IR 14 (Hong Kong Court of Final Appeal).

42 Cf. *Malhi v Abbey Life Assurance Co Ltd* [1996] LRLR 237.

43 *HIH Casualty & General Insurance Ltd v Chase Manhattan Bank* [2003] UKHL 6; [2003] 2 Lloyd's Rep 61.

44 *Property Insurance Co Ltd v National Protector Insurance Co Ltd* (1913) 108 LT 104.

45 *Schoolman v Hall* [1951] 1 Lloyd's Rep 139, at 143; *O'Kane v Jones (The Martin P)* [2003] EWHC 2158 (Comm); [2004] 1 Lloyd's Rep 389, [238]-[239]; *Doheny v New India Assurance Co Ltd* [2004] EWCA Civ 1705; [2005] Lloyd's Rep IR 251; *Synergy Health (UK) Limited v CGU Insurance plc* [2010] EWHC 2583 (Comm); [2011] Lloyd's Rep IR 500, [164]-[179]; *Bate v Aviva Insurance UK Ltd* [2013] EWHC 1687 (Comm); [2013] Lloyd's Rep IR 492, [22]; [2014] EWCA Civ 334; [2014] Lloyd's Rep IR 527 (CA).

example, an insurer who asks whether the assured has made any insurance claims over the previous five years may impliedly indicate that no disclosure is required of any insurance claims made by the assured ten years beforehand.

An insurer may also waive disclosure, within the meaning of section 18(3)(c), where the assured provides a summary of the material facts, if by reason of that summary, the insurer is reasonably put on notice of the possible existence of further material facts, and fails to ask for such information,[46] provided that the insurer can reasonably assume that the details which have not been disclosed will not vitiate or prejudice his or her assessment of the risk.[47] Any summary should include unusual or exceptional matters, because the insurer may not infer that such circumstances exist merely by reason of the assured's summary. Additionally, the insurer may waive disclosure having regard to the insurer's conduct based on the underwriter's own apparent knowledge. In this sense, the exception bridges section 18(3)(b) and (c).[48]

Further exceptions to the duty of disclosure may be found outside of section 18(3). Section 19 also includes an exception: where the assured uses a broker to place the insurance, the assured and the broker may be excused from disclosing a material circumstance, where the information came to the assured's knowledge too late to communicate it to the broker (section 19(b)). The assured may also be excused from providing disclosure not only in the circumstances provided for in the MIA 1906. For example, the assured may be relieved of the obligation of disclosure if the relevant circumstance is a matter which the insurer is not entitled to consider in the assessment of the risk, in particular certain matters falling within the scope of anti-discrimination legislation[49] or if the circumstance relates to a criminal conviction which is spent by the Rehabilitation of Offenders Act 1974.[50] Where the information attracts legal professional privilege, which privilege belongs to a person other than the assured, the assured may not have to disclose such information.[51]

2.2.4 Misrepresentation

To constitute an actionable misrepresentation, there is no requirement that the assured knew or ought to have known that the representation was untrue. The insurer will be able to rely on a material misrepresentation giving rise to a right

46 *Asfar & Co v Blundell* [1896] 1 QB 123, at 129–131.

47 *Container Transport International Inc v Oceanus Mutual Underwriting Association (Bermuda) Ltd* [1984] 1 Lloyd's Rep 476, at 496–498, 511–512 and 529–530; *WISE (Underwriting Agency) Ltd v Grupo Nacional Provincial SA* [2004] EWCA Civ 962; [2004] 2 Lloyd's Rep 483.

48 *Gandy v The Adelaide Marine Insurance Company* (1871) LR 6 QB 746, at 755 and 758; *Mann, MacNeal & Steeves Ltd v Capital & Counties Insurance Company Ltd* (1920) 5 Ll L Rep 424, at 427–428; *Greenhill* v *Federal Insurance Co Ltd* [1927] 1 KB 65, at 73; cf. *Sea Glory Maritime Co v Al Sagr National Insurance Co (The Nancy)* [2013] EWHC 2116 (Comm); [2014] 1 Lloyd's Rep IR 14, [170]-[178].

49 Sections 29 and 31, Schedule 3, Part 5 of the Equality Act 2010.

50 *Reynolds v Phoenix Assurance Co Ltd* [1978] 2 Lloyd's Rep 440, at 462; *Joseph Fielding Properties (Blackpool) Ltd v Aviva Insurance Ltd* [2010] EWHC 2192 (QB); [2011] Lloyd's Rep IR 238, [217]-[224].

51 *Quinn Direct Insurance Ltd v Law Society* [2010] EWCA Civ 805; [2011] 1 WLR 308.

of avoidance if he or she can establish that the representation was false. For this purpose, the representation must be first characterised either as a representation of fact or a representation as to expectation or belief. If the representation is one of fact, the representation will be true if it is "substantially correct, that is to say, if the difference between what is represented and what is actually correct would not be considered material by a prudent insurer".[52] For this purpose, the representation must be construed in order to determine its meaning and whether or not it is true. A representation may be made in answer to a question put by the insurer, in which case the insurer's question will also have to be construed (often *contra proferentem*).[53] If, however, the representation is as to a matter of expectation or belief, the representation will be true if it is made in good faith, that is honestly.[54] That is, if there has been a representation of expectation or belief, in order to establish that there has been a misrepresentation, the insurer will have to prove that the assured represented the expectation or belief dishonestly.[55]

2.2.5 Materiality

As regards the duty of full disclosure prior to the time of making the contract, the assured is bound to disclose "material" circumstances.[56] Similarly, the assured's insurance contract may be voidable if the assured has obtained it by making a "material" misrepresentation.[57] Whether the circumstance or representation is material is a question of fact.[58] By sections 18(2) and 20(2),[59] a circumstance or representation is material if it "would influence the judgment of a prudent insurer in fixing the premium, or determining whether he will take the risk". This test is often referred to as "the prudent insurer test" or "the prudent underwriter test". There was a time when it was thought that, at least in respect of certain classes of insurance, the test might be a "reasonable assured test". However, this is no longer possible given the terms of the MIA 1906. The characteristics of the prudent

52 Section 20(4) of the MIA 1906.

53 *R&R Developments Ltd v Axa Insurance UK plc* [2009] EWHC 2429 (Ch); [2010] 2 All ER (Comm) 527; *Involnert Management Inc v Aprilgrange Ltd* [2015] EWHC 2225 (Comm); [2015] 2 Lloyd's Rep 289, at [191]-[195].

54 Section 20(3) and (5) of the MIA 1906. *Economides v Commercial Union Assurance Co plc* [1998] QB 587; *Rendall v Combined Insurance Company of America* [2005] EWHC 678 (Comm); [2006] 1 Lloyd's Rep IR 732, para. 103; *Kamidian v Holt* [2008] EWHC 1483 (Comm); [2009] Lloyd's Rep IR 242, at [85]-[94], 138–141; *Zeller v British Caymanian Insurance Company Ltd* [2008] UKPC 4; [2008] Lloyd's Rep IR 545.

55 As regards representations of intention, see *St Paul Fire & Marine Insurance Co (UK) Ltd v McConnell Dowell Constructors Ltd* [1995] 2 Lloyd's Rep 116, at 127; *Limit No. 2 Limited v AXA Versicherung AG* [2007] EWHC 2321 (Comm); [2008] Lloyd's Rep IR 330, at [46]; [2008] EWCA Civ 1231; [2009] Lloyd's Rep IR 396, at [17]-[18].

56 Section 18(1) of the MIA 1906.

57 Section 20(1) of the MIA 1906.

58 Sections 18(4) and 20(7) of the MIA 1906. Expert evidence is often called to prove or disprove the materiality of a particular circumstance, but the court may well be able to judge materiality without the benefit of such evidence: *Synergy Health (UK) Ltd v CGU Insurance plc* [2010] EWHC 2583 (Comm); [2011] Lloyd's Rep IR 500, at [152]; *Bate v Aviva Insurance UK Ltd* [2014] EWCA Civ 334; [2014] Lloyd's Rep IR 527, at [35].

59 Cf. s. 152 of the Road Traffic Act 1988.

insurer are that the judgment of the prudent underwriter is to be "governed by the principles and calculations on which underwriters in practice act",[60] and the prudent underwriter must be experienced, rational, ordinary, prudent, intelligent, and fair and reasonable.[61]

In order to be material, the circumstance in question must have a particular effect on the prudent insurer's judgment in respect of determining whether he or she will enter into the contract of insurance on particular terms or determining the amount or rate of premium. Until 1994, there was a debate whether "influence" meant having a decisive impact or something less than that; and whether "judgment" meant formation of an opinion or the final decision. However, in *Pan Atlantic Insurance Ltd v Pine Top Insurance Ltd*,[62] the majority of the House of Lords held that a circumstance may be material even if it did not have a decisive impact on the insurer's final decision. Therefore, "influence" does not mean "decisively influence" such that the material circumstance must have an impact or effect on the decision of the prudent insurer whether or not he will take the risk or in fixing the premium. The circumstance is material if it has "an effect on the thought processes of the insurer in weighing up the risk". Materiality refers to "all matters which would have been taken into account by the underwriter when assessing the risk". It has also been said that a circumstance is material if being made aware of the circumstance "the prudent underwriter would have appreciated that it was a different . . . risk". This does not mean that the prudent underwriter must have appreciated that the risk was increased.[63]

Materiality (and inducement) has to be assessed by reference to the true state of affairs underlying the risk and not just by reference to what the insurer is actually told. It might be said that materiality of the non-disclosed or misrepresented circumstance has to be determined on the assumption that the assured has otherwise complied with his or her duty of full disclosure.[64] Where there are several non-disclosed facts, materiality of all of the circumstances not disclosed may be assessed in the round, rather than by reference to each of the individual circumstances.[65]

Where the parties agree that the truth of pre-contractual representations is warranted (often by means of what is known colloquially as a "basis clause"), any

60 *Ionides v Pender* (1874) LR 9 QB 531, at 539.

61 *Stribley v Imperial Marine Insurance Company* (1876) 1 QBD 507, at 514–515; *Tate & Sons v Hyslop* (1885) 15 QBD 368, at 377; *Associated Oil Carriers Limited v Union Insurance Society of Canton Limited* [1917] 2 KB 184.

62 [1995] 1 AC 501, 531, at 538. See also *Container Transport International Inc v Oceanus Mutual Underwriting Association (Bermuda) Ltd* [1984] 1 Lloyd's Rep 476, at 492.

63 *St Paul Fire & Marine Insurance Co (UK) Ltd v McConnell Dowell Contractors Ltd* [1995] 2 Lloyd's Rep 116, at 123–124.

64 *Drake Insurance plc v Provident Insurance plc* [2003] EWCA Civ 1834; [2004] 2 WLR 530, at [60]-[78], [131]-[142], [162]-[164], [179]-[182]; *Sea Glory Maritime Co v Al Sagr National Insurance Co (The Nancy)* [2013] EWHC 2116 (Comm); [2014] 1 Lloyd's Rep 14, at [162]-[169].

65 *Container Transport International Inc v Oceanus Mutual Underwriting Association (Bermuda) Ltd* [1984] 1 Lloyd's Rep 476, at 516 ("If a number of undisclosed facts taken together are such that they would influence the judgment of a prudent underwriter that is in my view sufficient even if no single one of them taken alone would do so"); *Joseph Fielding Properties (Blackpool) Ltd v Aviva Insurance Ltd* [2010] EWHC 2192 (QB); [2011] Lloyd's Rep IR 238, at [144].

misrepresentation will operate to discharge the insurer from liability automatically from the date of the breach, that is before inception, thereby avoiding the need to prove materiality or inducement, unless the contract provides otherwise.[66]

There are currently two unresolved issues concerning materiality. The first is the question whether, if fraud is proved, materiality is still a requirement or can the insurer establish that there has been a breach of the duty of utmost good faith or an actionable misrepresentation without proving materiality? The possibility of materiality being dispensed with in these circumstances is based on a number of *obiter* remarks made by the courts.[67] However, it is difficult to give credence to this view in circumstances where the MIA 1906 makes no distinction in this respect between fraudulent and non-fraudulent misrepresentations. The second is the question whether, in order to establish materiality, the relevant circumstance or representation must be objectively relevant to the risk or the insurer's net financial position under the insurance, in addition to satisfying the prudent insurer test, or whether the prudent insurer test is the only test to be satisfied. There are authorities in favour of both sides of this question.[68]

2.2.6 Inducement

In addition to establishing materiality, in order to be entitled to avoid the insurance contract by the assured's breach of the duty of full and accurate disclosure, it must be demonstrated that the insurer, in particular the underwriter who concluded the relevant insurance contract, was induced to enter into the insurance contract on the terms agreed by reason of the non-disclosure or misrepresentation.[69]

This means that the misrepresentation or non-disclosure must make an effective or material contribution to the actual underwriter's decision to agree to enter into the insurance contract on the terms actually agreed such that, if the non-disclosure or misrepresentation had not been made, the underwriter would not have agreed to enter into the insurance contract on the same terms. For this purpose, the test

66 *Genesis Housing Association Ltd v Liberty Syndicate Management Ltd* [2013] EWCA Civ 1173, [2014] Lloyd's Rep IR 318.

67 *Sibbald v Hill* (1814) 2 Dow 263, at 266–267; *The Bedouin* [1894] P 1, at 12; *Pan Atlantic Insurance Co Ltd v Pine Top Insurance Co Ltd* [1995] 1 AC 501, at 533.

68 *Glasgow Assurance Corp Ltd v Symondson & Co* (1911) 16 Com Cas 109, at 119–120; *Société Anonyme d'Intermediaries Luxembourgeois v Farex Gie* [1995] 2 Lloyd's Rep 116, at 149; *O'Kane v Jones (The Martin P)* [2003] EWHC 2158 (Comm); [2004] 1 Lloyd's Rep 389, at [222]. See also the High Court of Australia's decision in *Permanent Trustee Australia Ltd v FAI General Insurance Co Ltd* [2003] HCA 25; (2003) 77 ALJR 1070, at [32]-[33]; contra, *Sharp v Roarer Investments Ltd (The Moonacre)* [1992] 2 Lloyd's Rep 501. See P. MacDonald Eggers, "Pre-Contractual Duty of Utmost Good Faith – Materiality and Remedies", published as Chapter 3 in D.R. Thomas (ed.), *Marine Insurance: The Law in Transition*, (Informa, 2006), at paras. 3.1–3.34.

69 *Pan Atlantic Insurance Co Ltd v Pine Top Insurance Co Ltd* [1995] 1 AC 501; following *Berger & Light Diffusers Pty Ltd v Pollock* [1973] 2 Lloyd's Rep 442, at 463 and disapproving *Container Transport International Inc v Oceanus Mutual Underwriting Association (Bermuda) Ltd* [1984] 1 Lloyd's Rep 476, at 495, 510, 527–528; see also *Involnert Management Inc v Aprilgrange Ltd* [2015] EWHC 2225 (Comm); [2015] 2 Lloyd's Rep 289, at [210]-[217]; *AXA Versicherung AG v Arab Insurance Group (BSC)* [2015] EWHC 1939 (Comm); [2016] Lloyd's Rep IR 1, at [118]-[122].

of causation rests on a "but for" cause.[70] The underwriter must therefore be induced to agree to a particular course to which he would not have consented had he benefited from complete and accurate disclosure.[71] It is, therefore, not sufficient if the underwriter would have merely wanted to undertake further inquiries if he had been fully informed.[72]

It is sometimes said that inducement may be presumed if a material non-disclosure or misrepresentation is proved, if the underwriter cannot be called to give evidence or there is no reason to suppose that he or she acted other than prudently.[73] This "presumption" is not an inflexible rule of law, but merely a guide to the court in reaching any inference on the factual question whether or not the underwriter was induced. It is not a presumption of law, but an inference of fact.[74] It has been said that no such inference should be drawn if the underwriter is called to give evidence.[75]

2.2.7 Remedies

Section 17 of the MIA 1906 states that if either party fails to observe the utmost good faith, the other party may "avoid" the insurance contract. The remedy of avoidance is also referred to in sections 18(1) and 20(1) of the MIA 1906, dealing specifically with non-disclosures and misrepresentations respectively. By an avoidance of the insurance contract, the contract is unwound such that the parties are placed in the same position they would have been in had there been no contract of insurance. This requires the return of claims proceeds paid by the insurer to the assured and the return of premium paid by the assured to the insurer. However, at least with respect to marine insurance contracts, in the event of fraud by the assured, the insurer is entitled to retain the premium.[76]

In the event of avoidance, it is the contract of insurance which is avoided, not the insurance policy. The policy is the physical embodiment of the contract; indeed, the policy might encompass numerous contracts, especially in the case of composite

70 *Assicurazioni Generali SpA v Arab Insurance Group (BSC)* [2002] EWCA Civ 1642; [2003] Lloyd's Rep IR 131, at [62], [78], [215]-[221].

71 *Sugar Hut Group Ltd v Great Lakes Reinsurance (UK) plc* [2010] EWHC 2636 (Comm); [2011] Lloyd's Rep IR 198, at [23]-[25]; *Sealion Shipping Ltd v Valiant Insurance Co* [2012] EWHC 50 (Comm); [2012] 1 Lloyd's Rep 252.

72 *O'Kane v Jones (The Martin P)* [2003] EWHC 2158 (Comm); [2004] 1 Lloyd's Rep 389, at [235]; cf. *Moore Large & Co Ltd v Hermes Credit and Guarantee plc* [2003] EWHC 26 (Comm); [2003] Lloyd's Rep IR 315, [67], [75]; *Garnat Trading & Shipping (Singapore) Pte Ltd v Baominh Insurance Corporation* [2010] EWHC 2578 (Comm); [2011] 1 Lloyd's Rep 589, [144], [156]-[159]; [2011] EWCA Civ 773; [2011] 2 Lloyd's Rep 492.

73 *Marc Rich & Co AG v Portman* [1996] 1 Lloyd's Rep 430, at 442; *Sirius International Insurance Corp v Oriental International Assurance Corp* [1999] 1 All ER (Comm) 699.

74 *Assicurazioni Generali SpA v Arab Insurance Group (BSC)* [2002] EWCA Civ 1642; [2003] Lloyd's Rep IR 131, at [62]; *Laker Vent Engineering Ltd v Templeton Insurance Ltd* [2009] EWCA Civ 62; [2009] Lloyd's Rep IR 704, at [69]-[70].

75 *Sea Glory Maritime Co v Al Sagr National Insurance Co (The Nancy)* [2013] EWHC 2116 (Comm); [2014] 1 Lloyd's Rep 14; [2013] 2 All ER (Comm) 913, [56], [116].

76 Section 84(3)(a) of the MIA 1906.

policies, where there may be numerous assureds insured under the one policy.[77] Similarly, where there is more than one insurer subscribing to the policy, there is a separate contract of insurance between each insurer and assured.[78] Accordingly, if the assured failed to disclose a material circumstance to one insurer but not another, only the former would be entitled to avoid the insurance contract. Furthermore, it is possible that the one policy might contain a separate and distinct contract, relating to each separate item of insured property, even if there is only one assured, so that in the case of a fleet policy, there may be a separate insurance contract for each vessel which is a member of the fleet (depending on the terms of the policy).

The insurer's right to avoid the insurance contract may be lost by affirmation, that is when the innocent party elects to affirm the contract in full (actual, not constructive) knowledge of the facts giving rise to his or her right of avoidance and with knowledge of the insurer's legal right to avoid the insurance contract.[79] The affirmation consists of a statement of conduct on the part of the insurer which unequivocally communicates to the assured that the insurer has chosen to keep the insurance contract on foot. This can be done expressly or impliedly by conduct, for example where the insurer exercises a contractual right or performs a contractual obligation which is inconsistent with the avoidance of the contract.[80] An insurer may be entitled to a reasonable time to conduct its enquiries before making an election to affirm the contract.[81] The right to avoid may also be lost by equitable or promissory estoppel, namely where the insurer promises not to exercise the right of avoidance and the assured relies on that promise to his detriment.[82]

In addition, the right to avoid the insurance contract by reason of misrepresentation or non-disclosure, which is a right arising as a matter of law, may itself be excluded or limited (e.g. limited to cases of fraud) by the terms of the insurance contract itself.[83] It has been suggested by the Court of Appeal that the doctrine

---

77 *New Hampshire Insurance Company v MGN Ltd* [1997] LRLR 24; *Arab Bank plc v Zurich Insurance Co* [1999] 1 Lloyd's Rep 262, at 276–277.

78 Section 24(2) of the MIA 1906. See also *General Accident Fire and Life Assurance Corporation v Tanter (The Zephyr)* [1984] 1 Lloyd's Rep 58, at 66, 70, 72, 81.

79 *Insurance Corporation of the Channel Islands Ltd v McHugh* [1997] LRLR 94; [1998] Lloyd's Rep IR 151; *Persimmon Homes Ltd v Great Lakes Reinsurance (UK) plc* [2010] EWHC 1705 (Comm); [2011] Lloyd's Rep IR 101, at [111]-[116]; *Involnert Management Inc v Aprilgrange Ltd* [2015] EWHC 2225 (Comm); [2015] 2 Lloyd's Rep 289, at [157]-[161]. As to the circumstances in which the court might infer such knowledge, see *Moore Large & Co Ltd v Hermes Credit and Guarantee plc* [2003] EWHC 26 (Comm); [2003] Lloyd's Rep IR 315, at [92]-[100].

80 See, e.g., *WISE (Underwriting Agency) Ltd* v *Grupo Nacional Provincial SA* [2004] EWCA Civ 962; [2004] 2 Lloyd's Rep 483; *Scottish Coal Co Ltd v Royal & Sun Alliance Insurance plc* [2008] EWHC 880 (Comm); [2008] Lloyd's Rep IR 718. However, certain provisions may be separable from the insurance contract and may be unaffected by the avoidance of the main insurance contract, such as a jurisdiction or arbitration clause, unless that jurisdiction or arbitration agreement is itself the result of a misrepresentation or non-disclosure (*Fiona Trust & Holding Corporation v Privalov* [2007] UKHL 40; [2008] 1 Lloyd's Rep 254, paras. 17–18, 34).

81 *Sea Glory Maritime Co v Al Sagr National Insurance Co (The Nancy)* [2013] EWHC 2116 (Comm); [2014] 1 Lloyd's Rep 14, at [126].

82 See recently *IHC v Amtrust Europe Ltd* [2015] EWHC 257 (QB).

83 *HIH Casualty & General Insurance Ltd v Chase Manhattan Bank* [2003] UKHL 6; [2003] 2 Lloyd's Rep 61.

of utmost good faith might prevent an insurer from exercising a right to avoid where the insurer has demonstrated a lack of good faith in respect of a particular claim or in avoiding the policy. However, this appears to be at odds with a previous decision of the Court of Appeal.[84]

There is no monetary relief, such as compensatory damages, available for a breach of the duty of utmost good faith.[85] However, where the relevant facts also give rise to another cause of action occasioning a remedy in damages, such damages may be recoverable on that independent ground, such as damages in deceit, for breach of a duty of care in tort, or under the Misrepresentation Act 1967.[86]

2.2.8 Amendments or variations to the insurance contract

The duty of full and accurate disclosure is a duty which must be observed prior to and at the time of the conclusion of the insurance contract. However, where the contract of insurance is varied, this pre-contractual duty of disclosure revives, requiring the assured to disclose circumstances material to the amendment.[87] In the event of a material non-disclosure or misrepresentation inducing the insurer to agree to the variation on the terms actually agreed, the insurer would be entitled to avoid the variation, not the entire insurance contract.[88] By contrast, where the insurance contract is renewed, rather than varied, this is in effect a new contract attracting full disclosure pursuant to a fresh duty of utmost good faith.[89] There is a similar revival of the duty of disclosure, not in the case of variations, but in the case of the assured taking the benefit of a "held covered" clause in the insurance contract, by which the insurer will not be entitled to be discharged from liability or otherwise to terminate the cover, by reason of a breach of warranty or condition of the contract, provided that the assured provides prompt notice to the insurer of the breach and subject to the agreement of an additional premium. For the purpose of the agreement of that premium, the insurer is entitled to full and accurate disclosure.[90]

84 *Drake Insurance plc v Provident Insurance plc* [2003] EWCA Civ 1834; [2004] 2 WLR 530, at [87]-[88], [91]-[93], [145], [177]-[178]; contra *Brotherton v Aseguradora Colseguros SA* [2003] EWCA Civ 705; [2003] Lloyd's Rep IR 746, at [34], [44]-[48].

85 *Banque Keyser Ullmann SA v Skandia (UK) Insurance Co Ltd* [1990] 1 QB 665; [1991] 2 AC 249, 274; *The Good Luck* [1989] 2 Lloyd's Rep 238, at 263.

86 *Argo Systems FZE v Liberty Insurance (Pte)* [2011] EWHC 301 (Comm); [2011] 2 Lloyd's Rep 61, at [41]-[45]; [2011] EWCA Civ 1572; [2012] 1 Lloyd's Rep 129, at [35].

87 *Commercial Union Assurance Company Limited v The Niger Company Limited* (1922) 13 Ll L Rep 75, at 82; *Container Transport International Inc v Oceanus Mutual Underwriting Association (Bermuda) Ltd* [1982] 2 Lloyd's Rep 178, at 191–192.

88 *Manifest Shipping Co Ltd v Uni-Polaris Shipping Co Ltd (The Star Sea)* [1997] 1 Lloyd's Rep 360, 370; *K/S Merc-Scandia XXXXII v Lloyd's Underwriters (The Mercandian Continent)* [2001] EWCA Civ 1275; [2001] 2 Lloyd's Rep 563, at [22(2)].

89 *Stokell v Heywood* [1897] 1 Ch 459, at 464; cf. *Limit No. 2 Limited v AXA Versicherung AG* [2007] EWHC 2321 (Comm), at [67]; [2008] EWCA Civ 1231; [2009] Lloyd's Rep IR 396, at [20]-[21].

90 *Overseas Commodities Ltd v Style* [1958] 1 Lloyd's Rep 546; *Liberian Insurance Agency Inc* v *Mosse* [1977] 2 Lloyd's Rep 560; *Fraser Shipping Ltd v Colton (The Shakir III)* [1997] 1 Lloyd's Rep 586.

2.3 The Insurance Act 2015

2.3.1 Duty of utmost good faith

The 2015 Act was introduced with the promise of effecting change for the benefit of assureds in order to level the perceived imbalance of insurance law, which had previously favoured the insurer. The 2015 Act does not overhaul insurance law, rather it changes the law with respect to three distinct and discrete topics, namely the duty of fair presentation, the legal effect of breaches of warranties and other terms of the insurance contract, and the remedy for fraudulent claims. (This is to ignore a further reform introduced by way of amendment to the 2015 Act by sections 28-30 of the Enterprise Act 2016.) It achieves these aims by amending certain provisions of the MIA 1906, including the replacement of sections 18–20 of the 1906 Act. Whereas the 1906 Act was, largely, a codifying statute, the 2015 Act is a reforming statute.

As far as the duty of utmost good faith is concerned, the 2015 Act begins with two changes. First, it re-brands the pre-contractual duty of utmost good faith as the "duty of fair presentation".[91] Second, whilst it retains the name and concept of the duty of utmost good faith, the 2015 Act abolishes the remedy of avoidance for *any* breach of the duty of utmost good faith.[92] After the entry into force of the 2015 Act, section 17 of the 1906 Act will provide that "A contract of marine insurance is a contract based upon the utmost good faith."[93] In its Explanatory Notes, Parliament has stated that "[t]he intention of [s.] 14 is that good faith will remain an interpretative principle, with section 17 of the 1906 Act and the common law continuing to provide that insurance contracts are contracts of good faith".[94] It is unclear what role section 17, as modified, will play.

The 2015 Act replaces sections 18–20 of the MIA 1906,[95] by providing a fresh legislative regime for the assured's pre-contractual duty, now called the duty of fair presentation, with specified remedies for the breach of this duty of fair presentation, both in respect of contracts induced by the breach and in respect of contractual variations induced by the breach.[96] The 2015 Act does provide a remedy for the insurer in the event of the assured's presentation of a fraudulent claim,[97] which constituted a breach of the duty of utmost good faith.[98] However, a consequence of the abolition of the remedy of avoidance for any other breach of the duty of utmost good faith is that recognised categories of breach of the duty now have no remedy, unless another cause of action can be established. In particular,

91 Section 3(1) and (2) of the Insurance Act 2015.
92 Section 14(1) of the Insurance Act 2015.
93 Section 14(3)(a) of the Insurance Act 2015.
94 At para. 116.
95 Sections 18–20 of the 1906 Act are "omitted" by section 21(2) of the 2015 Act.
96 Sections 2(2) and 3, respectively, and Schedule 1, Part 1 and Part 2, respectively. There is no provision in the 2015 Act dealing with "held covered" clauses.
97 Section 12 of the Insurance Act 2015.
98 *Galloway v Guardian Royal Exchange (UK) Ltd* [1999] Lloyd's Rep IR 209. It has been questioned whether or not the presentation of a fraudulent claim is embraced by the duty of utmost good faith or whether it is subject only to an independent common law rule (*Agapitos v Agnew (The Aegeon)* [2002] EWCA Civ 247; [2002] 2 Lloyd's Rep 42). See the discussion in *Manifest Shipping Co Ltd v Uni-Polaris Shipping Co Ltd (The Star Sea)* [2001] UKHL 1; [2003] 1 AC 469.

previously recognised breaches of the duty of utmost good faith now no longer attract a remedy, namely: (a) breach of the insurer's pre-contractual duty of full and accurate disclosure,[99] (b) breach of the assured's post-contractual duty to abstain from fraud other than in respect of claims,[100] and (c) breach of the assured's duty of disclosure in respect of the operation of "held covered" clauses.[101] This chapter, however, will focus on the assured's duty of pre-contractual disclosure (the duty of fair presentation).

2.3.2 The assured's duty of fair presentation: no change

In many respects, the assured's duty of fair presentation under section 3 of the 2015 Act is the same as the assured's pre-contractual duty of utmost good faith as it applied pursuant to sections 18–20 of the MIA 1906. This reflects the Law Commission's conclusion, after a long review and after a consultation, that the duty of disclosure retained an important place in the insurance transaction, because of the inherent imbalance of knowledge between the parties. Nevertheless, there is a re-branding and re-packaging of the duty in that it is now called a duty of fair presentation and the duty has two alternative components as far as disclosure is concerned. By section 3(4) of the 2015 Act, the assured is required to disclose every material circumstance which the insured knows or ought to know, or, "failing that", to provide disclosure which gives the insurer sufficient information to put a prudent insurer on notice that it needs to make further enquiries for the purpose of revealing those material circumstances. By the earlier law, under section 18(1) of the 1906 Act, the duty of disclosure required of the assured every material circumstance which is known to the assured, but if the assured provides a summary of the risk to the insurer so as to put the insurer on notice that there may be undisclosed material information and, if the insurer fails to ask questions about that further information, he or she would have been taken to have waived disclosure (which is a recognised exception to the duty of disclosure under section 18(3)(c) of the 1906 Act).[102] Accordingly, the re-packaged duty represents a blend of the duty under section 18(1) and the exception of waiver under section 18(3)(c).

---

99 *Carter v Boehm* (1766) 3 Burr 1905; *Duffell v Wilson* (1808) 1 Camp 401; *Refuge Assurance Co Ltd v Kettlewell* [1908] 1 KB 545; affd [1909] AC 243; *Banque Keyser Ullmann SA v Skandia (UK) Insurance Co Ltd* [1990] 1 QB 665; [1991] 2 AC 249; *Aldrich v Norwich Union Life Insurance Co Ltd* [2000] Lloyd's Rep IR 1. This issue will be deliberated in the following chapter written by Professor Soyer.

100 *K/S Merc-Scandia XXXXII v Lloyd's Underwriters (The Mercandian Continent)* [2001] EWCA Civ 1275; [2001] 2 Lloyd's Rep 563. In *Agapitos v Agnew (The Aegeon)* [2002] EWCA Civ 247; [2002] 2 Lloyd's Rep 42, Mance LJ said that *The Mercandian Continent* applied to post-contractual fraud other than in respect of claims.

101 *Overseas Commodities Ltd v Style* [1958] 1 Lloyd's Rep 546; *Liberian Insurance Agency Inc v Mosse* [1977] 2 Lloyd's Rep 560; *Fraser Shipping Ltd v Colton (The Shakir III)* [1997] 1 Lloyd's Rep 586.

102 *Asfar & Co v Blundell* [1896] 1 QB 123, at 129–131; *Container Transport International Inc v Oceanus Mutual Underwriting Association (Bermuda) Ltd* [1984] 1 Lloyd's Rep 476, at 496–498, 511–512, 529–530; *WISE (Underwriting Agency) Ltd v Grupo Nacional Provincial SA* [2004] EWCA Civ 962; [2004] 2 Lloyd's Rep 483.

The exceptions to the duty of disclosure under section 3(5) of the 2015 Act are broadly the same as the exceptions under section 18(3) of the 1906 Act, with two differences. Section 3(5) provides that, in the absence of enquiry, the duty of fair presentation does not require the assured to disclose a circumstance if (a) it diminishes the risk, (b) the insurer knows it, (c) the insurer ought to know it, (d) the insurer is presumed to know it, or (e) it is something as to which the insurer waives information. These exceptions correspond to section 18(3)(a)–(c) of the MIA 1906. The first difference is the abolition of the exception in section 18(3)(d) by which the assured is excused from disclosing material circumstances where disclosure is superfluous by reason of the existence of a promissory warranty in the insurance contract. The reason for this change is that the effect of a breach of warranty has been altered by sections 10 and 11 of the 2015 Act. The second difference is that the scope of the exception based on the insurer's knowledge has been redefined under the 2015 Act (as to which, see below).

The assured's obligations in respect of misrepresentations are largely the same as they were under section 20 of the 1906 Act. What constitutes a false representation of fact and a false representation of expectation or belief under sections 3(3)(c) and 7(5) of the 2015 Act are the same as that under section 20(4) and (5) of the 1906 Act.

The test of materiality as adopted by sections 18(2) and 20(2) of the 1906 Act is continued by section 7(3) of the 2015 Act, which provides that "[a] circumstance or representation is material if it would influence the judgement of a prudent insurer in determining whether to take the risk and, if so, on what terms". Section 7(4) then proceeds to identify examples of circumstances or representations "which may be material", namely (a) special or unusual facts relating to the risk,[103] (b) any particular concerns which led the insured to seek insurance cover for the risk,[104] and (c) anything which those concerned with the class of insurance and field of activity in question would generally understand as being something that should be dealt with in a fair presentation of risks of the type in question. This is consistent with the existing case law.

In addition, the 2015 Act maintains the requirement that the insurer be induced by the assured's breach of fair presentation in order to be entitled to exercise one of the remedies allowed by the Act. This means that, had there been a fair presentation of the risk, the insurer would not have entered into the insurance contract at all or would have entered into the insurance contract but on different terms.[105] If there has been a breach of duty and if the insurer was induced by the breach of duty, the breach is identified by the 2015 Act as a "qualifying breach",[106] meaning that it is a breach which attracts a remedy under the Act.

103 This reflects the insurer being presumed to know the "normal risks" associated with the insured activity (*North British Fishing Boat Insurance Co Ltd v Starr* (1922) 13 Ll L Rep 206, at 210), but not being presumed to know any "unusual risks" (*Greenhill v Federal Insurance Co Ltd* [1927] 1 KB 65; *Marc Rich & Co AG v Portman* [1996] 1 Lloyd's Rep 430, at 442; affd [1997] 1 Lloyd's Rep 225).

104 Cf. *Fraser Shipping Ltd v Colton (The Shakir III)* [1997] 1 Lloyd's Rep 586, at 596.

105 Section 8(1) of the Insurance Act 2015.

106 Section 8(3) of the Insurance Act 2015.

2.3.3 *The assured's duty of fair presentation: fundamental changes*

A remarkable feature of the 2015 Act is that in seeking to reform what is perceived to be an onerous duty resting on the shoulders of the assured, much of that duty is largely unaffected by the reforms. However, there are fundamental changes to the assured's pre-contractual duty brought about by the 2015 Act. These changes relate to:

(a) The manner of the assured's disclosure.
(b) The abolition of the broker's duty of disclosure.
(c) The knowledge of the assured for the purposes of the duty of disclosure.
(d) The knowledge of the insurer as an exception to the duty of disclosure.
(e) The remedies for breach of the duty of fair presentation.

Of these changes, the most substantial are those relating to the parties' knowledge and the remedies for the breach. When one considers these particular changes, the question whether or not Parliament has achieved its objective of making the law less insurer-friendly becomes more pressing.

(a) Manner of the assured's disclosure

A small, but important, change introduced by the 2015 Act is that set out in section 3(3)(b). Under that sub-section, a fair presentation of the risk requires "disclosure in a manner which would be reasonably clear and accessible to a prudent insurer". This is important because it makes it clear that the assured will not discharge the duty of fair presentation by providing a large quantity of documentation, which includes pertinent information hidden in the mass of disclosed material. Thus, it will not necessarily be sufficient for the purposes of the duty, for example, for the assured to provide the insurer with a 600-page report, including material information in a footnote on page 517 of the report.

By the Explanatory Notes, Parliament observed that this change "is intended to target, at one end of the scale, 'data dumps', where the insurer is presented with an overwhelming amount of undigested information. At the other end, it is not expected that this requirement would be satisfied by an overly brief or cryptic presentation."[107]

(b) The abolition of the broker's duty of disclosure

The duty of disclosure which was borne by the assured's agent to insure, its insurance broker, under section 19 of the MIA 1906 has been removed. In its place is the requirement that the assured disclose not only information known to itself, but also information "known to one or more of the individuals who are responsible for the insured's insurance".[108] Section 4(8)(b) explains which persons who are responsible for the insured's insurance, namely an individual who "participates on behalf of the insured in the process of procuring the insured's insurance (whether the individual does so as the insured's employee or agent, as an employee of the

107 At para. 46.
108 Sections 4(2)(b) and 4(3)(b) of the Insurance Act 2015.

insured's agent or in any other capacity)". This encompasses information known to the assured's risk manager and insurance broker.[109] It may also encompass both producing and placing brokers.[110] Accordingly, there is no longer a requirement that the insurance broker disclose information which ought to be known to the broker; the assured now is obliged to disclose only information which is actually known to the insurance broker.[111]

(c) The assured's knowledge

The duty of fair presentation requires the assured to disclose information which the assured "knows or ought to know".[112] This duty entails a considerable burden on the assured, greater than that under the MIA 1906, whether the assured is an individual or an incorporated entity or unincorporated association and whether the knowledge which defines the scope of the assured's duty of disclosure is based on actual knowledge ("knows"),[113] or constructive knowledge ("ought to know").

Under section 4(2) of the 2015 Act, the assured who is an individual is obliged to disclose to the insurer what he or she actually knows and what is known to the "one or more of the individuals who are responsible for the insured's insurance". Other than extending the assured's duty of disclosure to information actually known to persons responsible for the assured's insurance, including the placing broker and others (by section 4(8)(b)), there is little change between the old and new law.

Under section 4(3) of the 2015 Act, the assured who is not an individual (namely, a company or an incorporated or unincorporated association) must disclose to the insurer information which is known to one or more individuals who are either (i) part of the assured's "senior management" or (ii) responsible for the assured's insurance. This has the potential effect of substantially increasing the actual knowledge of the assured which informs the duty of disclosure. Under the MIA 1906, a corporate assured will be taken to know that which is known to the individual or individuals, who is or are the directing mind and will of the company, which may include an internal insurance manager or may refer to a chief executive or managing director and the board of directors. However, under the 2015 Act, the actual knowledge of the corporate assured will extend not only to those responsible for the insurance within the assured's organisation, namely the internal insurance and risk managers, but also to the appointed brokers, including potentially the producing broker. Further, the knowledge of any one of these individuals will have to be disclosed.

In addition, where information is known to at least one individual who is part of the assured's "senior management", the assured must disclose that information. Section 4(8)(c) of the 2015 Act defines "senior management" to mean "those

109 Explanatory Notes, at paras. 51, 53.

110 However, information acquired by the broker through a business relationship other than with the assured will not be disclosable for this purpose: s. 4(4) and (5). This is similar to the position under the 1906 Act.

111 Explanatory Notes, at para. 58.

112 Section 4(1) of the Insurance Act 2015.

113 Actual knowledge includes blind-eye knowledge (s. 6(1)).

individuals who play significant roles in the making of decisions about how the insured's activities are to be managed or organised". This means that any information known to any one individual who plays a significant role in deciding how the assured's activities are managed or organised will have to be disclosed, including information known to each individual member of the company's board of directors, senior executives, such as chief executives, chief operating officers, treasurers or chief financial officers, personnel directors, and in the case of large corporations, heads of divisions of the company. Where a composite policy insures the activities of a group of companies, each individual occupying each of these positions in each of the members of the group will have knowledge which may have to be disclosed.

By the Explanatory Notes, Parliament states that the phrase "senior management" "captures those individuals who play significant roles in the making of decisions about how the insured's activities are to be managed or organised. In a corporate context, this is likely to include members of the board of directors but may extend beyond this, depending on the structure and management arrangements of the insured."[114] However, Parliament has also said that it expects this category of persons to be "construed relatively narrowly, but are capable of being applied flexibly". It is not clear how the express words of the provision can be restrictively interpreted to reduce the assured's obligation of disclosure in line with that under the MIA 1906. This represents a substantial addition to the corpus of information which must be disclosed by the assured, compared to the position prior to the introduction of the 2015 Act.

Under the 2015 Act, the assured's duty of fair presentation requires disclosure of not only information actually known to the assured, but also information which the assured ought to know. Section 4(6) and (7) of the 2015 Act defines what an assured ought to know, namely an assured ought to know what should reasonably have been revealed by a reasonable search of information available to the insured (whether the search is conducted by making enquiries or by any other means). This includes information held within the assured's organisation or by any other person (e.g. an agent or co-assured).

By its Explanatory Notes, Parliament suggests that this test of constructive knowledge reflects existing (i.e. pre-2015 Act) case law and that these provisions will be interpreted guided by existing case law.[115] However, by its terms, the test of constructive knowledge under the 2015 Act imposes a considerably broader duty of disclosure upon the assured, whether an individual assured or a corporate assured. In particular:

i) The duty is one of reasonable search. This suggests that the assured must positively look for information to disclose. The duty of disclosure under section 18 of the MIA 1906 requires the assured to disclose information which it ought to know in the ordinary course of business; it does not impose an active duty to acquire such information.

114 At paras. 54 and 55.
115 At paras. 56 and 57.

ii) The nature of the search is not exhaustively defined. It extends to making enquiries or "by any other means". This could require the assured to undertake documentary, archival or electronic searches as well as making enquiries with other persons.

iii) The sources of the information which the assured must search for is not limited to information held by the assured. Although such sources must be "available" to the assured, they include information held by "any other person", which may include agents, employees, co-assureds, commercial partners, contractors, and service-providers (including lawyers and other professional advisers).[116]

iv) Unlike the test of constructive knowledge under the MIA 1906, the test under the 2015 Act is not restricted to information which the assured "ought to know in the ordinary course of business". Under the 1906 Act, the assured need disclose only information which the assured ought to know in the ordinary course of the way in which the assured actually operates its business, whether or not that was done efficiently,[117] whereas under the 2015 Act, the duty of reasonable search suggests that the steps which the assured should take are to be defined by reference to the measures which any assured with the characteristics of the assured ought reasonably to pursue.

(d) The insurer's knowledge

By section 3(5)(b)–(d) of the 2015 Act, the assured is not obliged to disclose material circumstances to the insurer if the insurer knows the relevant circumstance, ought to know the relevant circumstance, or is presumed to know the relevant circumstance. The scope of the insurer's knowledge is defined further in section 5 of the 2015 Act.

Section 5(1) provides that an insurer actually knows a circumstance "only if it is known to one or more of the individuals who participate on behalf of the insurer in the decision whether to take the risk, and if so on what terms (whether the individual does so as the insurer's employee or agent, as an employee of the insurer's agent or in any other capacity)". This essentially provides that the insurer knows what the individual underwriter who decided to insure the relevant risk knows.[118] This is no different from the position under the 1906 Act.

Section 5(2) of the 2015 Act defines what an insurer ought to know: the insurer ought to know a circumstance only if (i) an employee or agent of the insurer knows it, and ought reasonably to have passed on the relevant information to the underwriter(s) concerned, or (ii) the relevant information is held by the insurer and is readily available to the underwriter(s) concerned. This is a restrictive test of constructive knowledge as far as the insurer is concerned. Under the 1906 Act,

116 As to the impact of legal professional privilege, see *Quinn Direct Insurance Ltd v Law Society* [2010] EWCA Civ 805; [2011] 1 WLR 308.

117 *Australia & New Zealand Bank v Colonial & Eagle Wharves Ltd* [1960] 2 Lloyd's Rep 241, at 252; *Simner v New India Assurance Co Ltd* [1995] LRLR 240, at 253–255; *ERC Frankona Reinsurance v American National Insurance Co* [2005] EWHC 1381 (Comm); [2006] 1 Lloyd's Rep IR 157, [173].

118 Explanatory Notes, para. 61.

what ought to have been known to the assured under section 18(1) and to the insurer under section 18(3)(b) was defined in the same terms: what the assured or insurer ought to have known "in the ordinary course of business". Under the 2015 Act, the constructive knowledge of the assured is broader and therefore increases the burden of disclosure upon the assured and the constructive knowledge of the insurer – setting the scope of the exception to the assured's duty of disclosure – is defined more narrowly under the 2015 Act:

i) The insurer is not expressed to be subject to a positive duty of reasonable search, to which the assured's duty is subject.[119]
ii) The insurer's constructive knowledge is defined only by reference to the information held by the insurer, whereas the assured's duty of constructive knowledge is defined to include information held "by any other person". It is unclear whether, by this test, information available to the insurer not only in electronic databases held by the insurer, but also those available to the insurer held by external organisations (such as public or subscription electronic databases) will fall within the 2015 Act definition of constructive knowledge.[120]

The difference in the definition of how the assured's constructive knowledge and the insurer's constructive knowledge are defined by the 2015 Act may have unintended or unexpected consequences, for example, where the insurer seeks to reinsure the risk which it has insured: as far as the direct insurance is concerned, what the insurer ought to know is more limited than what the insurer ought to know as a reinsured.

Section 5(3) of the 2015 Act defines what knowledge the insurer is presumed to have, namely matters which are common knowledge and matters which an insurer offering insurance of the class in question to insureds in the field of activity in question would reasonably be expected to know in the ordinary course of business. This definition of presumed knowledge appears to reflect the existing case law applicable under the 1906 Act.[121]

(e) Remedies

The 2015 Act reflects the recommendations made by the Law Commission that there remained a place for the duty of disclosure in the insurance transaction. Nevertheless, the Law Commission, with the backing of Parliament, considered

119 However, by para. 64 of the Explanatory Notes, Parliament has said that s. 5(2)(b) is intended to "*require the relevant underwriter to make a reasonable effort to search such information as is available to them within the insurer's organisation, such as in the insurer's electronic records*" (emphasis added).

120 *Sea Glory Maritime Co v Al Sagr National Insurance Co (The Nancy)* [2013] EWHC 2116 (Comm); [2014] 1 Lloyd's Rep 14, [170]-[178].

121 See *The Bedouin* [1894] P 1, at 12; *Cantiere Meccanico Brindisino v Janson* [1912] 3 KB 452; *Mann, MacNeal & Steeves Ltd v Capital & Counties Insurance Company Ltd* (1920) 5 Ll L Rep 424; *North British Fishing Boat Insurance Co Ltd v Starr* (1922) 13 Ll L Rep 206, at 210; *George Cohen Sons & Co v Standard* (1925) 21 Ll L Rep 30, at 38; *Fraser Shipping Ltd v Colton (The Shakir III)* [1997] 1 Lloyd's Rep 586, at 595–596; *Marc Rich & Co AG v Portman* [1996] 1 Lloyd's Rep 430, at 442; affd [1997] 1 Lloyd's Rep 225. In the Explanatory Notes, at para. 67, Parliament states that s. 5(3)(b) is intended to reflect s. 18(3)(b) of the MIA 1906 where it refers to "matters which an insurer in the ordinary course of his business, as such, ought to know".

that the duty required reform, which reforms are discussed above. However, the real difficulty with the duty of utmost good faith under the MIA 1906 is the inflexibility and harshness of the remedy for the assured's breach of that duty. It is not surprising, therefore, that the 2015 Act reformed the remedies available to the insurer in the event of the assured's breach of the duty of fair presentation. However, the even more curious aspect of the remedies available to the insurer under the 2015 Act is the fact that the changes to the remedies are not more substantial. Although they are more favourable to the assured than those under the MIA 1906, they remain potentially harsh as far as the assured is concerned. In particular, there is no room for the court to exercise a discretion (in the same way that the court has a discretion under the Misrepresentation Act 1967, although it is possible that the court may exercise such a discretion with respect to insurance contracts, even after the entry into force of the 2015 Act).[122]

Section 14 of the 2015 Act abolishes the general remedy of avoidance for breach of the duty of utmost good faith. In its place, the 2015 Act provides for a range of remedies for breach of the duty of fair presentation.[123] The applicable remedy under the 2015 Act depends on (i) whether the breach was "deliberate" or "reckless",[124] and (ii) the extent of the insurer's inducement by reason of the breach of duty on the part of the assured.[125]

If the breach was deliberate or reckless, the insurer is entitled to avoid the insurance contract, and the insurer may retain the premium paid by the assured, no matter what the extent of inducement, provided that the insurer was induced. However, if the breach was neither deliberate nor reckless, the remedies available to the insurer depend on the extent to which the insurer was induced by the breach to enter into the insurance contract. If the insurer would not have entered into the insurance contract at all, the insurer may avoid the contract but must return the premium to the assured.

If the insurer would have entered into the insurance contract in any event, but on different terms, where those terms were other than in respect of premium, the insurer may elect to treat the contract as if it had been written on those terms; and where the different terms represented a higher premium, the insurer may reduce the recoverable claim proportionately by reference to the increase in premium. The relevant proportion is defined as that represented by the premium actually charged divided by the premium which the insurer would have charged. For example, if the insurer in fact charged a premium of US$20,000, but would have charged US$30,000, had full and accurate disclosure been provided by the

122 In *Highlands Insurance Co v Continental Insurance Co* [1987] 1 Lloyd's Rep 109, at 117–118 and in *HIH Casualty & General Insurance Ltd v Chase Manhattan Bank* [2001] EWCA Civ 1250; [2001] 2 Lloyd's Rep 483, at [51], [116], it was questioned whether the court should exercise the discretion under s. 2(2) in respect of insurance contracts. It is difficult to see any justification for ruling out the exercise of that discretion in any circumstances.

123 Section 8 and Schedule 1 of the Insurance Act 2015.

124 These terms are defined in s. 8(5) of the Insurance Act 2015. A deliberate breach means one where the assured knows that it acted or failed to act in breach of the duty of fair presentation. A reckless breach is one where the assured did not care whether or not it acted or failed to act in breach of duty.

125 Schedule 1, Part 1 of the Insurance Act 2015.

assured, the insurer would be liable to pay only US$40,000,000 on an otherwise recoverable claim of US$60,000,000. As with avoidance and treating the contract as if it was written on different terms, the remedy of paying only a proportion of the assured's claim is dependent on the insurer electing to take up this remedy. As each of these remedies depends on the insurer's election, the insurer may lose the right to claim these remedies by election or affirmation or by estoppel.

The remedies for breaches of the duty of fair presentation which induce the insurer to agree to variations to an insurance contract are similarly dependent on whether the breaches were deliberate or reckless and on the extent of the insurer's inducement.[126] If there was a deliberate or reckless breach, the insurer may terminate the insurance contract from the date of the making of the variation and the insurer may retain all premium. If the breach was neither deliberate nor reckless and if the insurer would not have agreed the variation at all, the contract may be treated as if the variation had not been made and the insurer must return any extra premium paid. If the insurer would have agreed the variation but on different terms other than as to premium, the insurer may treat the contract as if it were varied on those terms. If the insurer would have charged a higher premium for the variation, the insurer may proportionately reduce any claim recoverable under the original or varied contract.

(f) Contracting out of the Insurance Act 2015

It is open to the parties to modify the duty of fair presentation and the remedies available for a breach of the duty by contract. However, under section 9 of the 2015 Act, basis clauses are no longer permitted, although specific pre-contractual representations can be warranted.[127] In addition, no contract can protect a contracting party from his or her own fraud.[128] The 2015 Act provides for a transparency requirement which must be complied with in the event that the parties agree, in their contract, to a modification of the default position under the 2015 Act. Under sections 16 and 17 of the 2015 Act, where the relevant contractual term puts the assured in a worse position as regards the duty of fair presentation, that contractual term will be of no effect, unless, having regard to the characteristics of the assured and the circumstances of the transaction (a) the term is clear and unambiguous as to its effect, and (b) either (i) the insurer takes sufficient steps to draw the term to the assured's attention before the contract or variation, or (ii) the assured (or its agent) had actual knowledge of the term.

2.4 Conclusion

The Insurance Act 2015 was introduced as a measure to make English insurance law, as it applied to the duty of full and accurate disclosure – now referred to as the duty of fair presentation – more proportionate and in line with modern insurance

126 Schedule 1, Part 2 of the Insurance Act 2015.

127 See Explanatory Notes, para. 84.

128 *HIH Casualty & General Insurance Ltd v Chase Manhattan Bank* [2003] UKHL 6; [2003] 2 Lloyd's Rep 61.

practice. The intention behind the 2015 Act was to allow remedies to the insurer for breach of that duty which were meritorious, meaning that they were proportionate to the nature and seriousness of the breach of duty.

The 2015 Act maintains the current state of the law, making a number of changes. The two most substantial changes reflect the scope of the assured's duty of disclosure and the remedies available for breach. The remedies have been described as more proportionate. It is true that the remedies scheduled under the 2015 Act are graduated taking into account the blameworthiness of the assured and the impact on the insurer in deciding whether and on what terms to enter into the insurance contract. However, these remedies lack flexibility and still pose serious consequences for an assured in breach of the duty of fair presentation, especially where the assured's breach is inadvertent and minor.[129] Nevertheless, this scale of remedies is better than the inflexible, harsh remedy available under the MIA 1906.

The other substantial change relates to the burden of disclosure resting upon the assured, by reference to the knowledge treated as that of the assured for the purposes of the duty of fair presentation and the knowledge treated as that of the insurer which operates as an exception to the assured's duty of disclosure. This change in the law renders the breadth of the assured's duty of disclosure substantially more onerous than the duty allows under the 1906 Act, or at the least it has the potential to render the duty of disclosure more rigorous than it was beforehand. In this respect at least, it is doubtful that the 2015 Act will achieve its aim in making the duty of fair presentation less insurer-friendly.

129 P. MacDonald Eggers, "Pre-Contractual Duty of Utmost Good Faith – Materiality and Remedies", published as Chapter 3 in D.R. Thomas (ed.), *Marine Insurance: The Law in Transition*, (Informa, 2006), at paras. 3.51–3.72. Also, see, B. Soyer, "Reforming Pre-Contractual Information Duties in Business Insurance Contracts: One Reform too Many?" (2009) *Journal of Business Law* 15, where difficulties in applying proportionate remedies in the context of commercial insurance contracts have been discussed.

CHAPTER 3

The insurer's duty of good faith: is the path now clear for the introduction of new remedies?

*Professor B. Soyer**

3.1 Introduction

It has long been established that in insurance law the duty of good faith is reciprocal[1] and the insurer is expected to act in good faith in his dealings with the assured in the same fashion as the assured is expected to observe good faith towards the insurer. The insurer's duty of good faith has been traditionally traced to s. 17 of the Marine Insurance Act (MIA) 1906[2] which stipulates in a general manner that: "A contract of marine insurance is a contract based upon the utmost good faith, and, if the utmost good faith be not observed by either party, the contract may be avoided by the other party."

The fact that the only remedy afforded by this section is "avoidance" of the contract creates enormous difficulties. At the pre-contractual stage, in most instances "avoidance" would be an impractical remedy for the assured, especially if a breach is detected after the insured property suffers a loss. The duty at the post-contractual stage is also not free from controversy. In this context, the remedy of "avoidance" is often deemed to be too harsh[3] and courts have been forced to resort to innovative construction techniques in order to impose restrictions on the scope of the post-contractual duty of good faith. Initially, on the premise that there is no justification for requiring the same high degree of openness post-contractually as is expected from parties at the pre-contractual stage, it was held in *The Star Sea* that only fraudulent failure to act in good faith, post-contract, gives rise to the right to avoid. Building upon that principle, in *K/S Merc-Skandia XXXII v Certain Lloyd's Underwriters (The Mercandian Continent)*,[4] Longmore LJ held that it would be appropriate to invoke the remedy of avoidance in a post-contractual context if the innocent party would otherwise be justified in accepting the conduct of the

* Director of the Institute of International Shipping and Trade Law, Swansea University.

1 Lord Mansfield in *Carter v Boehm* (1766) 3 Burr 1905, famously said: "The policy would equally be void, against the underwriter if he concealed; as, if he insured a ship on her voyage, which he privately knew to be arrived, and an action would lie to recover the premium."

2 Especially given that ss. 18–20 of the MIA 1906 devote their attention to specific pre-contractual duties of the assured and his intermediaries, the only provision in the Act that the insurer's duty could derive from is s. 17 of the MIA 1906.

3 This led Lord Clyde in *Manifest Shipping Co Ltd v Uni-Polaris Shipping Co Ltd (The Star Sea)* [2001] UKHL 1; [2003] 1 AC 469, at [6], to comment that limiting the scope of s. 17 to pre-contractual negotiations "appears to be past praying for".

4 [2001] EWCA Civ 1275; [2001] 2 Lloyd's Rep 563.

party in breach of the duty as a repudiatory breach of the policy. This approach presupposes that the need to observe good faith in the post-contractual context would normally be associated with a contractual obligation, and it attempts to align "avoidance" with contractual remedies that would be applicable when the clause in question is breached in a fraudulent fashion. Naturally, these authorities, originally designed to ameliorate the harshness of the remedy of avoidance, impose a serious constraint on the scope of the insurer's post-contractual duty of good faith, if not trivialising it.

One of the fundamental changes imposed by the Insurance Act 2015 ("the 2015 Act") is removal of the remedy of "avoidance" from the scope of s. 17.[5] In its new format, this section does nothing more than stipulate that "a contract of marine insurance is a contract based upon the utmost good faith". This was a necessary step to ensure that other reforms introduced by the 2015 Act, especially new proportionate remedies available to an insurer in case of breach of the assured's duty of fair presentation of the risk[6] and remedies afforded to the insurer in case of submission of a fraudulent claim,[7] are not undermined by the continued existence of reference to the remedy of "avoidance" in s. 17.

Evidently, the driving force behind the alteration to s. 17 of the MIA 1906 was the desire to tidy up insurer's remedies in cases of pre- or post-contractual breach of the good faith duty on the part of the assured. However, it is possible that the change in the relevant statutory provision might also have an impact on the position of the insurer, accelerating the organic development of the doctrine by the courts, given that the unpopular remedy associated with this section is out of the way. The objective of this chapter is, therefore, to evaluate and comment on the future development of the insurer's duty of good faith by taking into account relevant authorities decided prior to the 2015 Act coming into force, and general principles of law. Although the amended version of s. 17 in itself is not intended to give an insurer a cause of action,[8] it is submitted that reaffirmation of the underlying nature of insurance contracts as requiring utmost good faith can still play a vital role in the development of the insurer's duty of good faith by directing the attention of the courts to the common law position as it stood prior to the passing of the MIA 1906.

3.2 Pre-contractual duty of good faith of the insurer

At the outset, it needs to be stressed that, even before the introduction of the 2015 Act, the assured has always been in a strong position in a case where he is induced to enter into an insurance contract following a material misrepresentation on the part of the insurer at the formation stage. It is open to the assured in such an instance to rely on alternative courses of action. For instance, a fraudulent

5 See s. 14(3)(a) of the Insurance Act 2015.
6 See s. 8 and Schedule 1 of the Insurance Act 2015.
7 See s. 12 of the Insurance Act 2015.
8 See "Insurance Contract Law: Business Insured's Duty of Disclosure and the Law of Warranties", Joint Consultation Paper, (2012), LCCP 204/SLCDP 155 at p. 127.

misrepresentation made by the insurer to induce the latter to enter into the contract is likely to satisfy ingredients of the tort of deceit in line with the judgment of *Derry v Peek*.[9] When it comes to the measure of damages for the tort of deceit, the assured will be entitled to an award which would put him in the same position he would have been in had the tort been never committed. This would, therefore, enable the assured who enters into an insurance contract as a result of the fraudulent misrepresentation of the insurer, and finds out later that the policy has no practical use for him, to recover the cost of repair or cost of reinstatement in cases where the subject matter suffers a loss, on the premise that he has been deprived of the anticipated benefits from pursuing an alternative cause of action (e.g. purchasing another insurance policy).[10] Furthermore, the Misrepresentation Act (MA) 1967 provides an opportunity to the assured to sustain a claim for damages even in cases where the misrepresentation is merely negligent. The MA 1967 allows the assured to recover damages in the same measure as if he were suing for the tort of deceit,[11] so the measure of damages will be calculated favourably from the assured's perspective. Therefore, it is fair to say that revamping of s. 17 is unlikely to alter the current state of play in a case where the insurer fraudulently or negligently makes a misrepresentation as to the nature of the cover; although, admittedly, in practice instances of this nature are rather rare.

However, is the insurer under a duty to speak at the formation stage and, if so, could his silence on certain occasions be treated as a breach of his good faith obligation? For example, if the insurer is in possession of information relating to the assured's entitlement under the policy or sells an insurance product which he knows is unlikely to benefit the assured for a variety of reasons, would the insurer be in breach of the pre-contractual duty of good faith by opting to keep silent? And, more significantly, what remedy would be available to an assured in such an instance?

This was the central issue in *Banque Financière de la Cité v Westgate Insurance Co Ltd*.[12] Relevant facts of this rather complex case can be summarised in the following manner. A fraudster named Ballestero persuaded a consortium of Swiss banks to make loans of 26.25 million Swiss francs to four companies controlled by him. The primary security for the loan was a parcel of gemstones independently valued at 95 million Swiss francs. In fact, the parcel of gemstones later proved to be worthless. As secondary security, a credit insurance policy for 37 million Swiss francs was put forward which was specifically written to cover default by Ballestero's companies for the eventuality of the gemstones proving to be inadequate security. The banks instructed an insurance broker to arrange the credit insurance policy. The task of securing the policy was delegated to one of the employees of the broker's firm, Mr Lee. In the process of setting up the credit policies with various insurers, Mr Lee engaged in several fraudulent activities. In particular, he

9 (1889) 14 App Cas 337.
10 *Dadourian Group International v Simms* [2006] EWHC 2973 (Ch); [2006] ALL ER 351.
11 See *Royscot Trust Ltd v Rogerson* [1991] 2 QB 297 (CA).
12 [1990] 1 QB 665; [1987] Lloyd's Rep 69; [1990] 1 QB 665 (CA); [1991] 2 AC 249 (HL) (sub nom *Banque Keyser Ullman SA v Skandia (UK) Insurance Co Ltd*).

issued cover notes on behalf of some of the insurers undertaking second and third layers of the insurance several months prior to these policies being, in fact, obtained. By June 1980, the full amount of insurance had been obtained. In May 1980, however, an employee of one of the underwriters providing cover for the primary level became aware of Mr Lee's fraud but did not report this to the banks. Under the assumption that the loans were firmly secured, the banks continued making advances up to 80 million Swiss francs to the companies of Ballestero between August 1980 and March 1981. Mr Lee was asked to extend the current layers of credit insurance and arrange a fourth layer. The fourth layer had never been arranged; although continuing with his earlier practice, Mr Lee issued a cover note in respect of the new layer for the banks. Before Mr Lee's wrongdoings were discovered, the extent of the fraud perpetrated by Ballestero became apparent to the banks when his companies defaulted on repayment of the loans. In 1983, the banks brought actions against the insurance brokers and Mr Lee for negligence and fraud, respectively. The claim was settled by the insurance brokers to the extent of their liability insurance. When the banks turned to the credit insurers, to the extent that such policies were in place, the underwriters refused payment on the ground of Ballestero's fraud by virtue of a clause that appeared in the credit policies:

> The insurers shall not be liable hereunder for . . . any claim or claims arising directly or indirectly out of or caused directly or indirectly by fraud attempted fraud misdescription or deception by any person firm or company.

Running out of options, the banks then turned to the insurers on the premise that the insurers failed to inform them of other frauds committed by Mr Lee of which the insurers were aware. It was contended that, had there been full disclosure, the banks would have gone elsewhere for the additional insurance and would not have used the relevant brokerage firm and, particularly, Mr Lee. The damages sought from the insurers represented the advances made between August 1980 and March 1981.

The first instance judge and the Court of Appeal were receptive to the idea that the insurer is expected to disclose certain facts and circumstances to the assured at the pre-contractual stage. The source of this duty was traced to s. 17 of the MIA 1906; but given that this provision is silent as to the scope of such a duty, it was necessary to engage in a painstaking analysis of the scope of the insurer's duty of disclosure at the pre-contractual stage. In particular, the opinions expressed by the Court of Appeal can be viewed as providing insightful guidance on the matter. The first issue that needed to be settled was the nature of the materiality test in this context. On that matter, the first instance judge, Steyn J, took a very liberal stand. He was disposed to accept that the duty of the insurer at the pre-contractual stage should be viewed as an example of his general duty of "good faith and fair dealing" and accordingly the insurer should be expected to disclose every circumstance and fact which, if not disclosed, would influence the assessment process of the assured whether to conclude the contract of insurance or not.[13]

13 See [1987] 1 Lloyd's Rep 69, at 95.

Applying this test, Steyn J reached the conclusion that the leading underwriter was in breach of his pre-contractual disclosure obligation by not revealing the fraud of Mr Lee, because Mr Lee was a key figure in setting up the second and third layers of the cover and the banks relied on him heavily for their information concerning the transactions.[14]

The fundamental problem in Steyn J's analysis is the fact that the scope of materiality is so far-reaching that, if adopted, good faith and fair dealing would possibly require the insurers not only to disclose circumstances pertinent to the nature of the risk but also to provide advice as to the terms of the contract that the assured is about to enter, or even guidance as to the state of the market on a particular product. Naturally, these are the duties that one would expect an independent agent (i.e. a broker) to perform at the formation stage, but perhaps not an insurer. Also, defining "materiality" in this fashion would put the concept out of line with its counterpart that applies to the assured at the pre-contractual stage. In that context, the disclosure duty would not require the assured to give guidance to the insurer as to the nature of their business or the state of the market.[15] Pleasingly, the Court of Appeal has taken a more sober stand on the matter. Whilst concurring with Steyn J, that there had been a breach by the insurers of the duty of disclosure, the Court of Appeal has subscribed to a rather different and more precise materiality test. In the Court of Appeal's view, the insurer is expected to disclose at the pre-contractual stage all facts known to the insurer as long as such facts relate to "the nature of the risk sought to be covered or the recoverability of a claim under the policy which a prudent insured would take into account in deciding whether or not to place the risk for which he seeks cover with that insurer".[16] Tying the materiality requirement to factors that are relevant to the decision-making process of the assured, such as attributes of the risk and recoverability under the policy, the Court of Appeal has marked its boundaries in a clearer fashion compared to Steyn J's test.[17] Under this test, it is likely that the insurer

14 A desire to find a suitable remedy in all circumstances (*ubi jus ubi remedium*) was the driving force behind the judgment of Steyn J. His ruling seems to have been based on his appreciation of "justice and policy considerations". See particularly, [1990] 1 QB 665, at 706.

15 Courts have repeatedly held that the disclosure duty of the insurers at the pre-contractual stage is not extended to giving advice as to the state of the insurance market, in particular the losses facing the insurers on a particular type of product. Rix J, in *Norwich Union Life Insurance Society v Qureshi* [1999] Lloyd's Rep IR 263, at 272, expressed the view that the imposition of a duty of good disclosure on insurers in relation to the investments to be made by the assured would convert them into financial advisers. The Court of Appeal decided in similar fashion in joint cases *Aldrich v Norwich Union Life* and *Norwich Union Life v Qureshi* [2000] Lloyd's Rep IR 1.

16 [1990] 1 QB 665, at 772.

17 It should be stressed that the Court of Appeal's approach to materiality found considerable support at the House of Lords even though it was not necessary to apply it to solve the case. Lord Templeman [1991] 2 AC 249, at 280, who gave the only substantial speech in the House, described the reasons given by the court as "cogent". The House of Lords, viewing the matter in a different light, came to the conclusion that the case could be disposed of without considering whether the insurer was under a duty to disclose Mr Lee's fraud by reason of the obligations of an insurer to deal with the proposer of the insurance with the utmost good faith. Their Lordships found in favour of the insurers by employing a straightforward causation analysis. It was held that the losses suffered by the banks did not stem from the fraudulent activities of Mr Lee carried forward by the brokerage firm's failure to inform them. Mr Lee's fraud did not cause a claim under the policy to arise. It was the fraud

will be expected to disclose: the existence of fraud in connection with the risk undertaken; any defence which he is aware of and may rely on at a later stage;[18] information in relation to the state of the subject-matter insured that the insurer is privy to;[19] and even foreign illegality[20] or any proposed change in law that might have an impact on recovery under the policy.[21] The decision of the Court of Appeal, however, still left a sour taste in the mouths of the banks despite the victory on the point of materiality, as they failed in their quest to recover damages for the insurer's breach of good faith. The Court of Appeal took the stand that the relevant provisions of the MIA 1906 do not give rise to damages and it proved impossible to establish any other alternative cause of action (i.e. tort) for damages.

A number of observations as to the nature and scope of insurer's duty of good faith in the light of *Banque Financière* litigation are in order. First, it is indisputable that such a duty exists and s. 17 of the MIA 1906 has been viewed as the statutory basis for codifying the principles of equity law developed over the centuries prior to the enactment of the MIA 1906. Second, the first instance judge and the Court of Appeal, by drawing an analogy with the assured's pre-contractual duty of good faith, needed to engage in judicial lawmaking in order to define the degree of materiality required in this context, given that s. 17 is silent on the point. Last but not least, "avoidance" not only provides an impractical remedy for the assured but also has proved something of a stumbling block in allowing alternative remedies (notably damages), as its existence led the judges in the Court of Appeal to conclude that the judicial basis of the statutory duty stems from the jurisdiction exercised by the Court of Equity.[22]

It is submitted that removal of the remedy of "avoidance" from the equation presents a great opportunity to courts to develop the insurer's pre-contractual duty of good faith in an organic but systematic fashion in the years to come. Although the 2015 Act is silent on the insurer's duty of good faith, it is plausible to suggest that s. 17, which stipulates that an insurance contract, unlike other types of contracts, is a contract based on utmost good faith, could be of use in asserting that a duty, comparable with the pre-contractual duty of good faith of the assured, should be imposed requiring the insurer to act in a fair fashion to the assured when assessing the risk proposed to him. Here, it is not proposed that s. 17 should be viewed as the source of the insurer's duty of good faith. The duty should be

of the borrower, Ballestero, which caused the loss under the policy in the present case; but of course that kind of loss was excluded from the policy by express provision of the contract anyway.

18 This would have been the case in *Banque Financière de la Cité v Westgate Insurance Co Ltd* if the insurer had been aware of the fact that Ballestero was a fraudster, which would invalidate any claim made under the credit insurance policy due to the existence of the exclusion clause in the contract.

19 *Carter v Boehm* (1766) 3 Burr 1905.

20 An example would be where the kidnap and ransom insurer providing cover for a ship registered in a foreign country fails to disclose to the assured that payment of ransom would be illegal under the law of that state.

21 For a similar situation, see *Duffell v Wilson* (1808) 1 Camp 401.

22 See, in particular, the judgment of Slade LJ [1990] 1 QB 665, at 780. This stance seems to have been endorsed by the House of Lords [1991] 2 AC 249, at 280, per Lord Templeman. The parties in *Manifest Shipping Co Ltd v Uni-Polaris Insurance Co Ltd (The Star Sea)* [2001] UKHL 1; [2003] 1 AC 469 were prepared to proceed on the premise that good faith duties do not attract damages as a remedy.

traced back to the common law, and s. 17 in its amended format could be viewed as a stepping stone, offering a reminder of the common law position laid down by Lord Mansfield around 250 years ago to the effect that the duty of good faith is reciprocal in character.

At this juncture, one might rightly indicate that the decision in *Banque Financière* could stop such an assertion in its tracks. The author, however, disagrees. The reasoning of the court in *Banque Financière* was based on the fact that the only remedy stipulated in the MIA 1906 for breach of the duty of good faith was "avoidance". That was deemed adequate to establish a parallel between the good faith obligation in insurance contracts and equitable concepts such as duress and undue influence; although, when viewed from the historical setting, it is clear that the role of the Court of Chancery in the development of good faith in insurance law was rather secondary. For a considerable period of time and certainly until the judicature reforms, Chancery's attitude in insurance cases concerning non-disclosure or misrepresentation was to refrain from exercising jurisdiction in cases where the matters alleged by the bill afforded a defence to a claim on the policy at common law. In those cases, Chancery would send an insurer's claim for relief to the common law courts for trial.[23] It is, therefore, rather curious to suggest that the doctrine of good faith in insurance law emerges from the law of equity.[24] The fact that "avoidance" is not any more the only remedy stipulated by the relevant statute does not, of course, alter the origins of the doctrine, but it certainly opens the door for a fresh judicial analysis on the subject. Looking at the matter in that light, it could be easier for a court to disregard the finding of the courts in *Banque Financière* litigation on the origins of the duty.[25]

Although the duty could be traced to common law, with the aid of the remaining part of s. 17 of the MIA 1906, there still remain problems in identifying the scope of the duty and potential remedies in case of its breach. It is submitted that the assured's pre-contractual duty of good faith could be instrumental in determining the scope of the insurer's duty, given that s. 17 does not hint of any difference in the nature of these duties. If so, the insurer would presumably be required to disclose information relating to the nature and extent of the policy risks that are within the exclusive knowledge of the insurer, or information relating to the assured's entitlement under the policy. Put differently, drawing a parallel with the assured's pre-contractual duty of good faith, it is evidently necessary that a "materiality test" in this context be applied; and accordingly, the insurer's obligation to speak is

---

23 See *Wilson v Duckett* (1762) 3 Burr 1361 and *Duncan v Worrall* (1822) 10 Price 31.

24 The part of the judgment in *Banque Financière* linking the origins of the good faith doctrine to the law of equity has often been doubted. See, for example, R. Grime, "Counterclaims by Marine Insurers" published in D.R. Thomas (ed.), *Modern Law of Marine Insurance, Volume 2,* (2002, LLP) at pp. 275–275; P. MacDonald-Eggers, "Remedies for the Failure to Observe the Utmost Good Faith" [2003] LMCLQ 249, at p. 250; B. Soyer, *Marine Insurance Fraud,* (2014, Informa), at pp. 126–127.

25 There are powerful dicta doubting the conclusion that the Court of Appeal reached in *Banque Financière* to the effect that remedy in case of breach of the insurer's duty of utmost good faith was equitable in origin. For example, Lord Bingham MR in *Cox v Bankside Members Agency Ltd* [1995] CLC 671, at 680, said: "I cannot for an instant accept [counsel's] suggestion that breach of this duty [to act with good faith in conducting legal proceedings] by an insurer, once the policy is in force, gives the assured no right other than recession."

restricted to certain instances. There is no reason why the materiality test laid down by the Court of Appeal and endorsed by the House of Lords in *Banque Financière* could not be utilised, given that the introduction of the 2015 Act does not alter fundamentally the law's approach to parameters against which materiality is judged.[26]

The more difficult question is what the consequence of breach of the insurer's duty of good faith would be if it proves possible to create a mutual obligation of good faith. The 2015 Act, as opposed to ss. 18 and 20 of the MIA 1906, introduces proportionate remedies in case of breach of the duty of fair presentation by the assured. For example, if the assured negligently fails to disclose a material circumstance and it can be demonstrated that the insurer would have entered into the contract but would have charged a higher premium, the insurer may reduce proportionately the amount to be paid on a claim.[27] Even though a remedy of this kind is made available by analogy in this context, recovering part or all of the premium paid would in most instances not be an adequate remedy for the assured following fraudulent or negligent non-disclosure on the part of the insurer. The remedy that would provide a practical benefit to an assured who is induced as a result of non-disclosure of the insurer to purchase a worthless policy, or a policy that would not be of any benefit to him, is claiming damages. The prospect of a claim for damages was denied in *Banque Financière* but if it proves possible to demonstrate that the duty of good faith stems from common law, it remains a genuine possibility that courts could award damages to the assured in appropriate cases. In other common law jurisdictions courts have had no qualms in making damages available as a direct remedy for breach of utmost good faith principles.[28]

An alternative could be that s. 17 could be utilised in arguing that a novel tort should be created allowing the assured to recover damages in cases where the insurer at the pre-contractual stage fails to observe good faith. Such an attempt did not find a sympathetic ear in *Banque Financière*. However, removal of the remedy of "avoidance" from the ambit of s. 17 has potentially altered the equation. We now face a situation where the existence of a duty on the part of the insurer to observe good faith has been recognised by a statutory provision but, unlike the pre-contractual duty of the assured, no remedy has been specified in the relevant legislation in case of its breach. It is not an uncommon occurrence for the courts to introduce new torts in appropriate instances,[29] and there is no risk that this new tort might work against the assured (e.g. by allowing insurers to pursue assureds

26 Under s. 7(3) of the Insurance Act 2015, a circumstance or representation is deemed material "if it would influence the judgment of a prudent insurer in determining whether to take the risk and, if so, on what terms". This is almost identical to the test laid out by ss. 18(2) and 20(2) of the MIA 1906 – the provisions that were in force when the decision in *Banque Financière* was delivered.

27 See s. 8 and Schedule 1 of the Insurance Act 2015.

28 See, for example, *Stuart v Guardian Royal Exchange Assurance Co of New Zealand Ltd (No 2)* (1988) 5 ANZ Ins Cas 60–844.

29 For example, a new tort of "breach of confidence" has been introduced in *Fraser v Thames Television* [1984] QB 44; [1998] 2 All ER 101.

for damages even in cases of innocent non-disclosure)[30] given that the courts will be able to determine the boundaries of this tort. Ultimately, a policy decision needs to be made as to the desirability of a new tort allowing damages when the insurer is in breach of his obligation to observe good faith at the pre-contractual stage; but it is submitted that the conditions are rather different than they were 25 years ago when *Banque Financière* was decided, and the changes made to the MIA 1906 could pave the way for a different outcome on the matter.

3.3 Post-contractual duty of good faith of the insurer

3.3.1 Role of good faith doctrine in implying obligations on the insurer

It is commonly recognised that the good faith obligations of the parties do not come to an end after an insurance contract is concluded.[31] On several occasions, the courts have indicated that in cases where an insurer is granted a right to use his discretion by the contract, he is by virtue of the duty of good faith expected to exercise his discretion in a reasonable fashion without arbitrariness, capriciousness or perversity. In *Groom v Crocker*,[32] for example, there was no doubt that a liability insurer is under an implied duty to take into account the assured's interest in handling a claim and its defence. Sir Wilfrid Greene MR expressed the legal position in an emphatic fashion:[33]

> The right given to the insurers is to have control of proceedings in which they and the assured have a common interest – the assured because he is the defendant and the insurers because they are contractually bound to indemnify him. Each is interested in seeing that any judgment to be recovered against the assured shall be for as small a sum as possible. It is the assured upon whom the burden of the judgment will fall if the insurers are insolvent. The effect of the provisions in question is, I think, to give to the insurers the right to decide upon the proper tactics to pursue in the conduct of the action, provided that they do so in what they bona fide consider to be the common interest of themselves and their assured. But the insurers are in my opinion clearly not entitled to allow their judgment as to the best tactics to pursue to be influenced by the desire to obtain for themselves some advantage altogether outside the litigation in question with which the assured has no concern.[34]

---

30 This was a concern expressed by Slade LJ at the Court of Appeal [1990] 1 QB 665, at 780.

31 See *The Star Sea* [2001] UKHL 1; [2003] 1 AC 469 and *The Mercandian Continent* [2001] EWCA Civ 1275; [2001] 2 Lloyd's Rep 563.

32 [1939] 1 KB 194.

33 Ibid. at 203.

34 Similar sentiments have been echoed by Auld LJ in *Cormack v Washbourne* [2000] CLC 1039, at 1048. The same point was also made by Longmore LJ in *The Mercandian Continent* [2001] EWCA Civ 1275; [2001] 2 Lloyd's Rep 563 at [22] in the following fashion:

> Such other situations may arise under liability policies, particularly if the insurers decide to take over the insured's defence to a claim. Interests of the insured and the insurers may not be the same but they will be required to act in good faith towards each other. If for example the limit of indemnity includes sums awarded by way of damages, interest and costs, insurers may be tempted to run up costs and exceed the policy limit to the detriment of the insured. The insured's protection lies in the duty which the law imposes on the insurer to exercise his power to conduct the defence in good faith.

In a similar fashion, in the Scottish case *Fargnoli v GA Bonus plc*,[35] Lord Penrose expressed the view that mutuality of the obligation of good faith would require an insurer at the claims stage not to delay in bad faith an admission of liability for the settlement of claims which he would objectively be obliged to admit before a court to be valid, or which might prevent the insurer from advancing knowingly spurious defences to a claim or putting the assured to proof of what he already knows to be true. Lord Penrose was adamant that an insurer would be held to be in repudiatory breach of the contract in case of breach of this duty, again pointing to the prospect of the insurer's duty of good faith implying a contractual obligation on the assured.[36]

The general feeling is that such an obligation is imposed on the insurer as a matter of law, perhaps in this context as a direct result of the insurer's mutual obligation of good faith.[37] It is, however, worth noting that no mention is made of s. 17 of the MIA 1906 in the relevant authorities. That could be due to the fact that such an obligation is implied by law in most contracts in cases where a discretion is conferred upon one of the parties and, therefore, it is not unique to insurance law. For example, in *Socimer International Bank Ltd v Standard Bank London Ltd*,[38] where a contract for the sale of assets between banks entrusted the task of valuation to one party, the Court of Appeal noted that the decision-maker's discretion will be limited "as a matter of necessary implication", as the decisions would have an effect on both parties; accordingly, there is a "need for the absence of arbitrariness, capriciousness, perversity and irrationality".[39] Similarly, in *Paragon Finance plc v Nash*,[40] where the lender was given a discretion to vary the interest rate, it was held by the Court of Appeal that the discretion is subject to an implied term that "the rates of interest would not be set dishonestly, for an improper purpose, capriciously or arbitrarily".[41] It is evident from the authorities that the scope of an implied term will depend on the circumstances of the particular contract, and that could explain why in *Fargnoli v GA Bonus plc* the court indicated that the insurer must avoid acting in bad faith at the claims stage, while the degree of co-operation required from the insurer in *Groom v Crocker* was slightly more onerous. In any event, it is crystal clear that despite reference to the "mutual duty of good faith" in several cases, the source of this implied term in insurance contracts is not s. 17, so amendment to the statutory provision is unlikely to lead to any change. The case law on the subject will continue to evolve regardless.

A related but slightly different issue is the role that good faith could play in the process of implying a term into the insurance as part of the "business efficacy"

35 [1997] CLC 653, at 670–671.

36 Similar sentiments have also been echoed by HHJ Kershaw QC in *Transthene Packgaging Co Ltd v Royal Insurance (UK) Ltd* [1996] LRLR 32, at 39.

37 *Eagle Star Insurance Co Ltd v Cresswell & Ors* [2004] EWCA Civ 602; [2004] Lloyd's Rep IR 537, at [54] per Rix LJ.

38 [2008] EWCA Civ 116; [2008] 1 Lloyd's Rep 558.

39 Ibid. at [66] per Rix LJ.

40 [2001] EWCA Civ 1466; [2002] 1 WLR 685.

41 Ibid. at [36] per Dyson LJ. See also *Horkulak v Cantor Fitzgerald International* [2004] EWCA Civ 1287; [2005] ICR 402.

test. The courts are willing to add a term into a contract when they reach the conclusion that the contract in question will not work in the absence of such term, so it is necessary to imply that term to give efficacy to the contract in the business sense.[42] In a number of authorities the continuing duty of good faith has been regarded as an additional reason for implying a term into the contract in question. For example, in *Phoenix General Insurance Co of Greece SA v Halvanon Insurance Co Ltd*[43] it was held that in a reinsurance treaty the reinsurer had an implied right to the reassured's records insofar as they related to the covered business. Hobhouse J put it in the following way:[44]

> The relevant terms have to be implied primarily so that the reassured shall conduct his business in a proper and business-like fashion, but, for the present purpose, so that the reinsurer may also be able to find out what his rights are . . . there is no ground for curtailing the obligation which would probably be imported anyway by the duty of good faith and which could also be enforced by way of discovery and inspection in any subsequent litigation.

In similar fashion, in *Goshawk Dedicated Ltd v Tyser & Co Ltd*,[45] the Court of Appeal was prepared to imply a term into the contract between the Syndicates and the assureds giving the claimant, a Lloyd's Syndicate, a right to inspect and take copies of placing and claiming documents held by the brokers. Rix LJ, who delivered the judgment of the court, indicated that although the implication was to be made on the traditional basis that it is necessary for business efficacy, the doctrine of good faith that applies in the insurance context supported that conclusion.[46]

Although the two examples above relate to the insurer's rights against the assured, there is no doubt that in appropriate insurances – in particular, liability policies where the insurer assumes the control of the litigation – the continuing duty of good faith could form one of the justifications for implying a term into the contract setting out the obligations of the insurer. This is a role that the doctrine of utmost good faith has played prior to the amendment in s. 17 of the MIA 1906, and there is no reason to assume that the statutory amendment would lead to any change. The fact that the duty of good faith continues throughout the policy period in an insurance contract could be a critical factor in determining whether it is necessary to imply a particular term into the contract or not.

42 See *Liverpool City Council v Irwin* [1977] AC 239, at 254 and 262; and *Tai Hing Cotton Mill Ltd v Liu Chong Hing Bank Ltd* [1986] AC 80 at 106. The Privy Council in *Attorney General of Belize and others v Belize Telecom Ltd and another* [2009] UKPC 11 expressed the view that the proper test for deciding whether or not a term should be implied into a contract was whether it would spell out, in express words, what the contract, read against the relevant background, would reasonably be understood to mean. On that basis, it was stressed that the business efficacy test was no more than a reformulation of that question and therefore should not be treated as being a different or additional test.

43 [1985] 2 Lloyd's Rep 599.

44 Ibid. at 614.

45 [2006] EWCA Civ 54; [2006] 1 Lloyd's Rep 566.

46 Ibid. at [53]. See also *Bonner v Cox* [2005] EWCA Civ 1512; [2006] 2 Lloyd's Rep 152; and *Goshawk Dedicated Ltd v Tyser & Co Ltd* [2006] EWCA Civ 54; [2006] 1 Lloyd's Rep 566.

3.3.2 Using good faith to restrict rights of insurers

In a number of authorities, it has been indicated that the insurer might be precluded from exercising an apparent right (e.g. the right to avoid the policy) if it is evident that the insurer has not acted in good faith whilst exercising the remedy. It was Colman J in *Strive Shipping Corporation v Hellenic Mutual War Risks Association (Bermuda) Ltd (The Grecia Express)*[47] who first brought this debate into the limelight, by suggesting that the continuing duty of good faith might place constraints on the insurer's right to avoid an insurance policy due to the assured's pre-contractual breaches of utmost good faith.[48] In that case, insurers sought to avoid a marine policy on the grounds that at the time of renewal the assured failed to disclose the fact that there were suspicious circumstances which connected the assured with previous marine casualties. Colman J held that the previous losses were not, in fact, suspicious and thus not material. However, his additional observations on the matter were very interesting. He went on to say, *obiter dictum*, that even though the suspicious circumstances may have been material facts at the inception of the policy requiring their disclosure, it would be unconscionable and contrary to the insurer's continuing duty of good faith if the insurer were to be allowed to avoid the policy based on those facts which had not been disclosed and which had been proved at the date of the purported avoidance not to have been true.[49] If it proves possible to make an inroad into the equitable concept of "unconscionability", the corollary of such a development is that the courts might be given discretion to overturn a purported avoidance at a trial stage.[50]

A similar theme is apparent in *Drake Insurance plc v Provident Insurance plc.*[51] The primary focus of the case was a contribution action for double insurance between two insurers; but to determine the outcome of that action it was vital to identify whether one of the insurers, namely Provident, was entitled to avoid the motor insurance policy for non-disclosure of the assured, Dr Singh. When renewing his insurance policy, Dr Singh informed his brokers of the fact that his wife, who was a named driver on the policy, was involved in an accident. This was a non-fault incident, as the car had been hit in the rear by a third party; but the incident was recorded as a fault incident on the broker's computer system until the claim was settled in Dr Singh's wife's favour. However, Dr Singh forgot to inform his brokers that he had received an SP30 speeding conviction and that his wife's claim had now been settled in her favour. Under the ranking system

47 [2002] EWHC 203 (Comm); [2002] 2 Lloyd's Rep 88.

48 There are hints in some previous authorities that the right to avoid may be fettered by a requirement of good faith. Most emphatically in *Pan Atlantic Insurance Co Ltd v Pine Top Insurance Co Ltd* [1995] 1 AC 501, at 555, Lord Lloyd stipulated: "the obligation of good faith [is not] limited to one of disclosure. As Lord Mansfield said in Carter v. Boehm, at p. 1908, there may be circumstances in which an insurer, by asserting a right to avoid for non-disclosure, would himself be guilty of want of good faith."

49 Paras. [129], [133] and [154].

50 It was convincingly argued by Professor Clarke that good faith and unconscionability should act as bars to the remedy of avoidance in some instances: "Recession: A Bridge too Far for Insurance Good Faith?" [2012] LMCLQ 611.

51 [2003] EWCA Civ 1834; [2004] 1 Lloyd's Rep 268.

operated by Provident, the conviction of Dr Singh would not have affected the quote if the accident of Dr Singh's wife had been reclassified as non-fault. At a later stage, Provident became aware of the speeding conviction and sought to avoid the policy for non-disclosure. It was held by the Court of Appeal that Provident could not avoid the policy. Had Provident made further investigations prior to avoiding the policy, it would have become apparent to them that the earlier accident had not been the fault of Dr Singh's wife and ought to have been left out in fixing the premium, thereby rendering the conviction alone incapable of affecting the premium.

Few would disagree with the outcome of the case, but what makes the judgment rather interesting is the fact that there are fundamental differences in the reasoning adopted by the judges. Rix and Clarke LJJ based their decision on the finding that the insurer had not been induced by the non-disclosure of the speeding conviction to enter into the contract, given that the accident that Dr Singh's wife was involved in was a non-fault accident and therefore its non-disclosure could not have had any impact on the quote of the Provident under their grading system. This is a rational stand to take and was adequate to dispose the case before them. However, their Lordships went on to make observations on the impact of the insurer's continuing duty of good faith in this context. Their view was that the continuing duty of good faith would prevent the insurer from avoiding the contract if the insurer, with the knowledge (including knowledge in the shape of turning a blind eye) of the "non-fault" accident, nevertheless attempted to avoid the policy.[52] Adopting this test, their Lordships were satisfied that avoidance in the present case had not been made in bad faith. Pill LJ, on the other hand, took a rather different stance on the matter. In his view, the continuing duty of good faith required the insurer at least to make an enquiry of the assured, offering him an opportunity to update the insurer on the accident. He continued:[53]

> All that was required was a simple enquiry as to what had happened in relation to that accident. If more than lip service is to be paid to the principle that an insurer shall show the utmost good faith, the principle in my judgment required that enquiry to be made before the "wholly one-sided" remedy of avoidance was exercised.

The majority was sympathetic to the sentiments expressed in the judgment of Pill LJ, but felt that it was a bridge too far, and Clarke LJ stressed the fact that there was no authority for the proposition that an insurer owes a duty of care to the assured to take reasonable care to make proper inquiries before avoiding the policy.[54] One should also not lose sight of the fact that Mance LJ, *obiter dictum*, in *Brotherton v Aseguradora Colseguros SA (No 2)*[55] expressed the view that, even if there may be some support for the idea that the insurer's good faith can be taken into account where allegations that a prudent insurer would have wanted to know

52 Ibid. at [91] per Rix LJ, and at [177] per Clarke LJ. Interestingly, both of their Lordships indicated that their observations on the role of good faith should not be regarded as part of their judgment.

53 Ibid. at [177].

54 Ibid. at [145].

55 [2003] EWHC 335 (Comm); [2003] EWCA Civ 705; [2003] Lloyd's Rep IR 746 (CA).

about would have proven to be untrue by the time the insurer sought to avoid, this could not be applied in a case where reinsurers did not at the time of avoidance accept or know for certain of the incorrectness of the intelligence constituting the basis of their avoidance. Furthermore, he was of the view that the mere fact that a right to rescind has an equitable origin does not mean that its exercise is only possible if it is consistent with good faith or with a court's view of what is conscionable.[56]

It is undisputable that the law in this area is uncertain. Despite its long history, unconscionability is relatively underdeveloped in English law. The doctrine is a broad one covering all equitable intervention, whether based on dishonesty, breach of contract or the simple innocent receipt by a donee of trust property. It is possible that Colman J was suggesting that acting in bad faith when exercising the right of avoidance amounts to unconscionable conduct, allowing the court to protect the assured (who is in a vulnerable position) by preventing the insurer from utilising this self-help remedy.[57] Regardless of the juristic origin of the duty of disclosure in insurance law, in particular whether or to what extent the origin is equitable and what role the common law played, one feels that the two prerequisites of the equitable doctrine of unconscionability, namely, the complainant's weakness and the defendant's unconscionable conduct, could be satisfied especially if the insurer acting in bad faith attempts to rely on a self-help remedy (i.e. if he knows, or is in a position to know, that he should not rely on that remedy).

Equally, the common law is well equipped to deal with a situation where an insurer in contravention of the principle of fair dealing attempts to avoid an insurance contract in the knowledge that no right of avoidance arises in the circumstances. The general principles of common law would naturally prevent the insurer in those circumstances from avoiding the contract, given that it is one of the fundamental principles of common law that everyone must act honestly towards others with whom one deals. That principle is of universal application in the common law and it does not depend on the existence of a relationship between parties based on good faith; but the fact that an insurance contract is based on mutual utmost good faith might be a relevant factor in the minds of the judges who might be tempted to use the doctrine as a bar to the insurer's right to avoid the policy.[58]

Despite uncertainties surrounding the concept, it is submitted that the removal of "avoidance" as a remedy from the scope of s. 17 of the MIA 1906 is likely to yield positive results. This might allow courts to develop the concept further with the aid of the mutual duty of good faith by adopting entirely new remedies depending on different circumstances. It is true that with the introduction by the 2015 Act of proportionate remedies for breach of the assured's pre-contractual breach of good faith, instances in which the insurer will be allowed to "avoid" the contract

56 Ibid. at [34].

57 Conduct which is clearly against the "public policy" of the forum is sometimes described as "unconscionable conduct". See, for example, *Re Fuld (No 3)* [1968], at 698, per Scarman J.

58 This would also be consonant with the views of the majority, Rix and Clarke LJJ, expressed in *Drake Insurance plc v Provident Insurance*.

will be restricted. However, one might envisage situations where it might be necessary for the courts to intervene. For example, imagine that an insurer attempts to decline liability by using the erroneous description of the subject matter of insurance at a later stage in a case where he realises that the assured mistakenly misstated the identity of the insurance.[59] In that situation, it is possible that the insurer might be prevented from raising this defence on the premise that this would amount to breach of the insurer's duty of utmost good faith. It can also be possible that an insurer might be prevented from using its superior bargaining power to extract a disadvantageous settlement from the assured.[60]

In summary, authorities have been receptive to the idea of using the utmost good faith doctrine, without attempting to define its boundaries, to prevent an insurer from acting unreasonably at the post-contractual stage. The scope of the doctrine in this context is far from being clear, but it is, at least, indisputable that an insurer attempting to rely on a remedy in the knowledge that he has no such remedy in the circumstances will be prevented from doing so. Regardless of the origin of this legal remedy (i.e. whether it stems from common law or equity), it is an indisputable fact that no reference to s. 17 of the MIA 1906 has been made by judges who have elaborated the matter so far. On that basis, it is not fanciful to suggest that there is no reason why the concept will not be developed further by reference to the statement made in s. 17 of the MIA 1906, to the effect that an insurance contract is a contract based upon utmost good faith.

3.4 Concluding remarks

Although it has received widespread acceptance that the duty of utmost good faith is mutual in nature, the development of the insurer's duty of good faith has been hampered due to the fact that s. 17 has been viewed as the source of that duty, bringing the unfitting remedy of "avoidance" into play in case of its breach. It is submitted that the change introduced in the wording of this statutory provision could potentially open the door for the courts to engage in a more sober analysis of the origins and nature of this duty.

There is no obstacle any more for the courts which might be minded to penalise an insurer who fails to draw the attention of the assured to limitations of coverage offered by the policy by tracing the origins of the concept of good faith to common law, as its historical setting suggests.[61] This would still require the judges to utilise by analogy the rules set out by the 2015 Act on the assured's duty of fair presentation in determining the scope of the doctrine, but this should not pose any problem. More fundamentally, this kind of analysis will facilitate the introduction of new remedies, such as damages, which will yield a practical benefit to an

59 In that case, the insurer could potentially argue that the policy has never attached. See *AF Watkinson & Co Ltd v Hullett* (1938) 61 LILR 145.

60 See the comments of Rix J in *Royal Boskalis Westminister NV v Mountain* [1997] LRLR 523, at 600.

61 See, for example, *Kelly v New Zealand Insurance Co Ltd* 1996 9 ANZ Ins Cas 61–317 (FCWA).

assured who is harmed by his insurer's failure to observe good faith at the pre-contractual stage.

In the post-contractual context, the duty could be useful in determining whether there is a need to imply a term in the contract to protect the interests of the assured. In a similar vein, an insurer who decides to rely on a contractual right in an unreasonable fashion[62] might be prevented from doing so by general principles of common law, and even perhaps through the intervention of equity principles.

These developments should not be viewed as extraordinary or exceptional. In other types of contracts where parties are expected to observe good faith, courts seem to be happy to contemplate various remedies in case of breach of such obligations. For example, in partnership contracts, parties acting in bad faith could be prevented from pleading what would otherwise amount to a defence to a claim.[63] In insurance contracts, the law should have developed in a similar fashion, but for many years s. 17 and the remedy of "avoidance" has halted any attempt to develop the doctrine of utmost good faith of the insurer. Now the path has been cleared, and one should not be surprised to see the doctrine evolving at the hands of the judiciary in the years to come.

62 See, for example, *Massoud v NRMA Insurance* (1995) 62 NSWLR 657.
63 *Clements v Hall* (1858) 2 De. G & J 173.

CHAPTER 4

The future of warranties and other related terms in contracts of insurance

*Professor Malcolm Clarke**

4.1 Introduction

When the Insurance Act 2015 comes into force on 12 August 2016 for contracts concluded after that date,[1] it will affect warranties and similar clauses in insurance policies. In particular, the Act banishes "basis" clauses.[2] Although basis clauses were well established in the courts as being what the parties intended, it was difficult to square them with the notion underlying the parol evidence rule, that a document such as an insurance policy which looks like the whole of the contract should be treated as the whole of the contract and as being therefore exclusive of matters not recorded in the policy. It was also difficult to square them with the expectations of reasonable insurance applicants; hence, as far back as 1942 basis clauses were described as "traps" for the unwary.[3]

Now, by section 9(2) of the 2015 Act, a representation by an applicant even for non-consumer insurance "is not capable of being converted into a warranty by any provision" of the contract.[4] Moreover, the effect of section 10 of the Act is that for certain periods of time (and for both consumer and non-consumer contracts) breach of warranty will suspend rather than discharge the insurer's liability.[5]

Although insurers defended them with determination,[6] few outside the industry will lament the demise of the common law warranty; warranties have been a

* Emeritus Professor of Law, Cambridge University.

1 The Act is the outcome of nine years of consultation by the Law Commission and Scottish Law Commission. The provisions in the 2015 Act affecting consumer insurance will be mandatory while the Act provides a default statutory regime for non-consumer insurance contracts.

2 Enforced e.g. in *Provincial Insurance Co Ltd v Morgan* [1933] AC 240, at 252; and recently in *Genesis Housing Association Ltd v Liberty Syndicate Management Ltd* [2013] EWCA Civ 1173. An example, taken from *Dawsons v Bonnins Ltd* [1922] 2 AC 413, is a policy clause that refers to a proposal of a given date, "which proposal shall be the basis of the contract and be held as incorporated herein".

3 *Zurich General Accident & Liability Ins Co Ltd v Morrison* [1942] 2 KB 53, at 58 (CA).

4 For consumers the law was changed by the Consumer Insurance (Disclosure and Representations) Act 2012, notably section 6; and note also the Australian Insurance Contracts Act 1984 (Cth), section 24: an insurer may not elevate a statement made by the insured about the existence of a state of affairs to the status of warranty.

5 "The notion of suspension of the risk draws on a line of common law authority which drew a distinction between a warranty proper, breach of which rendered it irremediable, and a term which merely described the risk run by the insurer so that the insurer was only liable if the risk was as described": R.M. Merkin and M. Hemsworth, *Motor Insurance* (2nd edn), (Sweet & Maxwell, 2015), 2–103.

6 See e.g. *Thomson v Weems* (1884) 9 App Cas 671, at 683, *per* Lord Blackburn.

troublesome feature of English insurance law.[7] When assessing the scope of cover it has been often difficult to distinguish them from exceptions or exclusions.[8] Moreover, the absolute nature of common law warranties[9] was such that if, for example, a warranty of temperance had been broken in January, the life insurer could refuse to pay if the insured died in March completely sober.[10] Unsurprisingly, insurance lawyers in other parts of Europe were determined to eschew anything like the English warranty.[11]

The absolute character of the common law has already been eroded by the *Insurance: New Conduct of Business Sourcebook* (ICOBS). Rule 8.1.1 states that insurers must not "unreasonably reject a claim (including by terminating or avoiding a policy)"; and that "rejection of a consumer policy-holder's claim is unreasonable, except where there is evidence of fraud, if it is for . . . breach of warranty or condition" unless the breach and claim are factually connected.

4.2 The Insurance Act 2015, part 3

Part 3 of the Act (sections 9 to 11) is headed "Warranties and other terms". Warranties are not defined, the assumption apparently being that the likely reader knows the much cited dictum of Lord Mansfield that a warranty is "a condition on which the contract is founded",[12] or that of Lord Goff that a warranty is any term of an insurance contract which, properly construed, is "a condition precedent to the liability or further liability of the insurer".[13]

Section 9 applies to representations made by the insured, and section 9(2) provides that such a "representation is not capable of being converted into a warranty by means of any provision of the non-consumer insurance contract" to which the Act applies, "or of any other contract (and whether the representation to form the basis of the contract or otherwise)".

7 Entire books have been published on them, such as B. Soyer, *Warranties in Marine Insurance*, now in its second edition (Routledge, 2006). A new edition of this book is expected to be published in 2016.

8 See M. Clarke, *The Law of Insurance Contracts* (Informa Law, 2016), 20–1.

9 See Clarke, above, 20–3.

10 *Thomson v Weems* (1884) 9 App Cas 671, at 685, *per* Lord Blackburn. Cf. the USA where the trend has been not to grant "forfeiture" unless there was causal connection between breach of warranty and loss. Most states have "antitechnical" statutes, whereby "policy provisions; misrepresentations; warranties; conditions" do not defeat the policy unless breach contributed to loss. Even in England, recently a clause has been given a "sensible" construction, with the effect that a causal connection was required between breach and loss: *Bennett v Axa* [2003] EWHC 86 (Comm); [2004] Lloyd's Rep IR 615.

11 See J. Basedow *et al.* (eds), *Principles of European Insurance Contract Law* (2nd edn), (Schmidt, 2015), Art. 4:101. The authors grasped the nettle and provided for "precautionary measures": a precautionary measure is "a clause in the insurance contract, whether or not described as condition precedent to the liability of the insurer, requiring the policy holder or the insured, before the insured event occurs, to perform or not to perform certain acts"; and it was then stipulated that a "clause . . . that in the event of non-compliance with a precautionary clause the insurer shall be entitled to terminate the contract, shall be without effect" unless the breach was done "with intent to cause the loss or recklessly and with knowledge that the loss would probably result": Art. 4:102(1).

12 *Bean v Stupart* (1778) 1 Doug 11, at 14.

13 *Bank of Nova Scotia v Hellenic Mutual War Risks Assn (Bermuda) (The Good Luck)* [1992] 1 AC 233, at 263.

This leads to section 10, sub-headed "Breach of warranty", which provides in section 10(1) that any "rule of law that breach of a warranty (express or implied) in a contract of insurance results in the discharge of the insurer's liability under the contract is abolished". The rest of section 10 sets out the revised consequences of breach; see below, 4.3.

Section 11 of the Act is sub-headed "Terms not relevant to the actual loss". These are terms "other than a term defining the risk as a whole,[14] if compliance with it would tend to reduce the risk [of] (a) loss of a particular kind, (b) loss at a particular location, [or] (c) loss at a particular time" (section 11(1)). In relation to such terms, section 11(2) provides that if "a loss occurs, and the term has not been complied with, the insurer may not rely on the non-compliance to exclude, limit or discharge its liability under the contract" if the insured latter shows that "the non-compliance with the term could not have increased the risk of the loss which actually occurred in the circumstances in which it occurred": section 11(3).

The purpose of section 11 is to ensure that the absolute rule at common law cannot be revived.[15] However, that is not certain, or beyond argument. Suppose breach of a term about the storage of waste outside a supermarket and then a fire caused by an electrical fault inside the supermarket. The insured would argue that there was no (causal) connection between the breach outside and the fire inside, whereas the insurer might argue that the term was aimed at preventing fire, wherever it might occur on the premises; so, the insured gets nothing unless it can prove that the breach "could not have increased the risk of the loss which actually occurred", i.e. the fire inside.

Given the (high) profile of the common law (absolute) rule, some commentators expected (and have been searching for) a causal connection requirement in the 2015 Act,[16] even implicitly, extrapolating from section 11. However, given the (high) profile of the rule, a change in the law by implication is surely unlikely. Indeed, although an express causal rule was suggested by the Law Commission in the past, having thought about it again, in 2014 the Law Commission rejected the idea, accepting opposition "on the grounds of increased investigation costs, complex litigation, uncertain outcomes, and difficulties of proof".[17] Moreover, the Commission accepted that "a causation test would not be appropriate for all warranties, since some may be relevant to the loss without having a causal connection with it. For example, a past claim does not cause (or even contribute to) a future claim, but it may be highly relevant to the insurer's assessment of the likelihood

14 For example, travel insurance worldwide, except travel in the USA.

15 Section 11 "prevents reliance by the insurers on specific risk clauses which are not risk defining": R.M. Merkin and M. Hemsworth, above, 3–63; and defeats the "whilst" cases, such as that whereby the insurer is not liable while the insured is under the influence of liquor, provided that the insured can show that non-compliance could not have increased the actual loss: section 11(3).

16 Especially in Europe; see J. Basedow *et al.* (eds), *Principles of European Insurance Contract Law* (2nd edn) (Schmidt, 2015), Art. 4:103 note 2.

17 Law Com No 353/Scots Law Com No 238, para 14.24. It noted (para 14.26) the experience of such a rule in New Zealand and the "difficulties" found there with the rule.

of future claims."[18] That is correct but it is also reminiscent of the respect for the language used to justify warranties in centuries past.[19] Underlying this debate, it is submitted, is the question of the appropriate allocation of risk. The fair presentation rule (section 3 of the Act) requires care on the part of applicants, but there is nothing requiring care by insurers in deciding who or what to cover – nothing in the Act. So, the question remains: can they really be allowed to use breach of warranty as an excuse for terminating cover during the insurance period because of "the likelihood of future claims"?[20]

On the question of carelessness on the part of a representee (here the insurer), people are usually referred (in general contract law) to *Redgrave v Hurd.*[21] However, *Redgrave v Hurd* can be explained on the basis that the representor in that case (a doctor) should himself have been much better informed than the misrepresentee (buying the doctor's practice) about relevant documents in the doctor's possession, so the carelessness of the misrepresentee could be excused. In cases such as *Redgrave v Hurd*, courts are "balancing the equities"[22] case by case; the question in each case is whether the risk should be allocated to the representor or the representee. The answer depends on various factors, notably which party was actually or potentially better informed. In the world of insurance today, that will often be the insurer. This being so, surely, insurers should not be allowed to terminate cover prematurely because their policyholder turns out to be likely to make more claims than expected.

4.3 Breach of warranty

The Act does not abolish warranties but seeks to mitigate the consequences of their breach. Section 10(2) provides that an insurer has no liability for "any loss occurring or attributable to something happening, after a warranty (express or implied) in the contract has been breached but before the breach has been remedied". According to section 10(3), however, section 10(2) does not apply in three situations.

The first is where "the warranty ceases to be applicable to the circumstances of the contract" because the circumstances have changed. This exception can be traced back to one in the Marine Insurance Act 1906, section 34(1).[23] "According to the drafter of the [1906] Act, if, during war, a warranty to sail with a convoy at a future time from some foreign station was inserted, the intervention of peace before the period at which the ship was so to sail would excuse the necessity of

---

18 Ibid.

19 See *Thomson v Weems* (1884) 9 App Cas 671, at 683, *per* Lord Blackburn; and *Dawsons Ltd v Bonnin* [1922] 2 AC 413, at 423 *per* Viscount Haldane.

20 *Shaw v Robberds* (1837) 6 Ad & E 75, at 84, *per* Lord Denman CJ; *Cornish v Accident Ins Co* (1889) 23 QBD 453, at 457, *per* Lindley LJ (CA).

21 (1881) 20 Ch D 1, CA; *contra,* e.g. *McInerney v Lloyds Bank Ltd* [1974] 1 Lloyd's Rep 246, at 254, *per* Lord Denning MR (CA).

22 *Butterworth's Law of Contract* (4th edn, 2010) 4.42. See, e.g. *Peekay Intermark Ltd v ANZ Banking Group Ltd* [2006] EWCA Civ 386; [2006] 2 Lloyd's Rep 511; and *Kyle Bay Ltd (t/a Astons Night Club) v Underwriters* [2007] EWCA Civ 57; [2007] Lloyd's Rep IR 460, at [35], *per* Neuberger LJ.

23 See the Law Commission Report No. 353, para 17.64.

compliance."[24] This relatively clear example, which derives from "the celebrated maxim *cessante ratione, cessat lex*",[25] has been given both before and since; however, "it may not be so obvious why the insurer required the warranty",[26] and whether the circumstances have sufficiently changed. The maxim *cessante ratione, cessat lex* has never been easy to apply.

The second situation is where "compliance with the warranty is rendered unlawful by any subsequent law", a matter of interpretation of the law in question.[27]

The third is where "the insurer waives the breach of warranty". Waiver is a much litigated area of insurance contract law,[28] and precedent (a decision of the House of Lords in 1991) indicated what was meant by waiver: where one party clearly abandons or relinquishes a contractual right, such as the right to exercise a remedy; here, the right to terminate the contract for breach of warranty.[29] However, the picture of precedent in the insurance context was later clouded when commentators (on another decision of the House of Lords) saw "waiver by estoppel".[30]

4.4 Breach remedied?

If a warranty has been broken,[31] doubt may well arise over whether, as stipulated in section 10(2), it has been remedied. A "clean January" does say something about the rest of the year, but suppose a warranty against the consumption of narcotics – when can it be said that a breach has been remedied? Clearly, sometimes it will not be possible; the Law Commission gave the example of a house warranted to be of construction XX where it is not.[32]

According to section 10(5), a breach "is to be taken as remedied (a) in a case falling within subsection (6), if the risk to which the warranty relates later becomes essentially the same as that originally contemplated by the parties, (b) in any other case, if the insured ceases to be in breach of the warranty".

Clearly, (b) may not answer the narcotics question; and (a) does not help either because cases only fall within subsection (6) if the warranty requires something to be done "by an ascertainable time" and, as it stipulates in section 10(5), the relevant risk "later becomes essentially the same as that originally contemplated". If an insurer has thought fit to include a warranty about narcotics, how likely is that?

24 B. Soyer, *Warranties in Marine Insurance* (2nd edn), (Routledge, 2006) at 5.13.

25 Soyer, above.

26 F.D. Rose, *Marine Insurance: Law and Practice* (2nd edn), (Informa, 2012) at 9.47.

27 Sometimes tricky; see E. Peel (ed), *Trietel: The Law of Contract* (13th edn), (Sweet & Maxwell, 2011) ch. 11; and Clarke, above, 24–1 ff.

28 See Clarke, above, 23–11.

29 See Clarke, above, 23–11 ff., which refers to *The Kanchenjunga* [1990] 1 Lloyd's Rep 391, at 397 (HL).

30 *The Good Luck*, above; see, for example, Clarke, above, 20–7.

31 As regards whether a warranty has been broken, something that may not be clear, see Clarke, above, 20–B1 and 20–5A.

32 Law Com Report No 353, para 17.49.

4.5 Conclusion

The insurer must respond, in accordance with its insurance contract, if insured loss occurs before the breach of warranty or after the breach has been remedied: section 10(4).[33] However, in the interim, section 10(2) applies: the insurer has no liability. The old common law idea, articulated by Lord Blackburn, has not changed. It is still "competent to the contracting parties, if both agree to it . . . to make the existence of anything a condition precedent to the inception of any contract; and if they do so, non-fulfilment is a good defence".[34] Thus the German soccer player in London wondering about seeking insurance in the UK for the Porsche he needs to go to his training ground is unlikely to get any more encouragement from his lawyer now than in the past.

33 Where "the risk is not altered following a remedy of a breach, we see no reason why the insurer should not be back on risk and liable for any loss": Law Com Report No 353, para 17.37.

34 Lord Blackburn in *Thomson v Weems* (1884) 9 App Cas 671, at 683, cited with approval by Viscount Haldane in *Dawsons Ltd v Bonnin* [1922] 2 AC 413, at 423.

CHAPTER 5

Remedies for fraudulent claims under the Insurance Act 2015

Simon Rainey QC and David Walsh***

5.1 Introduction

Fraud on the part of an insured in the making of a claim under a policy of insurance is a problem which has long bedevilled the insurance industry. It has reached epidemic proportions, particularly in the consumer field, leading to the creation in 2012 of the Insurance Fraud Enforcement Department and of the Association of British Insurers' own fraud database in its Insurance Fraud Register. The Association of British Insurers reported that insurers uncovered over 118,500 fraudulent claims in 2013.[1] The value of these claims was £1.3 billion; many more will, of course, have gone undetected.

From the fully fledged scheme to engineer a wholly false claim at one end of the spectrum to the seemingly irresistible temptation to an insured who has an otherwise good claim for an accident or event covered under the policy to "add" to the claim or to bolster the claim with some further "supporting" documentation at the other, the ingenuity of the dishonest insured is amply demonstrated in the authorities.

It was, therefore, unsurprising that the Law Commission's review into the law governing business insurance contracts included an assessment of the law related to fraudulent claims and particularly the remedies available to underwriters in such circumstances. The Commission's review was timely, not only because of the prevalence of insurance fraud but also because a number of cases have demonstrated the considerable uncertainty as to the insurer's remedies in the case of a fraudulent claim and as to the legal basis upon which the entitlement to that remedy falls to be determined.

In one sense, the position ought to have been straightforward. A contract of insurance is one *uberrimae fidei*, with insured and insurer owing to each other mutual duties of the utmost good faith both before the contract of insurance is concluded and thereafter in the performance of the contract. The perpetration

* Barrister at Quadrant Chambers, London; Honorary Professor of Business, Law and Economics at the University of Swansea, former visiting research fellow at the Institute of International Shipping and Trade Law, University of Swansea.

** Barrister at Quadrant Chambers, London.

1 ABI, "Insurance cheats feel the heat: value of fraudulent claims uncovered by insurers hits record level" (30 May 2014) (https://www.abi.org.uk/News/News-releases/2014/05/Insurance-cheats-feel-the-heat-value-of-fraudulent-claims-uncovered-by-insurers-hits-record-level) (last visited 1 February 2016).

of a fraud upon the insurer by the insured to extract money from the insurer in circumstances where it is not properly due under the contract, whether wholesale or partial and whether by the use of fraudulent devices to mislead the insurer or not, is the clearest possible instance of bad faith and of breach of that obligation.

Section 17 of the Marine Insurance Act 1906 (referred to herein as "the 1906 Act") dealt with this situation expressly and imposed unambiguously one simple albeit draconian remedy: "A contract of marine insurance is a contract based upon the utmost good faith, and, if the utmost good faith be not observed by either party, the contract may be avoided by the other party." *Fraus omnia corrumpit* or taints and vitiates all[2] and the insured has only himself to blame if the contract of insurance is avoided *ab initio* and all benefits received by him have to be disgorged to the insurer.

However, the very nature of the sole and absolute remedy in section 17 has led to the uncertainty as the courts sought to temper the remedy by fashioning a less radical result related more directly to the penalisation of the fraudulent claim itself and to find plausible intellectual routes for doing so notwithstanding the terms of section 17: for this reason, "[j]udges have struggled to characterise the rule [against fraudulent claims] in a way which escapes the full consequences of avoidance under section 17".[3]

This led to some juggling of the palpable bad faith involved in the making of a fraudulent claim on the one hand against the apparent availability in just such a case of the remedy of avoidance on the other. As Mance LJ expressed the position in one of the leading recent cases grappling with the consequences of fraud in the making of a claim, *Agapitos v Agnew (The Aegeon)*:[4]

> It has been said that the more cases there are endorsing a particular proposition, the shakier it may be (cf. Posner, The Problems of Jurisprudence, Harvard University Press, p. 83). The waves of insurance litigation over the last 20 years have involved repeated examination of the scope and application of any post-contractual duty of good faith. The opacity of the relevant principles – whether originating in venerable but cryptically reasoned common law cases or enshrined, apparently immutably, in s. 17 of the Marine Insurance Act, 1906 is matched only by the stringency of the sanctions assigned.

Therefore, far from being the straightforward, albeit stringent, solution that it might appear, section 17 had been seen as fettering the courts in their attempt to arrive at more just and proportionate sanctions for the making of a fraudulent claim. As it has been put:

2 See per Lord Bingham in *HIH Casualty & General Insurance Ltd v Chase Manhattan Bank* [2003] 2 Lloyd's Rep 61 at [15]: "fraud is a thing apart. This is not a mere slogan. It reflects an old legal rule that fraud unravels all: *fraus omnia corrumpit*. It also reflects the practical basis of commercial intercourse. Once fraud is proved, 'it vitiates judgments, contracts and all transactions whatsoever'." (Unravelling is a common paraphrase although not the precise translation of *corrumpere*.)

3 LC Issues Paper 7, para. 4.18. See also, B. Soyer, *Marine Insurance Fraud*, (Informa Law, 2014), at 3.87–3.88.

4 [2002] EWCA Civ 247; [2002] 2 Lloyd's Rep 42 at [1].

> The traditional elasticity of the common law, with its ability to attribute just solutions to individual disputes, has been constrained by the manner in which the principle of good faith has been codified by the Marine Insurance Act 1906, section 17 . . . There can be little doubt that, had the remedy for breach of good faith been codified more flexibly, the contours of contemporary law relating to fraudulent claims would be very different and much clearer.[5]

The resultant position, summarised by Mance LJ as "the present imperfect state of the law, fettered as it is by section 17",[6] was the understandable impetus behind the Law Commission's desire for reform in this area.[7]

The widespread reaction of those participating in the Law Commission's consultation[8] was that the need for simple and clear statutory provisions prescribing the remedies available to insurers for fraudulent claims was overwhelming. Out of 25 responses that addressed the question as to the need for legislative reform, all but four agreed that the law was unnecessarily complex and, of these, all but two thought that it would be helpful to introduce legislation to clarify insurers' remedies.

As the Law Commission noted, amongst those consultees who considered that the law was sufficiently clear on the decided case law as it stood, it was striking that, even then, there was a divergence of viewpoint as to *what* the law was:

> Interestingly, the consultees who argued that the law was clear disagreed about what the legal position was. An academic commentator thought that the remedy was clearly forfeiture of the claim, stating that "the common law rule following especially [*The Aegeon*] is a clear and incontrovertible part of English law". By contrast, two respondents argued that the "clear" legal position included the right to avoid: the remedies of avoidance and forfeiture continued to exist alongside each other.[9]

The lengthy process of review and consultation conducted by the Law Commission has culminated in legislation clarifying the position.[10] Sections 12 and 13 of the Insurance Act 2015 (referred to herein as "the Act") now provide a statutory framework for the remedies available to the insurer where the assured presents a fraudulent claim.

This chapter examines: first, the state of the law concerning the remedies for fraudulent claims prior to the introduction of the Act; second, the provisions of sections 12 and 13; and last, an assessment of the likely impact of those provisions.

5 D.R. Thomas, "Fraudulent insurance claims: definition, consequences and limitations" (2009) LMCLQ 485 at 515.

6 *Agapitos v Agnew (The Aegeon)* [2002] EWCA Civ 247; [2002] 2 Lloyd's Rep 42 at [45].

7 Answering Mance LJ's hope in *Agapitos v Agnew* that the post-contractual application of section 17 in the context of the making of claims be re-considered by the House of Lords or Parliament; see [13].

8 See, generally, LC Summary of Responses 2012.

9 LC Consultation Paper 201, paras. 7.6 and 7.7.

10 The Law Commission did not tackle the question of what constitutes a fraudulent claim and it has instead been left to the courts to determine. The remedies in the Act apply once fraud has been determined in accordance with common law principles. This issue is not, therefore, covered in this analysis.

5.2 The law on remedies for fraudulent claims pre-Act

5.2.1 The effect of the fraud upon the claim to which it relates

It has long been clear that the claim to which a fraud relates is wholly irrecoverable. The leading cases are *Levy v Baillie*,[11] *Goulstone v Royal Insurance Co*[12] and *Britton v Royal Insurance Co.*[13] In both *Goulstone* and *Britton*, the law was summarised in directions given to the jury by, respectively, Pollock CB and Willes J.

In *Goulstone*, where the alleged fraud on the insurers consisting of a misrepresentation as to the true value of furniture and chattels insured under a fire policy was bound up with a previous fraud by the assured upon creditors as to the value of his assets generally, Pollock CB directed the jury in these terms: "the question is whether the claim was fraudulent, i.e., whether it was wilfully false in any substantial respect",[14] the jury being directed that if that were made out the claim was to be dismissed as the assured would have "forfeited all benefit under the policy".

In *Britton*, where the assured under a fire policy was alleged to have set the fire himself, Willes J gave the following direction (emphasis added):[15]

> Of course, if the assured set fire to his house, he could not recover. That is clear. But it is not less clear that, even suppose that it were not wilful, yet as it is a contract of indemnity only, that is, if the claim is fraudulent, it is defeated altogether. That is, suppose the insured made a claim for twice the amount insured and lost, thus seeking to put the office off its guard, and in the result recover more than he is entitled to, that would be a wilful fraud, and the consequence is that he could not recover anything. This is a defence quite different from that of wilful arson. It gives the go-by to the origin of the fire, and it amounts to this – that the assured took advantage of the fire to make a fraudulent claim. The law upon such a case is in accordance with justice, and also with sound policy. The law is, that a person who has made such a fraudulent claim *could not be permitted to recover at all.* The contract of insurance is one of perfect good faith on both sides, and it is most important that such good faith should be maintained. It is the common practice to insert in fire policies conditions such that *they shall be void in the event of a fraudulent claim*; and there was such a condition in the present case. Such a condition is only in accordance with legal principle and sound policy. It would be most dangerous to permit parties to practise such frauds, and then, notwithstanding their falsehood and fraud in the claim, to recover the real value of the goods consumed. And if there is wilful falsehood and fraud in the claim, *the insured forfeits all claim upon the policy.*

It will be noted that the passage often cited from the direction is the opening passage, which is phrased in terms which relate only to the claim being made under the policy and to which the fraud itself relates and to that particular claim being "forfeited". However, while perhaps wider than was required for

11 7 Bing 349.
12 1 F & F 276.
13 4 F & F 905.
14 1 F & F 276 at 279.
15 4 F & F 905 at 910.

the case before him, concerned only with the recovery of a particular claim, Willes J went further (mirroring the common forms of clause then in use: see above). Read as a whole, the direction, like that of Pollock CB in shorter terms, is capable of being interpreted in a wider sense, as extending the vitiating effect of the fraud to any claim and to any benefit receivable or received under the policy. Similarly, the direction speaks in terms of the policy being void and can be read as being to the effect that, by reason of the duty of the utmost good faith which attaches to it, the common law treats a policy of insurance as subject to the same remedy of avoidance as was commonly inserted by express terms.

Subsequent cases confined the effect of *Goulstone* and *Britton* to a rule, (a) of common law separate and distinct from the duty of utmost good faith and section 17 of the 1906 Act,[16] and (b) which relates only to the claim itself, without any wider effect upon recovery generally under the policy or in respect of other claims independent of that which is tainted by the fraud.

In *Agapitos v Agnew*[17] the Court of Appeal had to consider the effect of the rule as to forfeiture of a claim made fraudulently (either in circumstances where no loss had been suffered at all or where an otherwise valid claim was exaggerated to claim a greater indemnity than was due) in the case where fraudulent means or devices ("fraudulent devices" for short) were used by the assured to promote a claim, which claim would otherwise have been in all other respects valid. Mance LJ, analysing the law to be derived from *Goulstone* and *Britton*, summarised it in terms which confined the operation of the forfeiture to the particular claim made as follows (emphasis supplied):[18]

> I turn to examine the scope of the rule and the section more closely. Where there is a fraudulent claim, *the law forfeits not only that which is known to be untrue, but also any genuine part of the claim*. In contrast, where the use of fraudulent devices occurs, the whole claim is by definition otherwise good. The present appeal raises for consideration whether, as a matter of policy, the underlying rationale of the fraudulent claim principle should extend to invalidate not merely the whole of a claim where part proves good, but the whole of a claim where the whole proves otherwise good. The word "proves" of course assumes that all aspects of the litigation proceed to trial, which, although common, is not inevitable. The effect of the fraudulent claim principle is that, once it is determined (which it may be by trial of a preliminary issue) *that part of a claim was false, the rest is forfeit, without it being essential to determine whether or not that rest itself related to genuine loss.*

The Court of Appeal held that similar principles applied to claims affected by the use of fraudulent devices as applied to claims made fraudulently because no loss or only a lesser loss than that being claimed for had been sustained.

---

16 In *Manifest Shipping Co Ltd v Uni-Polaris Shipping Co Ltd (The Star Sea)* [2001] UKHL 1; [2003] 1 AC 469, hereafter *The Star Sea,* and Lord Hobhouse's explanation of the purpose and origin of the principle as that of a separate rule of law at [51].

17 [2002] EWCA Civ 247; [2002] 2 Lloyd's Rep 42.

18 At [19].

5.2.2 The effect of the fraud upon the contract of insurance: a right to avoid?

The clarity of the position as regards the effect of the fraud on the claim to which it relates is to be contrasted with the uncertainty which surrounded the effect of the fraud on the contract of insurance as a whole.

As seen above in the citation of the directions given by Pollock CB and Willes J in the fire insurance cases of *Goulstone* and *Britton,* respectively, the early cases dealing with fraudulent claims tackled the matter in wide terms, speaking of forfeiture of "all claim" or all "benefit" under the policy. The justification for the principle was the duty of the utmost good faith. However, as noted by Lord Hobhouse in *The Star Sea,*[19] there was no reference by either judge to the concept of *avoidance* of the contract of insurance as such, although such concept was a very well established incident of that duty, but only to an arguably different and more limited concept of *forfeiture* of the claim or claims which may be made by the assured.

In *The Star Sea*[20] the House of Lords reinterpreted the post-contract duty of good faith, as set out in section 17 of the 1906 Act. The House of Lords distinguished between the pre-contract and post-contract duty of good faith, holding that while the duty to disclose information pre-contract was a strict one, after the conclusion of the contract the duty of good faith was flexible and varied according to context and the circumstances.

In terms of avoidance as the remedy for fraud in the presentation of the claim, the leading speech of Lord Hobhouse of Woodborough adopted an analysis which militated against the availability of the remedy simply on the grounds that it was extreme and justifiable only in the pre-contractual context.[21]

The point was not, however, conclusively determined. As one leading textbook puts it, if a fraudulent claim amounts to a breach of the duty set out in section 17, then avoidance remains, at least arguably, an available remedy as a matter of law and by virtue of the statutory provision itself.[22]

In *The Mercandian Continent,*[23] the Court of Appeal held that the remedy of avoidance was in principle available for post-contractual breaches of the duty of good faith in section 17 but only in limited circumstances where it could be shown that the fraud was material to the liability of the insurer and the effect of the fraudulent claim was the same as a repudiatory breach. In this way, the disproportionate results which would arise from the blanket application of the right to avoid in any and every case where the duty of utmost good faith was broken by the making of a fraudulent claim would be rendered "less offensive than they would otherwise be".[24]

19 [2001] UKHL 1; [2003] 1 AC 469 at [64].
20 [2001] UKHL 1; [2003] 1 AC 469.
21 At [51].
22 J. Birds & B. Lynch and S. Milnes, *MacGillivray on Insurance Law* (13th edn), (Sweet and Maxwell, 2015), at para. 21-067.
23 [2001] EWCA Civ 1275; [2001] 2 Lloyd's Rep 563 (CA).
24 Per Longmore LJ at [36].

In *Agapitos v Agnew*, the Court of Appeal expressed the tentative view that on the authorities taken as a whole, the rule relating to the forfeiture of the claim had now been classified as a separate common law rule, falling outside section 17 of the 1906 Act and, therefore, falling outside the remit of the remedy of avoidance of the contract of insurance *ab initio*. As Mance LJ put it:[25]

> my tentative view of an acceptable solution would be: [. . .] (d) To treat the common law rules governing the making of a fraudulent claim (including the use of fraudulent device) as falling outside the scope of s. 17 (as advocated, though more generally, by Howard N. Bennett in the article to which I have already referred[26]). On this basis no question of avoidance ab initio would arise.

However, Mance LJ recognised that the position was undecided following *The Star Sea* notwithstanding the evident distaste at least on the part of Lord Hobhouse and the majority for the availability of avoidance for fraud in the making of the claim. He approached the problem before him on the basis that the position was possibly either that avoidance was simply not available at all or that if it was, then its availability was severely limited by the general considerations applicable to the post-contractual application of section 17 as laid down in *The Mercandian Continent*.[27]

Some later cases adopted an approach which appeared to proceed upon the implicit assumption that there is no retrospective remedy for a fraudulent claim and that the making of a fraudulent claim *after* a valid claim which has been met has no effect upon the insurer's liability for that claim.[28] If the applicable analysis was one of breach of section 17 and if the claim was wholly fraudulent (so as to satisfy the requirements for post-contractual operation of section 17 set out in *The Mercandian Continent*), then such cases would most naturally give rise to the invocation of the retrospective avoidance of the policy and the recovery of all previous paid claims together with it.

Accordingly, the law in this area prior to the introduction of the Act was at best unsettled and at worst confused and incoherent. Although it was possible to discern certain likely or predictable results (such as the difficulty in seeking to impugn prior valid claims, paid or yet to be paid at the time of the fraudulent claim), the potential availability of section 17 hovered over the law. Some commentators approached the matter pragmatically taking the cases as establishing, not very clearly but at least sufficiently, that there is now a single doctrine under which the fraudulent claim fails entirely and the insurer may terminate the contract with prospective effect but

25 *Agapitos v Agnew (The Aegeon)* [2002] EWCA Civ 247; [2002] 2 Lloyd's Rep 42 at [45]. Mance LJ's approach in *The Aegeon* was recently approved by the Court of Appeal in *Versloot Dredging BV v HDI-Gerling Industrie Versicherung AG (DC Merwestone)* [2014] EWCA Civ 1349; [2015] 1 Lloyd's Rep 32, though that decision is, at the time of writing, on appeal to the Supreme Court.

26 H. Bennett, "Mapping the doctrine of utmost good faith in insurance contract law" [1999] LMCLQ 165 at 177.

27 *Agapitos v Agnew (The Aegeon)* [2002] EWCA Civ 247; [2002] 2 Lloyd's Rep. 42 at [21].

28 See, e.g. *Axa General Insurance Ltd v Gottlieb* [2005] EWCA Civ 112; [2005] Lloyd's Rep IR 369.

that past valid claims remain enforceable;[29] others taking their stand on section 17 and the absence of clear authority, regarded there to be two separate and free-standing doctrines, those of the forfeiture of fraudulent claims and the breach of section 17 with the different remedies which attached.[30]

5.2.3 The effect of the fraud on the contract of insurance: termination upon the occurrence of the fraud and the fate of subsequent claims

Given that the pre-Act position on non-avoidance has only relatively recently become even tolerably clear, it was perhaps unsurprising that the effect on the contract of such a claim, absent avoidance, was not mapped out with any precision either. As it has been put in Arnould: "It is also uncertain whether, if the policy subsists when the fraudulent claim is made, the policy can survive even if the claim fails being tainted by fraud. The logical conclusion [. . .] would be that the policy theoretically could survive going forwards, but the point has yet to be decided."[31]

The approach of the courts to such a question was likely to be the adoption of an ordinary contractual analysis. In other words, treating a fraudulent claim as a breach of the contractual duty of good faith and, at least in most circumstances given the gravity of such a breach and the place of the contractual duty of good faith in a contract of insurance, as a repudiatory breach of the contract which entitles the insurer to terminate the contract with prospective effect, if it so elects.

Support for this result can be derived from the speech of Lord Hobhouse in *The Star Sea*.[32] As part of his consideration of the legal effect of a fraudulent claim, Lord Hobhouse distinguished between three possible analyses, based on or proceeding by analogy from: (a) the basic principle as to utmost good faith, enshrined in section 17 of the Marine Insurance Act 1906, with a remedy of avoidance *ab initio*; alternatively, (b) the application of general contractual principles, including repudiation; and (c) the existence of a special *sui generis* common law rule relating to fraudulent insurance claims.[33] As seen above, his view was that fraudulent claims were the subject of a special rule.[34] In the context of the wider effect on the policy, he stated:

> Having a contractual obligation of good faith in the performance of the contract presents no conceptual difficulty in itself. Such an obligation can arise from an implied or inferred contractual term. It is commonly the subject of an express term in certain

29 M. Clarke, *Law of Insurance Contracts* (4th edn), (LLP, 2002), at para. 27.2C3: "In the event of a fraudulent claim the claim fails entirely. Moreover, the contract is terminable at the option of the insurer. As to the future, the effect is to terminate the primary duties, but secondary duties, such as a duty to arbitrate an earlier honest claim, remain. As to the past, any outstanding honest claims remain enforceable. The insured claimant is unable to recover premium paid. However, the insurer can recover insurance payments on account of the latest loss made prior to the fraud."

30 J. Birds & B. Lynch and S. Milnes, *MacGillivray on Insurance Law* (13th edn), (Sweet and Maxwell, 2015), at para. 21–067.

31 J.C.B. Gilman et al (eds), *Arnould: Law of Marine Insurance and Average* (18th edn), (Sweet & Maxwell, 2013), at para. 18–52.

32 *Manifest Shipping Co Ltd* v *Uni-Polaris Co Ltd (The Star Sea)* [2001] UKHL 1; [2003] AC 469.

33 See [2001] UKHL 1; [2003] AC 469 at [53], [61] and [66].

34 At [62].

> types of contract such as partnership contracts. Once parties are in a contractual relationship, the source of their obligations the one to the other is the contract (although the contract is not necessarily exclusive and the relationship which comes into existence may of itself give rise to other liabilities, for example liabilities in tort). The primary remedy for breach of contract is damages. But the consequences of breach of contract are not confined to this. The contractual significance of the breach may go further. It may also amount to a breach of a contractual condition which will excuse or suspend the other party's obligation to continue to perform the contract. It may be a repudiatory breach, or evidence a renunciation, which entitles the other party to terminate the contract and sue for damages. However any such release only applies prospectively and does not affect already accrued rights.[35]

Having stressed that the alternative analysis based on section 17 led to an anomalous and disproportionate result which was not sanctioned by authority and would have been an extremely improbable contractual term for the parties to a contract of insurance to have agreed,[36] Lord Hobhouse suggested that a "coherent scheme" was to treat the duty of good faith differently in its pre- and post-contractual application applying, implicitly, the contractual analysis just explained by him in the post-contractual context:[37]

> A coherent scheme can be achieved by distinguishing a lack of good faith which is material to the making of the contract itself (or some variation of it) and a lack of good faith during the performance of the contract which may prejudice the other party or cause him loss or destroy the continuing contractual relationship. The former derives from requirements of the law which pre-exist the contract and are not created by it although they only become material because a contract has been entered into. The remedy is the right to elect to avoid the contract. The latter can derive from express or implied terms of the contract; it would be a contractual obligation arising from the contract and the remedies are the contractual remedies provided by the law of contract. This is no doubt why judges have on a number of occasions been led to attribute the post-contract application of the principle of good faith to an implied term.

Lord Hobhouse's speech was endorsed by Lords Steyn and Hoffmann. However, they also agreed with the speech of Lord Scott who appeared to have viewed the matter more in terms of a limited right to avoid, rather than a right to terminate for repudiatory breach.[38]

These indications were subsequently picked up in *Axa Insurance v Gottlieb*[39] by Mance LJ who, in confining the rule relating to fraudulent claims to the invalidation of the claim itself (however composed and irrespective of interim payments pre-fraud) excluding any effect on separate prior claims, and after referring back to Lord Hobhouse's reference to contractual remedies, stated tentatively as follows:[40]

> To my mind, there is no basis or reason for giving the common law rule relating to fraudulent claims a retrospective effect on prior, separate claims which have already been settled under the same policy before any fraud occurs. It is unnecessary to reach

35 At [50].
36 At [51].
37 At [52].
38 At [110].
39 *Axa General Insurance Ltd v Gottlieb* [2005] EWCA Civ 112; [2005] Lloyd's Rep IR 369.
40 At [22].

> any conclusion in this case on the common law position relating to separate claims which are still unpaid at the time of the fraud, though there seems to me some force in the argument that the common law rule relating to fraudulent claims should be confined to the particular claim to which any fraud relates, while the potential scope and operation of more general contractual principles might in some circumstances also require consideration (cf. paragraph 18(ii) above).[41]

While it might have been argued that the duty of utmost good faith in a post-contractual context justified a remedy of immediate termination of the contract of insurance with the consequence that all subsequent claims are invalidated, there has been no suggestion in the cases that this approach would be applied. No ordinary principle of general contract law visits a repudiatory breach of contract with that consequence.

Therefore, although wholly undeveloped, the law was probably as summarised by Professor Clarke: "In the event of a fraudulent claim the claim fails entirely. Moreover, the contract is terminable at the option of the insurer."[42] As such, the making of a fraudulent claim had no effect upon the contract of insurance unless and until the insurer elected to terminate; that termination operated for the future only and accrued rights were unaffected.

5.2.4 The insurer's right to damages in respect of fraudulent claims

The contract of insurance is a contract like any other but no case[43] has suggested that the making of a fraudulent claim constitutes a breach of contract entitling the insurer to damages. The costs borne by an insurer in investigating a fraudulent claim may be substantial. Leaving aside separate remedies in deceit the insurer has no clearly established right to recover such costs from the insured in damages.

It is clear that no claim can be made by the insurer for breach by the insured of the duty of good faith pre-contract, at least where the breach consists of non-disclosure. In *Banque Financière de la Cité v Westgate Insurance*[44] the Court of Appeal, reversing the decision of Steyn J, held that there was no basis for claiming damages as the duty of good faith provided its own remedy, that of avoidance and no other.[45]

As it has been put, "[m]any of the reasons given for that decision are less than overwhelming but, anyway, being concerned with the duty of good faith at the

41 Mance LJ had summarised at [18] Lord Hobhouse's view as follows: "(ii) general contractual principles, including repudiation (and possibly, in view of the insurance context, breach of warranty in the insurance sense)".

42 M. Clarke, *Law of Insurance Contracts* (4th edn), (LLP, 2002), at para. 27.2C3. See also his description of "view A" earlier in 27.2C3: "According to view A, the contract is 'terminated'. Termination by the insurer is optional and, if exercised, it operates for the future. The corollary is clear but worth articulating. Termination does not occur unless the insurer makes a clear election; and it does not discharge the insurer from the outstanding duty, if any, to pay past non-fraudulent claims."

43 Save in the general terms of a contractual analysis: see e.g. *Orakpo v Barclays Insurance Services* [1995] LRLR 443, 451 (CA).

44 [1988] 2 Lloyd's Rep 513 (CA).

45 At 550, per Slade LJ giving the judgment of the court.

time of contracting, they do necessarily rule out an action to recover damages for breach of the duty or of a related duty occurring later in the relationship".[46] The Court of Appeal's analysis was additionally, it is suggested, founded on a case of an *innocent* breach of the duty of good faith by inadvertent but nevertheless material non-disclosure in circumstances where no fraud was alleged. This played a large part in the court's reasoning.[47]

A similar approach was adopted in *Banque Keyser Ullman SA v Skandia (UK) Insurance Co Ltd*[48] and subsequent cases have confirmed that these decisions lay down a general principle but only for cases where fraud is not in issue.[49]

The case law, therefore, left open the question of a separate remedy in damages for a breach of the duty of good faith post-contract by the making of a fraudulent claim. However, it is fair to say that the general approach in the cases seems inimical to such a remedy. The view is perhaps taken that there are sufficient remedies in tort for deceit if required.

Some support for this is to be found in the case of *London Assurance v Clare*.[50] A claim was made following a fire which was found by a special jury to have been accidental, although the claim made for loss of stock following the fire was found to be wholly fraudulent. The insurers claimed the considerable costs of a detailed investigation which led them to reject the claim. Goddard J rejected the claim in these terms (emphasis supplied):[51]

> With regard to the claim for damages, that seems to me to be a very novel claim, and, so far as the learned Counsel on either side know, no such claim has ever been put forward before. *It is put, not as damages for fraud, for which I think there might be something to be said, but it is put as damages for breach of contract.* Mr. Vos argues that there is an implied term of the contract, even if there is not an express term, that the assured should put in an honest claim and not a fraudulent claim, and he says, therefore, that if it turns out that a person has put in a fraudulent claim, the insurers are entitled to recover all the expenses to which they have been put in investigating that claim, as damages for a breach of contract.
>
> With regard to that, I have great difficulty in seeing how that can be so. The claim was a claim which the deceased was entitled to put in because he had had a fire, and it is not suggested that it was an incendiary fire. Once the claim was in, the assurance companies could decide for themselves whether they would pay or whether they would not. They chose-rightly, as it has turned out, to investigate it, and by the investigation which they made they discovered that the claim was fraudulent. They repudiated the contract, and they did not pay, thereby getting, of course, a great advantage because they did not have to pay what they would have had to pay if the claim had not been fraudulent. They pay nothing, and any part of the expenses that they have been put to which is properly regarded as costs, no doubt the Taxing Master will take into account when he is dealing with the question of costs; but to treat this sum as damages for a breach of contract seems to me to be going beyond anything that has ever

46 M. Clarke, *Law of Insurance Contracts* (4th edn), (LLP, 2002), at para. 27.2C5.

47 See per Slade LJ at 551: "In our judgment, it would not be right for this Court by way of judicial legislation to create a new tort, effectively of absolute liability, which could expose either party to an insurance contract to a claim for substantial damages in the absence of any blameworthy conduct."

48 [1991] 2 AC 249.

49 See e.g. *Aldrich v Norwich Union* [2000] Lloyd's Rep IR 1 (CA) at 8.

50 (1937) 57 Ll L Rep 254.

51 At 270.

been done before, and no authority has been suggested or cited to me which would suggest that the courts have ever applied the principle of damages for breach of contract to such a matter.

In *Insurance Corporation of the Channel Islands Ltd v McHugh*[52] allegations of deceit were pleaded by the insurers but not pursued at trial. Mance J dismissed the claim on the basis that it had not been argued but acknowledged that it could be arguable in principle.

5.3 The provisions of the Insurance Act 2015 concerning remedies for fraudulent claims

As alluded to above, the relevant provisions are found in sections 12 and 13 of the Act. Section 12 deals with the general position and section 13 outlines how the general rules apply in the context of group insurance. Therefore, for the vast majority of cases it will be section 12 that is relevant and that will be the focus here.

In very broad summary, section 12 provides that where a fraudulent claim is made, the insurer is not liable to pay it, that it can recover any sums paid to the insured in respect of the fraudulent claim and that it is entitled to terminate the contract of insurance. Termination of the contract of insurance does not affect any claims arising before the fraudulent act but it does entitle the insurer to keep any premium paid and refuse liability for any claim arising after the fraudulent act.

The effect of section 13 can also be summarised shortly: where a policy provides cover for other beneficiaries that are not co-assureds and one of those beneficiaries presents a fraudulent claim, the insurer is only entitled to exercise its rights under section 12 in relation to the fraudulent beneficiary. In other words, section 13 treats the claim by the fraudulent beneficiary as if it were one made on a separate contract of insurance between the insurer and that beneficiary. One can see how this regime avoids unjust applications of section 12 in situations where group insurance schemes are most common, for example employers taking out health insurance for the benefit of their employees.

5.3.1 The effect of the fraud upon the claim to which it relates

Section 12(1)(a) of the Act states that if the insured makes a fraudulent claim[53] under a contract of insurance, underwriters are not liable to pay the claim. Section 12(1)(b) follows logically in that it provides that underwriters may recover any sums paid to the insured in respect of that claim.

52 [1997] LRLR 94.

53 J. Birds & B. Lynch and S. Milnes, *MacGillivray on Insurance Law* (13th edn), (Sweet and Maxwell, 2015) notes at para. 21–069 that "the courts are likely to construe the words 'makes a fraudulent claim' in s.12(1) as embracing a situation where the insured used a fraudulent device to bolster a valid (and correctly quantified claim), in line with the common law's approach of regarding fraudulent devices as a sub-species of fraudulent claims".

Thus, statutory effect has been given to the common law remedy of forfeiture, as established in the existing cases. This means that if a policyholder commits a fraud in relation to a claim, the whole claim is forfeited. There is, therefore, no change to the law, save to clarify that the remedy of forfeiture is a free-standing rule which relates solely to the claim to which the fraud relates.

5.3.2 The effect of the fraud upon the contract of insurance

Section 12(1)(c) provides that an insurer may, by notice to the insured making a "fraudulent claim", treat the contract as having been terminated with effect from the time of the "fraudulent act". The "fraudulent claim" is to be distinguished from the "fraudulent act". The latter is intended to be the behaviour that makes a claim fraudulent, which may be after the initial submission of the claim.

If the insurer does treat the contract of insurance as having been terminated, then section 12(2)(a) states that the insurer is entitled to refuse all liability in respect of a "relevant event" occurring after the time of the fraudulent act and it need not return any premium paid. A "relevant event" is defined in section 12(4) as whatever gives rise to the insurer's liability under the contract of insurance (that turning on the terms of the policy).[54]

This had not always been the Law Commission's stance. The Commission's starting point was to identify two possible approaches to the problem as a matter of principle:[55]

(1) The fraud is characterised as a breach of the contract, which gives the insurer the right to terminate cover. However, the policy continues to exist until termination, and any claim arising between the date of the fraud and the date of termination must be paid.
(2) The presentation of the fraudulent claim automatically brings the contract to an end, invalidating any claim which arises after the fraud but before the fraud is discovered.

Basing itself on the perceived view as to the likely position in English law, the Commission's initial proposal in Issues Paper 7 was that valid claims arising between the date of the fraud and the termination should be paid, this being in line with normal contract principles, in which terminating a contract only brings a contract to an end after the termination. The Commission expressed a relatively strong view to this effect: "This outcome is in line with general contract principles and we think it is correct."[56]

The responses in the primary consultation following that Issues Paper, however, were strongly in favour of the second solution, that of immediate termination upon

54 In the case of a liability policy, the relevant event will be the assured giving the insurer notice of the claim (claim A). If, at a later stage, when submitting another claim the assured acts fraudulently (claim B), the assured would have a contingent right to seek indemnity for claim A despite a subsequent fraud in relation to claim B.

55 LC Consultation Paper 201, para. 6.53.

56 LC Issues Paper 7, para. 7.37.

the making of the fraudulent claim. The chief reasons were as follows. First, as a matter of principle, it was felt that the insured's actions had undermined the contractual relationship, bringing the insurer's obligations to an end. Fraud undermined the necessary trust and good faith between the parties. Second, as a matter of practice, a rule which required the insurer to take action to terminate the contract would encourage premature allegations of fraud. If termination is not to take place until the claim has been refused, insurers will feel that their hand is being forced to make "knee jerk" allegations of fraud in order to avoid more claims. Third, as a matter of practice, insurers frequently include express policy terms which specify that, following a fraud, subsequent claims will not be covered. The denial of subsequent claims appears, therefore, already to be a matter to be common market practice. Bringing the law into line with the standard policy wordings was effectively recognised in the jury direction of Willes J in *Britton* in any event.

These responses led the Law Commission to change its proposal as formulated in Consultation Paper 201 into one of a right of termination for fraudulent claims with automatic invalidity of any claims made after that claim, albeit made before the insurer's termination. In other words, on discovery of the fraud the insurer would be entitled to terminate the contract with retrospective effect on any claim made after the fraud, unless it waived that right or was deemed to have waived it having failed to take action after discovering a fraud.[57]

While the Consultation Paper proposal provided that the termination required the act of the insurer terminating the contract and did not envisage automatic termination, the matter was put rather loosely. The Commission stated merely:[58] "That said, on discovery of a fraud, the insurer is expected to take some action to communicate the finding to the insured and terminate the cover. If an insurer has evidence of fraud and takes no action, it will be taken to have waived its defence to a subsequent claim."

This provoked some concern amongst consultees, even those in favour of the proposal (74% of those who responded)[59] as to when and how termination should be effected. The judges of the Court of Session appositely remarked that clarity in this regard was essential:[60]

> [it] should be made clear in any legislation whether this forfeiture is to happen automatically, as a matter of law, or whether it will happen only if the insurer elects to terminate or rescind the insurance cover on discovery of the fraud. The latter is, we suggest, consistent with the need for both parties to the contract to know where they stand.

The Act reflects the Law Commission's revised view and takes into account the need for underwriters to communicate their decision on termination to the insured. Section 12(1)(c) requires the insurer to give notice of its decision to the assured.

57 LC Consultation Paper 201, para. 8.11; see also L Summary of Responses 2012, para. 2.18.
58 LC Consultation Paper 201, para. 8.13.
59 LC Summary of Responses 2012, para. 2.14.
60 LC Summary of Responses 2012, para. 2.19.

Section 12(3) states that if the insurer treats the contract of insurance as having been terminated, it does not affect the rights and obligations of the parties with respect to a "relevant event" occurring before the time of the fraudulent act.

These provisions, therefore, represent an endorsement of the modern trend of the authorities in that they remove any question of the appropriate remedy being one of avoidance under section 17 of the 1906 Act and recognise that fraud does not affect any previous valid claim where the loss arises before the fraud takes place, whether or not the claim has been paid.

5.3.3 The insurer's right to damages in respect of fraudulent claims

Before its primary consultation, the Law Commission tentatively suggested that where the insurer suffers loss as a result of the insured's making of a fraudulent claim, damages should be available to compensate the insurer.[61] However, its reason for doing so appears to have been more the wish to create a fully-fashioned set of remedies rather than any actual perceived need on the part of the insurance industry or greater reason of public policy.[62]

The responses to the proposal were mixed. In particular, there was concern at the practicality of such a right with consultees feeling that it would be too difficult to assess the costs where the investigations are carried out internally. Insurers might instead outsource these investigations to third parties to be able to present the court with an invoice setting out the full costs of the investigation. This could have the effect of increasing overall investigation costs, which would be passed on in increased premiums if not recovered in full. Some argued that investigation of claims should be considered an inherent cost of the insurer's business.

Taking these points into consideration, the Commission decided that there was not a sufficiently strong case for reform. The law, therefore, remains unchanged in this regard.

5.4 The likely impact of section 12 of the Act

5.4.1 The effect of the fraud upon the claim to which it relates

Whilst the statutory embodiment of the forfeiture rule ought not to create any vastly different results in the cases from the position prior to the introduction of the Act, it is not difficult to see where arguments on section 12(1)(a) will arise.

There is still a view in certain quarters that a rule that the whole of the claim is forfeit in circumstances where the claim is good in part is anomalous since it deprives the assured of a good legal right as a sanction for fraud in relation to an

61 LC Issues Paper 7, para. 7.41: "we see no reason why the fraudster should not pay in these circumstances".

62 Recording as it did in Issues Paper 7 at para. 7.40: "If an insurer incurs the cost of investigating a fraudulent claim, should the fraudster be liable for those costs? This has not proved to be a major issue in the case law. The costs of investigating claims are rarely substantial, and tend to be lower than the savings which accrue from not paying the legitimate element of a fraudulent claim."

element of claim which, on account of the fraud, is already irrecoverable where no corresponding rule existed for other partially fraudulent claims (e.g. in relation to personal injuries). In their response to the Consultation Paper, certain judges of the Commercial Court[63] considered that:

> It is difficult to bring to mind any other area of the law in which we have a policy of penal non-damages, ie depriving a party of the damages to which they are legally entitled as a result of some deliberately false aspect of the claim or evidence advanced to support it. Yet insurers are not unique in facing exaggerated claims. Exaggerated claims are commonplace in many types of civil claim, as are fraudulent devices to support valid claims. For example personal injury claimants regularly exaggerate their injuries. One wonders why an assured whose house burns down loses his buildings and contents entitlement to hundreds of thousands of pounds because he falsely claims for extra laptops, when a personal injury claimant whose dishonesty about his injuries may be grosser and more reprehensible still gets his true entitlement.

This concern may now be compared with the decision of the Supreme Court in *Fairclough Homes Limited v Summers*[64] in which the court, dealing with a grossly exaggerated and fraudulently maintained claim for personal injuries, held that while the court had a jurisdiction to strike out such a claim including that part of it which was good as a sanction for the fraud, this would be extremely rarely justified.[65]

The element of deterrence in insurance law has always been paramount. As Lord Hobhouse of Woodborough explained in *The Star Sea*:[66] "The fraudulent insured must not be allowed to think: if the fraud is successful, then I will gain; if it is unsuccessful, I will lose nothing." However, whilst deterring fraud is of course a noble policy objective, it must be said that the efficacy of the forfeiture rule in achieving this end is doubtful.[67] This is perhaps why other justifications for the distinction between the treatment of fraudulent insurance claims and (for example) fraudulent personal injury claims has been required; for example, the fact that the personal injuries claimant does not owe the defendant any duty of good faith.[68]

Any lingering doubts about whether (and on what basis) the forfeiture rule is justified could have an impact on the way in which section 12(1)(a) of the Act is applied. Specifically, the Act does not define "the claim" that underwriters are not liable to pay; it has been left to the courts to decide how broadly "the claim" should be characterised based on the facts and circumstances of each case.

It may be that arguments about how broadly "the claim" should be defined in a particular case chime with familiar debates in an aggregation context about the meaning of an "event", "accident" or "occurrence". Or it may be that the focus is more on the way the quantum of the claim is presented. Either way, it is conceivable

63 Gloster; Burton; Beatson; Christopher Clarke; Flaux and Popplewell JJ.

64 [2012] UKSC 26; [2012] 1 WLR 2004.

65 Per Lord Clarke of Stone-cum-Ebony JSC at [49].

66 [2001] UKHL 1; [2003] 1 AC 469, at [62].

67 See e.g. the illuminating article by J. Davey and K. Richards "Deterrence, human rights and illegality: the forfeiture rule in insurance contract law" [2015] LMCLQ 314.

68 *Versloot Dredging BV v HDI-Gerling Industrie Versicherung AG (DC Merwestone)* [2014] EWCA Civ 1349; [2015] 1 Lloyd's Rep 32, [76].

that the flexibility given to the courts on this issue will leave room for judges to reflect any general misgivings about the anomalous nature of the forfeiture rule by applying a restrictive definition of "the claim" which is forfeited by the insured.

5.4.2 The effect of the fraud upon the contract of insurance

Perhaps unsurprisingly, the vast majority (94%) of consultees had no difficulty with the clarification that section 17 has no role to play in this area.[69] This demonstrates, as the Law Commission found[70] and as the dearth of modern authority confirms, that attempted avoidance by insurers on the grounds of a fraudulent claim is an extreme rarity of hypothetical interest only to the insurance market, with no insurer supporting its use and those few who spoke in favour of its retention doing so on the basis of a remedy of last resort in exceptional cases only (no examples of which were proferred). It therefore seems unlikely that this aspect of the Act will have any impact upon the way cases are decided.

The clarification that fraud does not affect any previous valid claim simply recognises the position which would otherwise follow absent a right of retrospective avoidance and will give statutory effect to the approach already clearly established in the cases: see, for example, *Axa General Insurance Ltd v Gottlieb*. Any obscurity arising out of expressions in the older cases such as forfeiture of "any claim" and "all benefit", if not already dispelled in the modern case law, is also removed. As the Law Commission remarked: "Avoidance of past claims is unprincipled and impractical, and appears unnecessarily harsh. Instead, valid past claims should be unaffected by a subsequent fraud. This reflects the approach already taken by the courts and by good market practice."[71]

On the status of genuine claims made following a fraudulent claim but prior to the insurer giving notice of termination, the Act probably strikes the right note in section 12(1)(c). The approach certainly avoids the obvious pitfall of the alternative that was initially being considered by the Commission, which undoubtedly would have encouraged insurers to terminate the contract on the slightest suspicion of fraud. However, the consequence of this is that, at least within the Act, there is no obvious time pressure on the insurer to make his election swiftly. One can envisage this causing difficulty where the insurer refuses to pay a fraudulent claim, does not give notice of termination but then thinks better of it when a substantial genuine claim is presented later in the same policy year. In those circumstances would the insurer be permitted to give notice of termination in relation to the fraudulent claim in order to avoid paying the later genuine claim? It may be that the answer to this question is to be found in the doctrines of waiver and estoppel but that would probably depend on the nature of the exchanges between the insurer and insured around the declinature of the fraudulent claim.

69 See LC Summary of Responses, 2012.
70 LC Consultation Paper 201, para. 7.14.
71 Ibid., para. 7.16.

5.5 Conclusions

Although certain insurance lawyers, well versed in the cases and commentaries, might possibly have taken the view that, while there were areas of potential argument, the law pre-Act was probably clear enough, that does not seem to have been the view of the insurance industry.

The Law Commission's aim to end the "disjuncture between the common law rule and section 17"[72] by providing for a clear statement of remedies in the case of fraudulent claims was plainly desirable. It is suggested that, at least in this respect, the Act is not mere "reform for the sake of tidiness"[73] but a sensible exercise in distilling and, where obscure, clarifying the uncertain position left by the existing case law.

As Sir Mackenzie Chalmers wrote in 1901, when composing a digest of the law, the codifier must needs grapple, not only with the situation where there is a plethora of reported cases all in one direction, but also the situation relating to issues or "points of apparently equal importance [where] the decisions are meagre and not always satisfactory" or are "untouched by authority and the rule depends upon established commercial usage".[74] This, the Act, by section 12, appears satisfactorily to have resolved.

72 LC Issues Paper 7, para. 7.3.

73 Lord Justice Aikens, "The post-contract duty of good faith in insurance contracts: is there a problem that needs a solution?", speech to BILA on 8 February 2010. This speech was later published in (2010) *Journal of Business Law* 379.

74 Introduction to the first edition of the *Digest of the Law Relating to Marine Insurance* (Williams Clowes, 1901) (co-authored with D. Owen).

CHAPTER 6

Late payment of claims: better, but by no means perfect

*Professor Andrew Tettenborn**

We frequently hear how often people with no connection with the UK elect for English law to govern their insurance arrangements. When asked why, the general reply from international operators is that it is because, unlike other systems, the English approach to insurance is generally down-to-earth, pragmatic and business-friendly. Very often, indeed, that is true. But one also has to remember that at times this same English law can be astonishingly stupid, perverse and doctrinaire. The question of liability – or rather lack of liability – for late payment of insurance indemnity claims is a case in point. Its sorry history forms the background to this chapter; its recent statutory reform by the revised Insurance Act 2015, the subject of it.

6.1 Late payment: the common law background

If insurance exists to shoulder risks which the assured cannot afford to bear from his own resources, implicit in this is the need to cushion these risks not only in due course but on time. This is because in commercial life cash-flow and the ability to continue trading are vital. When unexpected events do serious harm to cash-flow and stop a business in its tracks, any businessman will confirm that delay in making up the deficiency can cause grievous losses and, indeed, may quite plausibly have the effect of tipping an insured over into insolvency. Unfortunately, the common law in England always acted in sublime disregard of this fact of commercial life. Even though in *Sempra Metals Ltd (formerly Metallgesellschaft Ltd) v Inland Revenue Commissioners*[1] in 2008 it finally accepted that late payment of a debt could give rise to damages in the same way as any other breach of contract, until legislation intervened in 2015, it flatly denied an assured any recourse against an underwriter for late payment of a claim, except to the extent of the court's statutory power to award pre-judgment interest on sums adjudged due. It did not matter that the actual loss might be much greater than the interest foregone; that it was foreseeable; or that the delay in payment was the underwriter's fault.

The reason for this was a noxious combination of two principles. One was the long-standing rule that there could be no liability in a defendant to compensate

* Professor of Commercial Law, Institute of International Shipping and Trade Law, Swansea University.

1 [2007] UKHL 34, [2008] 1 AC 561.

for the late payment of damages due from him: a rule that applied not only to unliquidated damages computed by a court, but also, as a result of the decision in *President of India v Lips Maritime Corp'n*,[2] to liquidated damages whose payment at a particular time was mandated by the terms of a contract.[3] Although judicially abrogated in a number of Commonwealth jurisdictions,[4] this principle remained unaffected in England despite the decision in *Sempra Metals*[5] above, allowing general damages for late payment of *primary* payment obligations. The second principle at work was an equally long-standing technicality: namely, the rule that an underwriter's duty to pay out on an indemnity policy was construed not as a primary promise to pay the established amount of the assured's loss, but rather as a secondary liability to indemnify for consequences – that is, to pay damages triggered by the eventuation of the insured risk.[6]

The logical conclusion from these two propositions, that late payment of insurance monies could in the nature of things engender no cause of action, was duly drawn in the leading authorities of *The Italia Express*[7] in 1991 and *Sprung v Royal Insurance (UK) Ltd*[8] in 1996. In the former case, marine insurers faced with a total loss delayed payment for three and a half years on the basis of an unfounded suspicion of scuttling. Hirst J denied any claim for either loss of profits or ship value inflation in the intervening period. In *Sprung*, vandals trashed the premises of a small Liverpool business. The insurers prevaricated, as before, and only paid the reinstatement costs after (again) some three-and-a-half years. The Court of Appeal approved the decision in *The Italia Express*, and hence dismissed as misconceived the owner's claim for losses of about £75,000 allegedly resulting from his insurers' sloth, a sum reflecting allegations of lost profits and a vanished opportunity to sell his business as a going concern.

Two later decisions took this perverse logic right to its limits. In one, in 2005, it was held that the bar on damages for late payment continued to apply to a fire policy even where the assured was covered not only against fire damage itself, but also specifically for loss of profits pending the actual reinstatement of his premises by his insurers.[9] And a year later, in *Tonkin v UK Insurance Ltd*,[10] the same result was held to follow even where insurers had *expressly* promised to pay with due

2 [1988] AC 395.

3 In *Lips* the liquidated damages took the form of demurrage. See also *Mandrake Holdings Ltd v Countrywide Assured Group plc* [2005] EWCA Civ 840 (contractual promise to indemnify for loss: same result).

4 Notably Australia: see *Hungerfords v Walker* (1989) 171 CLR 125, 149 (Mason CJ and Wilson J), and *Tasmania v Shaw (No 2)* [2002] TASSC 12, (2000) 12 Tas R 1.

5 [2007] UKHL 34, [2008] 1 AC 561.

6 See the old case of *Luckie v Bushby* (1853) 13 CB 864; also *Chandris v Argo Insurance Co* [1963] 2 Lloyd's Rep 65, 73 (Megaw J), *Firma C-Trade SA v Newcastle Protection & Indemnity Association, The Fanti* [1991] 2 AC 1, 35 (Lord Goff), *The Italia Express* [1992] 2 Lloyd's Rep. 281, 285–292 (Hirst J), and *International Energy Group Ltd v Zurich Insurance plc* [2015] UKSC 33, [2015] 2 WLR 1471 at [89] (Lord Mance).

7 [1992] 2 Lloyd's Rep 281.

8 [1997] CLC 70.

9 *Normhurst Ltd v Dornoch Ltd* [2004] EWHC 567 (Comm), [2005] Lloyd's Rep IR 27.

10 [2006] EWHC 1120 (TCC), [2006] 2 All ER (Comm) 550.

expedition[11] but then inexcusably dragged their feet. This latter conclusion looks peculiar, but in fact it was entirely in accordance with *President of India v Lips Maritime Corp'n*,[12] which had ruled out damages for failure to pay liquidated damages at a particular time, not because of the inferred intent of the parties, but because a claim of this sort was a legal impossibility.

The rule of no recovery for late payment has few, if any, supporters. A number of civil law systems reject it outright.[13] It never applied in Scotland, for the simple reason that an insurance indemnity is not regarded in Scots law as a liability in damages.[14] It has been got rid of in some jurisdictions. The tendency in the US is to reject it.[15] Australia, for example, effectively disowned the rule against damages for late payment of damages in 1989,[16] with the result that there was then no objection to compensation for late payment of insurance monies.[17] In Canada, there is some indication that claims for late payment may be able to be brought insofar as such payment is a breach of the duty of good faith.[18] But in England this never happened. The liberalisation of damages for late payment of debts in *Sempra Metals Ltd (formerly Metallgesellschaft Ltd) v Inland Revenue Commissioners*[19] left undisturbed the rule on late payment of damages;[20] the characterisation of insurance payments as damages remains as it was,[21] from which it follows that the bar on recovery remains.[22] Indeed, two cases suggest that the rule goes even further

11 "Caring for You: We will always try to be fair and reasonable whenever you have need of the protection of this Policy. We will also act quickly to provide that protection."

12 [1988] AC 395.

13 For example, German law, besides providing for automatic pre-judgment interest in insurance cases at 4% (see VVG, § 91), expressly preserves the general right to damages for late payment under BGB § 288.4 ("*Die Geltendmachung eines weiteren Schadens ist nicht ausgeschlossen*"). An example comes in BGH, 19 September 1984, VersR 1984, 1137, IVa ZR 67/83 (fire insurance on factory; late payment; recovery of debt rescheduling costs). See W. van Boom, "Do insurers have to pay for bad behaviour in settling claims?" (2011) 2 Jo Eur Tort L 77, 89 ff.

14 *Strachan v Scottish Boatowners' Mutual Insurance Association* 2010 SC 367, esp. at 371–372 (Lord Eassie); see also *Scott Lithgow Ltd v Secretary of State for Defence* 1989 SC (HL) 9, 20 (Lord Keith).

15 See e.g. *Reichert v General Insurance Co*, 442 P.2d 377, 68 Cal.2d 822 (1968) (California); *Royal College Shop, Inc v Northern Insurance Co of NY*, 895 F.2d 670 (1990) (10 Cir CA, applying Kansas law).

16 *Hungerfords v Walker* (1989) 171 CLR 125, 149 (Mason CJ and Wilson J); *Tasmania v Shaw (No 2)* [2002] TASSC 12, (2000) 12 Tas R 1. See also in Canada *Alberta (Minister of Public Works, Supply & Services) v Nilsson,* 2002 ABCA 283, (2003) 220 DLR (4th) 474 at [218]-[219].

17 "A claim for general damages for unreasonably tardy payment arising from or the belated recognition of an entitlement to insurance indemnity is by no means heterodox" (Kirby P in *CIC Insurance Limited v Bankstown Football Club Ltd* (1995) 8 ANZ Ins Cas 61, 232 at 75, 566). See e.g. *Moss v Sun Alliance Aust Ltd* (1990) 55 SASR 145; *Maxwell v Highway Hauliers Pty Ltd* (2013) 275 FLR 64, (2013) 45 WAR 297.

18 *702535 Ontario Inc v Non-Marine Underwriters* (2000) 184 DLR (4th) 687.

19 [2007] UKHL 34, [2008] 1 AC 561.

20 See *Sempra Metals Ltd (formerly Metallgesellschaft Ltd) v Inland Revenue Commissioners* [2007] UKHL 34, [2008] 1 AC 561, esp. at [228] (Lord Mance).

21 *International Energy Group Ltd v Zurich Insurance plc* [2015] UKSC 33, [2015] 2 WLR 1471 at [89] (Lord Mance).

22 Thus, *The Italia Express* and *Sprung v Royal Insurance* were cited with apparent approval by Lord Mance in *International Energy Group Ltd v Zurich Insurance plc* [2015] UKSC 33, [2015] 2 WLR 1471 at [89]; see also the Scots decision in *McLean (or Toremar) v CGU Bonus Ltd* [2009] CSOH 78 at [109] (Lord Brodie). Note also M. Clarke, "Compensation for failure to pay money due: a 'blot on English common law jurisprudence' partly removed" [2008] JBL 291.

and bars damages claims against anyone at all for losses resulting from late payment,[23] though it is difficult to see why this should be so,[24] and the authority is not all one way.[25]

6.2 The reforms in general

There would have been a simple and elegant way of getting rid of the rule against damages for late payment: namely, a brief statutory provision stating that for the purpose of the law of damages all promises of indemnity in insurance contracts should be regarded as giving rise to liquidated debts payable within a reasonable time after a claim was made (as is the case in Scotland).[26] The result of that would have been that the courts would have been left to work out the consequences of late payment, and in particular when damages were available for it, in the light of the decision in *Sempra Metals Ltd (formerly Metallgesellschaft Ltd) v Inland Revenue Commissioners*.[27] In fact, however, this was not done. This was because the Law Commission had addressed the problem in its 2014 Report entitled "Insurance Contract Law: Business Disclosure; Warranties; Insurers' Remedies for Fraudulent Claims; and Late Payment".[28] Like almost all earlier commentators, it found no attraction in the rule against damages for late payment. Nevertheless, in recommending its repeal it firmly took the view that a fairly detailed provision was necessary in order to make clear precisely when an insurer would be in breach and what the result would be. It accordingly proposed a draft section on late payment in its proposed Insurance Bill. In fact, when the bill was first taken up, the provisions on late payment were not incorporated, and when it became the Insurance Act 2015 ("the 2015 Act"), it entirely omitted them. But the opportunity was smartly grasped to make good the deficiency by inserting amendment provisions in the Enterprise Act 2016. As a result, s. 13A of the 2015 Act[29] now contains the original Law Commission proposals on liability, with s. 16A enacting supplementary provisions on contracting-out.[30]

23 See *Ramwade Ltd v Emson & Co Ltd* [1987] RTR 72 and *Verderame v Commercial Union Assurance Co Plc* (1992) [1955–95] PNLR 612 (both negligence claims against brokers: held, no claim for losses resulting from receipt of payout late from broker rather than timeously from underwriter). A similar conclusion was reached, before the Australian re-think, in the old Australian case of *Norwest Refrigeration Services Pty Ltd v Bain Dawes (WA) Pty Ltd* (1984) 157 CLR 149.

24 See, generally, A. Tettenborn, "The Negligent Broker: Three Problems in the Assessment of Damages" in Thomas (ed), *The Modern Law of Marine Insurance, Vol. Four* (Informa 2016), 75–78.

25 For a contrary decision see *Arbory Group Ltd v West Craven Insurance Services* [2007] Lloyd's Rep IR 491; [2007] PNLR 23.

26 See above, Note 14.

27 [2007] UKHL 34, [2008] 1 AC 561.

28 Law Com No 353/Scot Law Com No 238, 2014 Cm 8898. Strictly speaking one should refer to the Law Commissions, this being a joint product of the English and Scottish Commissions.

29 These particular provisions are effective from 4 May 2017. Most of the rest of the Act comes into force on 12 August 2016.

30 See the Enterprise Act 2016, ss. 22–23. There is also a long-stop limitation period, which did not appear in the Law Commissions' proposals, preventing any claim for damages for late payment being brought more than one year after full payment, or settlement, of the amount due under the main claim: see s. 24, inserting a new s. 5A into the Limitation Act 1980.

The two sections run as follows:

13A. Implied term about payment of claims

(1) It is an implied term of every contract of insurance that if the insured makes a claim under the contract, the insurer must pay any sums due in respect of the claim within a reasonable time.
(2) A reasonable time includes a reasonable time to investigate and assess the claim.
(3) What is reasonable will depend on all the relevant circumstances, but the following are examples of things which may need to be taken into account –
 (a) the type of insurance,
 (b) the size and complexity of the claim,
 (c) compliance with any relevant statutory or regulatory rules or guidance,
 (d) factors outside the insurer's control.
(4) If the insurer shows that there were reasonable grounds for disputing the claim (whether as to the amount of any sum payable, or as to whether anything at all is payable)
 (a) the insurer does not breach the term implied by subsection (1) merely by failing to pay the claim (or the affected part of it) while the dispute is continuing, but
 (b) the conduct of the insurer in handling the claim may be a relevant factor in deciding whether that term was breached and, if so, when.
(5) Remedies (for example, damages) available for breach of the term implied by subsection (1) are in addition to and distinct from –
 (a) any right to enforce payment of the sums due, and
 (b) any right to interest on those sums (whether under the contract, under another enactment, at the court's discretion or otherwise).

. . .

16A. Contracting out of the implied term about payment of claims:
Consumer and non-consumer insurance contracts

(1) A term of a consumer insurance contract, or of any other contract, which would put the consumer in a worse position as respects any of the matters provided for in section 13A than the consumer would be in by virtue of the provisions of that section (so far as relating to consumer insurance contracts) is to that extent of no effect.
(2) A term of a non-consumer insurance contract, or of any other contract, which would put the insured in a worse position as respects deliberate or reckless breaches of the term implied by section 13A than the insured would be in by virtue of that section is to that extent of no effect.
(3) For the purposes of subsection (2) a breach is deliberate or reckless if the insurer

(a) knew that it was in breach, or
(b) did not care whether or not it was in breach.

(4) A term of a non-consumer insurance contract, or of any other contract, which would put the insured in a worse position as respects any of the other matters provided for in section 13A than the insured would be in by virtue of the provisions of that section (so far as relating to non-consumer insurance contracts) is to that extent of no effect, unless the requirements of section 17 have been satisfied in relation to the term.

(5) In this section references to a contract include a variation.

(6) This section does not apply in relation to a contract for the settlement of a claim arising under an insurance contract.

The broad aim is not difficult to see. Insurers are legally obliged to pay claims within a reasonable time; there is to be potential liability in damages for foreseeable loss suffered by the insured if they do not. As for waiver of this duty, this is impermissible for consumers, but possible for businesses, provided the waiver is clear and unequivocal, except in the case of deliberate and cynical foot-dragging.

So far, so good. Unfortunately, the devil, as ever, is in the detail. As will appear below, the drafting of ss. 13A and 16A is not as happy – or as clear – as it might be. There are a worrying number of points that need extended discussion.

6.3 The reforms discussed

6.3.1 The scheme of reform: an implied duty to pay claims on time

The central point of the new regime is s. 13A(1), imposing an implied contractual duty to pay claims within a reasonable time. It is not actually stated that the insurer's failure to do this gives rise to a right to damages, but this is clearly meant to be inferred, and indeed s. 13A(5) refers expressly to the possibility. Admittedly, if the section is taken absolutely (*au pied de la lettre)*, it could be said that this inference is not justified. This is because on the common law authorities there could be no liability to compensate for late payment of damages even if there *was* a contractual duty to pay them on time,[31] this reasoning being directly applied to indemnity insurance in *Tonkin v UK Insurance Ltd*;[32] and if an express contractual duty to pay on time made no difference, the same must follow with an implied statutory term. In practice, however, it is inconceivable that the courts would accept a pettifogger's point of this sort, however logical, that led to the conclusion that s. 13A had no effect whatever. In short, despite this instance of

31 Indeed, this was the very point of the demurrage case of *President of India v Lips Maritime Corp'n* [1988] AC 395, where there was argued to be such a promise, and also of the later indemnity case of *Mandrake Holdings Ltd v Countrywide Assured Group plc* [2005] EWCA Civ 840.

32 [2006] EWHC 1120 (TCC), [2006] 2 All ER (Comm) 550. True, Evans LJ suggested in *Sprung v Royal Insurance* [1997] CLC 70, 76 that a breach other than late payment, such as delay in consideration of the claim, that caused late payment might give a different result: but this seems doubtful.

curiously sloppy drafting,[33] it seems a foregone conclusion that they will indeed decide that Parliament intended to abolish the rule against compensation for late payment in the insurance context, and act accordingly.

Although s. 13A does not say so, presumably it only applies to policies governed by the law of a UK jurisdiction, so that where English courts or arbitrators have to deal with an insurance contract governed by the law of some other jurisdiction, any remedy for late payment will be limited either to that provided by that contract or to interest under s. 35A of the Senior Courts Act 1981 (or its county court or arbitration equivalent).[34]

6.3.2 The core duty: the obligation to pay within a reasonable time (s. 13A(2), (3))

The new duty to pay timeously appears in the legislation in the form of a statutory term implied in all insurance contracts, under which all claims are to be paid within a reasonable time. Much of the working-out of this is likely to be fairly uncontroversial, even if it requires the kind of painstaking analysis inherent in any open-ended standard. Clearly, what is a reasonable delay may vary almost infinitely according to the circumstances. A claim for £10 million may well justify more scepticism, and closer investigation, than one for £5,000. In the nature of things, reinsurance of asbestos liability risks is more complex and takes longer to sort out following a casualty, than buildings insurance on a burnt-out retail unit; business interruption insurance is less straightforward to deal with than buildings insurance; and so on and so forth. A less-than-clear-cut claim raising the need for detailed investigation will naturally take longer to appraise and settle than an open-and-shut case of damage clearly within the policy terms; again, where there has to be detailed argument on the amount of the assured's recoverable loss, this may quite understandably take longer to establish than a simple case of the total loss of a truck. If the assured has connections with a country under sanctions, or issues may arise as to money laundering, then this must all be factored into the equation. To this extent the enumeration in s. 13A of features relevant to reasonableness, such as the type of insurance, the complexity of the claim, or the impact of statutory or regulatory rules, is largely an exercise in stating the obvious.

Nevertheless, the clarity of s. 13A goes only so far. There are a number of issues which it does not address nearly so pellucidly.

First, the concept of a "reasonable time" contains within it an awkward potential ambiguity. Is it concerned with the time taken to pay, or with the conduct of the insurer in taking that time? In other words, in deciding whether the claim has been paid within a reasonable time, does the court simply have to look to such a time

33 The Law Commission report, para. 28.5, simply assumes that creating an implied term of this sort will necessarily allow damages at large for breach of contract.

34 Cf. *Maher v Groupama Grand Est* [2009] EWCA Civ 1191, [2010] 1 WLR 1564 (interest as damages under the *Sempra* decision governed by the law applicable to the claim). The result would, it is suggested, be the same under Rome I: see *Chitty on Contracts* (31st ed, Sweet & Maxwell 2012), 3-340.

as is objectively reasonable, given the nature and complexity of the claim, the possible need for investigation and appraisal, and the degree of essential co-operation provided (or perhaps, more to the point, not provided) by the assured? Or is the criterion the broader one of whether the insurer in question has acted unreasonably, in the sense of having been at fault for any delay? The point can matter where events peculiar to the insurer but not directly germane to the investigation intervene: for example, a major fire at the relevant company office or, for that matter, political interference such as sanctions legislation in the insurer's home state. Although matters of this kind are not due to the insurer's negligence, they may, nevertheless, cause delays to payment to rise above what is objectively reasonable.

There is something to be said on both sides here. Arguably, the sanction of damages for breach of contract, as against mere payment of interest in the court's discretion, should be limited to cases where the delay is due to actual fault on the part of the insurer. The open-ended reference in s. 13A to "all the relevant circumstances", and the mention of "factors outside the insurer's control", might seem to support this view; and the same goes for a reference by the Law Commission in its report to sanctions problems affecting the insurer as possible exempting factors.[35]

On the other hand, one can always look at it from the other side. Many insureds might be less than ecstatic at the idea that their premium buys them the right, not to reasonably swift payment in the event of an insured peril, but merely to the benefit of the insurer's best efforts to make it.[36] Furthermore, the presence of the provision in s. 13A(4) exonerating an insurer from liability where it reasonably disputes liability lends some support to the objective interpretation. Since reasonably disputing liability to pay a sum can hardly amount to culpable non-payment of it, this defence would be idle if there could only be liability in damages in the first place if the insurer was somehow at fault. Although the matter remains far from clear, it is suggested that the objective view is marginally preferable, and that some risks should be regarded as something the insurer should bear even if, strictly speaking, beyond its control. For example, imagine that in the case of an English policy governed by English law an insurer faces proceedings by (say) an alleged creditor of the assured in some other jurisdiction aimed at preventing payment to the assured. It is by no means clear that s. 13A intends that the assured should have to wait for months or years without compensation while matters of this sort are sorted out, merely because they arise independently of the insurer's fault.

Second, if this is right, presumably it also means that an insurer is intended to be liable not only for its own unreasonable foot-dragging and that of its employees,

35 Report, para. 28.37.

36 Compare the situation in Australia, where s. 57 of the Insurance Contracts Act 1984 (Cth) exacts a fixed, fairly painful, rate of interest as from "the day as from which it was unreasonable for the insurer to have withheld payment". Here, it has been said that what is reasonable must take account "not only of the chance of fraud, a not uncommon visitation on insurers, or other disentitlement of the insured, but also of the existence of the insured's apparent contractual rights attendant on a disaster bearing vitally on its commercial well-being" (see *Protean (Holdings) Ltd v American Home Assurance Co* (1986) 4 ANZ Ins Cas 74,051 at 75,059 (Marks J). See also *Settlement Wine Co Pty Ltd v National & General Insurance Co Ltd* (1994) 62 SASR 40, 70, where Perry J said that reasonableness "should be determined objectively" as "a question of fact"; and *Tropicus Orchids Flowers and Foliage Pty Ltd v Territory Insurance Office* (1998) 148 FLR 441, 489 (Mildren J) (same).

but also for the negligence of independent contractors engaged by it. Take, for example, the case where, following a factory fire, underwriters engage independent investigators to examine the cause of the casualty and independent loss adjusters to appraise the assured's damage from it; and assume that, through idleness or incompetence, those persons take three times as long as they should to prepare the necessary report. In such a case, the insurer should not be able to hide behind the fact that it was not itself at fault: a position reflecting the general contractual rule that even if personally blameless a contractor is liable for the negligence of independent contractors employed by him.[37]

Third, when s. 13A requires reasonably prompt payment of "any sums due in respect of the claim", does this of necessity refer to the *whole* of the sum payable under the policy, or is it possible to split the payout into different parts?[38] The point matters a lot. Imagine the case of a £100,000 claim under a business interruption policy following a major flood, where the quantification of the amount due depends (as it nearly always will) on a close analysis of the policyholder's accounts to fix the exact amount of profits lost. Now add a further factor: while getting a final figure will reasonably take three months, it is clear that on the most conservative reckoning the claim is good for £40,000. Is the insurer entitled to do nothing until the global sum due has been quantified, and only then pay the entire amount; or must it make a payment on account of £40,000 immediately, on pain of possible liability in damages for lost business opportunities if it fails to do so? It is to be hoped that the section will be construed as providing for different "reasonable times" for different tranches of a claim, since otherwise there would be scope for highly arbitrary results. To take an extreme case, if 95% of a £100,000 claim was clearly justified but the other 5% required extensive investigation, it would be a curious case of the tail wagging the dog if the insurer could withhold anything at all until the whole matter was completely sorted out.[39] But the meaning of s. 13A is entirely unclear here, and this matter will probably have to be sorted out for the benefit of insurance lawyers at the expense of some hapless litigant.[40]

6.3.3 Disputed claims: s. 13A(4)

The Law Commissions understandably wished to preserve the right of an insurer to dispute a claim without being potentially open to a claim for large damages for paying it late. Hence, we have s. 13A(4) of the 2015 Act, stating that there is no

37 *Photo Production Ltd v Securicor Transport Ltd* [1980] AC 827, 848 (Lord Diplock); *Woodland v Swimming Teachers Association* [2013] UKSC 66, [2014] AC 537 at [7] (Lord Sumption).

38 The Law Commissions' report is unhelpful here, stating simply that "The sums due in respect of the claim" encompass sums which are 'due' either by virtue of an agreement between the parties or because they have been determined by a court to be payable by the insurer" (para. 28.16).

39 As is the case with disputed claims, where it is made clear under s. 13A(4) that the insurer's protection where a claim is disputed in part is limited to the part genuinely in contention; see below.

40 The Law Commissions might have dealt with this, but skated round the issue, merely stating that there was no general duty to make a payment on account, but that any payment if made might go to mitigate any loss: see paras. 28.63–28.65.

liability as such where the insurer shows that a claim is disputed on honest and reasonable grounds, provided that the insurer's conduct in handling the claim is otherwise reasonable. It is made clear, moreover, that for these purposes a claim is severable: hence, if only part of it is reasonably disputed, the protection only applies to that part, with potential liability in damages if there is no payment on account of the undisputed residue.[41]

The burden of proof here is stated to be on the insurer,[42] though presumably this requirement will only bite in cases where the assured first shows that payment has been delayed for what would otherwise be an unreasonable time.[43]

The proviso to s. 13A(4) is, however, important. This says that although delay due to a reasonable dispute is not as such unreasonable, the conduct of the insurer in handling the claim may be a relevant factor in deciding whether that term was breached and, if so, when. Since logically this provision can only apply in cases where the claim is indeed reasonably disputed, the best analysis of it seems to be that it is intended to deny the insurer the benefit of the s. 13A(4) "safe harbour" insofar as it is guilty of some other culpable delay which adds to the period during which the assured has to wait.[44] The Law Commissions gave the examples of dilatory investigation by an insurer who otherwise had good reason to query a claim, or persistence in a denial of liability following the appearance of convincing evidence of a claim's legitimacy.[45] Another example might be prior delay in payment, followed by the raising of a genuine ground of dispute at a late stage, in which case there might be liability for the unreasonable delay up to the time the dispute was raised. Yet another might arise from delays to payment caused by "stonewalling", or some similar failure by the insurer to provide reasonable details of its objection to payment at the request of the insured.

A more difficult issue is what happens if matters actually come to litigation (or arbitration). Insofar as it remains reasonable to dispute liability, the safe harbour presumably continues to apply. But what if it does not? Is unreasonableness in the conduct of the litigation, or for that matter over-optimism in appealing an adverse judgment, to be dealt with as a breach of s. 13A giving rise to damages, or should it be regarded as a matter for the court alone? An analogy with the duty of utmost good faith might suggest the latter;[46] in that context it seems clear that, once matters have come to court, the duties arising from the insurance contract should be subsumed in those owed to the court, which has very adequate powers to deal with unreasonable litigants.[47] On the other hand, the structure and scheme of s. 13A(4) would, when looked at closely, appear to dictate the opposite result. This

41 "[T]he insurer does not breach the term implied by subsection (1) merely by failing to pay the claim *(or the affected part of it)* while the dispute is continuing" (italics supplied).

42 "If *the insurer shows that* there were reasonable grounds" (italics supplied).

43 Report, paras. 28.84–28.85.

44 In so far as both causes, unreasonable handling and reasonable dispute, led concurrently to the same degree of delay, presumably any claim for damages for unreasonable handling would fail on causation grounds.

45 Report, para. 28.51.

46 See *The Star Sea* [2001] UKHL 1, [2003] 1 AC 469 esp. at [75]-[77] (Lord Hobhouse).

47 "The battle lines have been drawn and new remedies are available to the parties. The disclosure of documents and facts are provided for with appropriate sanctions; the orders are discretionary within

subsection aimed at protecting insurers raising a reasonable dispute presupposes the existence of what would otherwise be an unreasonable delay making those insurers liable for damages. The defence provided for is carefully limited, and insofar as it does not apply, then (whether in litigation or otherwise) the default position should return, with the insurer liable on principle to compensate the assured.

6.3.4 Damages[48]

Once failure to pay within a reasonable time is shown, the Law Commissions' view is straightforward: any liability would be for ordinary contractual damages calculated and constricted in the same way as they are under the general law of contract.[49] They would thus be subject to the standard rules of causation, remoteness, mitigation and so on.

Little need be said about the first of these requirements. Presumably, it is enough that the late payment was a substantial rather than necessarily an exclusive cause of the loss:[50] so, for example, where there is a claim for loss of business, the insurer will not be able to escape by saying that a contributory cause was a general downturn in commercial confidence. Nevertheless, proof that late payment was even a substantial occasion of a given loss may provide quite a high hurdle for claimants – at least if the experience of claims for late payment generally is any guide.[51] In a suitable case, it is doubtless possible for a claim to be split with some, but not all, losses following late payment to be regarded as actually caused by it.[52]

As regards the rule of remoteness, this is worth a closer look. In practice, this is a factor that may well put a considerable limit on what is recoverable under the 2015 Act. The criterion under *Hadley v Baxendale*[53] is, one has to remember, what was foreseeable at the time of the conclusion of the contract. In the insurance context, this means what might have been envisaged as a plausible consequence of late payment of claims as at the time the relevant policy was taken out (or last renewed). It follows that, while general loss of profits may well be foreseeable,[54]

the parameters laid down by the procedural rules." *The Star Sea* [2001] UKHL 1, [2003] 1 AC 469 at [75] (Lord Hobhouse).

48 See, generally, S. Drummond, "Damages for consequential loss when the insurer fails to pay" (2005) 16 Ins LJ 128, concerning the position in Australia.

49 "We are satisfied that the general law of calculation of contractual damages is sufficiently well developed and well understood as to require no definition in statute", Report, para. 28.54.

50 This is the case generally in breach of contract cases: e.g. *Heskell v Continental Express Ltd* [1950] 1 All ER 1033, 1047 (Devlin J); *Banque Keyser Ullmann SA v Skandia (UK) Insurance Co Ltd* [1990] 1 QB 665, 716 (Steyn J).

51 Compare *Fortis Bank SA/NV v Indian Overseas Bank* [2011] EWHC 538 (Comm), [2011] 2 Lloyd's Rep 190; *Paros Plc v Worldlink Group Plc* [2012] EWHC 394 (Comm), both decisions concerning liability for late payment of debts under *Sempra Metals Ltd (formerly Metallgesellschaft Ltd) v Inland Revenue Commissioners* [2007] UKHL 34, [2008] 1 AC 561.

52 See *Fast Ferries One SA v Ferries Australia Pty Ltd* [2000] 1 Lloyd's Rep 534, 541–542 (late payment of debt; claimant's interest costs recoverable for only part of delay, since residue of interest charges due to claimant's own foot-dragging in progressing the claim).

53 (1854) 9 Ex. 341.

54 Cf. the Australian decision in *Brescia Furniture Pty Ltd v QBE Insurance (Australia) Ltd* [2007] NSWSC 598 (late payment of reinstatement cost after fire: general loss of profits allowed). But this

the loss of particularly profitable business opportunities only becoming apparent during the currency of the policy are likely to be too remote even if shown to result from late payment; and so also with heavy losses, such as unusually expensive types of borrowing to which an unpaid insured may resort.[55] On the other hand, the limiting effect of *Hadley v Baxendale* should not be overstated. Indeed, there may be a sting in the tail for insurers as regards small and medium enterprises. If such a business suffers a disaster, it is not unlikely in the nature of things that in the absence of swift payment the business itself will collapse. This is particularly significant because of the demise in 2003 of what was left of the rule that damages were not available for losses due to a claimant's lack of ready cash.[56] If this is right, we may well see a surprisingly large number of claims against insurers for the consequences of insolvency or personal bankruptcy. Such claims can in practice be considerable, and because of s. 16A there will be limited scope for insurers to avoid them by contractual stipulation.

Mitigation may well also play a part in putting limits to such claims. Claims for borrowings consequent on non-payment will presumably be subject to close scrutiny over whether funding could have been obtained more cheaply elsewhere: again, a business with ample resources to reinstate losses at its own expense without undue disturbance of its cash-flow might be expected to do so, and to that extent be barred from claiming loss of profits if it did not, pending payment. On the other hand, the duty to mitigate is not applied too harshly against claimants; and one expects that in most cases it will not be regarded as unreasonable to wait for a payout before incurring expense.[57]

On the general issue of the measure of recovery, there are a fair number of specific issues that may arise.

First, there is the question of the specificity with which any loss will have to be shown in order to give rise to a claim for damages. Clearly, insofar as payments such as interest on borrowings are actually proved in cash terms there will be no difficulty in recovering them: so too with loss of profits established with incontrovertible balance sheet evidence. But matters are often untidier than this. There is no doubt that, once the 2015 Act is bedded in, courts will be asked to draw inferences and make more impressionistic awards of general profits, or compensate late receipt with a general award of compound interest. How far is this possible? In Australia, where liability under general contract law for late payment is fairly well-established, awards of compound interest as general damages have been made,[58]

---

will not always be so: cf. *Ferrcom Pty Limited v Commercial Union Assurance Co of Australia Limited* (1989) 5 ANZ Ins Cas 60–907 (lost hire profits from unrestored crane following late payment unforeseeable).

55 Cf. the *Sempra* decision in *Sear v Kingfisher Builders Ltd* [2013] All ER (D) 106 (Jan).

56 See the well-known decision in *Lagden v O'Connor* [2003] UKHL 64, [2004] 1 AC 1067, finally putting to rest what was left of *The Liesbosch* [1933] AC 449.

57 Cf. the tort case of *Dodd Properties Ltd v Canterbury City Council* [1980] 1 WLR 433; also the Australian late insurance payment case of *Brescia Furniture Pty Ltd v QBE Insurance (Australia) Ltd* [2007] NSWSC 598 at [490] (Hammerschlag J).

58 For example, *Tropicus Orchids Flowers & Foliage Pty Ltd v Territory Insurance Office* (1998) 148 FLR 441, esp. at 494–495.

as have awards based on fairly unspecific inferences of lost profits.[59] Whether this will necessarily follow in England is more doubtful, however. The nearest analogy is damages for late payment of debts under *Sempra Metals Ltd v Inland Revenue Commissioners*;[60] and here the tendency is to say that claims must be proved with some specificity. General claims for lost profits and the like were specifically discountenanced in *Sempra Metals* itself;[61] and subsequent authorities have tended to echo this,[62] though not universally.[63] It remains to be seen how far these authorities will be followed in cases under the Insurance Act 2015.

Second, whatever the position as regards money losses, there is the related topic of claims for other losses. In jurisdictions that permit damages for late payment of insurance monies, these have been held to include damages for distress where this is foreseeable,[64] not to mention general damages for loss of use of a wrongfully unrepaired vehicle which an indigent insured is unable to repair until paid.[65] There seems no reason why at least the latter should not also be allowed cases under the Act. The former, however, is more problematical. In England, unlike most Commonwealth jurisdictions, damages for distress resulting from breach of contract are available not on the basis of foreseeability, but only in contracts aimed wholly or partly at protecting peace of mind.[66] It must be open to some doubt whether a court would be prepared so to categorise insurance contracts, even in the hands of a consumer.

Third, if matters come to litigation, a court making an award of damages for late payment must presumably take care to disregard any expenses connected with litigation which could otherwise be awarded as costs.[67]

Fourth, what happens where losses are suffered partly because of late payment of insurance monies but partly also because of contributory negligence by the insured? It would seem likely that this is irrelevant. This is because contributory negligence only affects contractual duties that parallel tort duties;[68] and, at least

59 *Settlement Wine Co Pty Ltd v National & General Insurance Co Ltd* (1994) 62 SASR 40 (inferences of extra borrowing costs reducing profitability).

60 [2007] UKHL 34, [2008] 1 AC 561.

61 See *Sempra Metals Ltd v Inland Revenue Comm'rs* [2007] UKHL 34, [2008] 1 AC 561 at [17] (Lord Hope, [94]-[96] (Lord Nicholls), [216] (Lord Mance).

62 See (interest) *Dyson Technology Ltd v Curtis* [2010] EWHC 3289 (Ch), *JSC BTA Bank v Ablyazov (Granton Action)* [2013] EWHC 867 (Comm); (profits) *Cassa di Risparmio della Repubblica di San Marino SpA v Barclays Bank Ltd* [2011] EWHC 484 (Comm) [2011] 1 CLC 701.

63 A notable exception is *Equitas Ltd v Walsham Bros & Co Ltd* [2013] EWHC 3264 (Comm), [2014] PNLR 8 where, in a case of late accounting by a broker, Males J was prepared to presume compound interest losses of 1% over LIBOR without specific proof (see [123]-[126]).

64 *Gaunt v Gold Star Insurance Co Ltd* [1991] 2 NZLR 341 (failure to pay for vehicle repairs on time: $NZ1000 distress damages).

65 See the Scottish decision in *Davidson v Guardian Royal Exchange Assurance Ltd* [1979] 1 Lloyd's Rep 406.

66 *Johnson v Gore Wood* [2002] 2 AC 1, 37–38, (Lord Bingham), 48–50 (Lord Cooke), 56 (Lord Hutton), 68 (Lord Millett); *Farley v Skinner (No 2)* [2001] UKHL 49, [2002] 2 AC 732, 746 (Lord Steyn), 752–753 (Lord Clyde), 757 (Lord Hutton), 767 (Lord Scott).

67 See *Seavision Investment SA v Evennett, The Tiburon* [1992] 2 Lloyd's Rep 26, 34 (Scott LJ).

68 *Forsikringsaktieselskapet Vesta v Butcher* [1986] 2 Lloyd's Rep 179, (on appeal) [1989] AC 852; *Clerk & Lindsell on Torts* (21st ed, Sweet & Maxwell 2014), 3-54.

at first sight, the insurer's duty to pay on time seems to be purely contractual. Nevertheless, the matter cannot be regarded as entirely beyond doubt.[69]

Fifth, what is the position of third party victims as regards liability insurance? Generally, they will not be able to take advantage of s. 13A, however disgracefully late they are paid. This is because the victim is not a party to the insurance contract and, therefore, cannot sue for breach of it.[70] On the other hand, if the insured happens to be insolvent, it is submitted that the position may possibly be different (however arbitrary this distinction may be). This is because, from the moment of insolvency, the insurer's duty to pay the amount of the insured's liability ceases to be owed to the insured and is transferred by operation of law to the victim:[71] and if the contractual right to receive this money is transferred, then the conclusion seems inescapable that this carries with it the right in the victim to sue for damages if it is not paid when it should be.[72]

6.3.5 The independent nature of the liability in damages

Section 13A(5) makes the point that any damages available under the section are in addition to, and separate from, the duty to pay the actual indemnity provided for under the policy. They are also independent of any other right to interest inhering in the policyholder, whether under the insurance contract itself, under another enactment, at the court's discretion, or otherwise.

The effect of this is mostly straightforward. If a policy provides expressly for payment of interest this does not pre-empt the right to damages if the policyholder's loss is greater than the amount of interest awarded. Similarly, if a policyholder is only partially compensated by any damages awarded for late payment there is no reason why he should not recover pre-judgment interest as regards the residue of his loss.[73] Again, damages under s. 13A may be available even if interest under s. 35A of the Senior Courts Act 1981 is not (for example, if the full amount of the claim is paid at the last minute before proceedings are commenced).[74]

Nevertheless, it seems pretty clear that the independence of the damages remedy cannot be taken entirely literally. Thus, when pre-judgment interest is awarded on sums due, presumably there will have to be a balancing reduction in any damages

69 This is because of the decision of Males J in *Equitas Ltd v Walsham Bros & Co Ltd* [2013] EWHC 3264 (Comm), [2014] PNLR 8, regarding it as arguable that a contractual duty to pay money within a reasonable time may give rise to liability in tort in the event of negligent late payment. That case concerned a reinsurance broker's duty to pay over reinsurance proceeds, but the principle, if good, could equally apply to an insurer's duty to pay a policyholder.

70 Theoretically, a liability insurance contract could give a victim the right to sue direct under the Contracts (Rights of Third Parties) Act 1999. But this rarely, if ever, happens.

71 See the Third Parties (Rights against Insurers) Act 2010, s. 1(2).

72 The Report, paras. 28.12–28.13, says this on the 2010 Act: "[A] third party recipient of rights against an insurer under the Act would only be able to claim for a loss if the insured would have been required to compensate the third party for the loss *and* the insurer would then have been required to compensate the insured for paying the loss. We think this would arise rarely in the context of remedies for late payment." With respect, this is difficult to understand.

73 Accepted by Steel J in *Fast Ferries One SA v Ferries Australia Pty Ltd* [2000] 1 Lloyd's Rep 534, 542.

74 See *President of India v La Pintada* [1985] AC 104.

for late payment, on the basis that the interest goes to reduce the loss which those damages go to compensate: indeed, any other result would lead to blatant double-dipping.[75] Conversely, if a policyholder claims (or has already received) compensation for late payment, it is suggested that a court will, in its discretion, trim any pre-judgment interest award in order to avoid double recovery.[76]

What is more awkward is the relation between the right under s. 13A and recoveries under a separate business interruption policy. Suppose a trader with both machinery and business interruption cover suffers a fire destroying his entire corpus of machinery. Imagine further that the machinery insurer unreasonably pays the costs of replacement three months late, causing a diminution in profits. It would seem that even if the interruption cover responds to a lost profits claim for the entire period, this will not affect any claim for damages against the machinery insurer.[77] Admittedly in many cases this will not result in over-compensation because a business interruption insurer is presumptively subrogated to any lost profits claims against third parties.[78] Nevertheless, it is worth noting that the disregard of insurance recoveries applies even where there is no subrogation,[79] which may conceivably be relevant in this regard.[80]

6.3.6 Contracting-out

Section 16A, on contracting-out, is largely straightforward. No escape at all is to be allowed in consumer insurance: elsewhere contracting-out by clear words is permitted, except where the insurer knew that it was in breach of the duty of timeous payment, or did not care whether or not it was in breach (s. 16A(3)). Two points are, however, worth making here.

First, there is some room for argument as to whose knowledge counts. Presumably that of mere independent contractors will not do since, even if there is liability for the acts of such parties,[81] their knowledge is not that of the insurer itself. But accepting that the relevant awareness must be that of the insurer, is this a case where ordinary rules of vicarious liability for employees apply, or must

75 Report, para. 28.17.

76 This is true under the general law: see *Nykredit Mortgage Bank plc v Edward Erdman Group Ltd (No 2)* [1997] 1 WLR 1627. A similar principle has been applied in the context of late payment of insurance monies in Australia: *Moss v Sun Alliance Australia Ltd* (1990) 55 SASR 145.

77 Under the principle in *Bradburn v Gt Western Ry Co* (1874) LR 10 Ex 1, that insurance recoveries are out of account in damages claims. This applies equally to insurance-related damages claims: see e.g. *FNCB v Barnet Devanney (Harrow) Ltd* [2000] PNLR 248 (brokers) and *Brown v KMR Services Ltd* [1995] 4 All ER 598 (underwriting agents).

78 "The insurer is subrogated to any claim *of any character* which the insured is entitled to bring in proceedings against a third party to diminish his loss", *McGillivray on Insurance Law* (13th ed, Sweet & Maxwell 2015), 24–036 (italics supplied). For an example see *Brit Inns Ltd v Brit Inns Ltd (In Liquidation) v BDW Trading Ltd* [2012] EWHC 2143 (TCC), (2012) 145 Con LR 181.

79 See *Portman Building Society v Bevan Ashford* [2000] PNLR 344.

80 Notably if the machinery and business interruption policies are with the same insurer. It must be arguable that in such a case the insurance proceeds disregard continues to apply: yet the insurer can hardly be subrogated to a claim against itself.

81 After the decision in *Woodland v Swimming Teachers Association* [2013] UKSC 66, [2014] AC 537 an insurer might well find itself facing liability for the acts of persons such as coverholders or third party administrators appointed to carry out the insurer's functions.

the knowledge be imputable to the insurer through some "directing mind and will"? The Law Commissions seem to have accepted the former solution, giving the example of a claims handler shelving hard work until later in order to secure a bonus.[82] But there is a good deal to be said in favour of the latter view. For one thing, it is more consistent with the wording of s. 16A(5), which refers to an insurer that "knew that it was in breach", rather than simply to a breach committed knowingly or some such. Furthermore, such a reading would reflect the general common law position on exoneration for fraud, this being barred in the case of fraud committed by those in charge of a company but freely permitted in the case of employees' misconduct.[83] Furthermore, if the knowledge of mere employees counts, the consequences could be wide-ranging. The right to exoneration could disappear as a result of the misbehaviour of one possibly very junior maverick claims handler. The adoption of a vicarious liability standard might also cause difficulties where a team of claims handlers delays dealing with a claim for a time that is in fact unreasonable, and it is then shown that one member thought this was the case but was overruled by his colleagues who disbelieved him. Indeed, the loss of the right to exclude liability could go further and embrace mere idleness, as where a lazy employee in the claims department consistently puts off work despite having a strong suspicion that it is seriously overdue. In none of these cases is it obvious that the insurer is guilty of such wrongdoing as ought to invalidate a freely-agreed exemption clause.

Second, while it seems clear that no exoneration will be allowed in the case of intentional delay to a claim in the knowledge that it is good, or deliberate delay in investigation for no good reason, one suspects that outside these cases conduct depriving the insurer of the right to limit will be difficult to show. What is a reasonable time is a congenitally vague standard, on which opinions can differ enormously. Assuming that the relevant knowledge must extend to the unreasonableness as well as to the simple fact of the delay, one suspects that such knowledge will be rare in practice and even where present almost impossible to prove.

6.4 Conclusion

The conclusion to this chapter can be very briefly stated. There is no doubt that s. 13A of the 2015 Act is an advance on the previous law; that it fills an important lacuna; and that it brings English insurance law closer into line with provisions elsewhere. Nevertheless, the sheer length of this chapter shows that there still remains a surprising degree of uncertainty on the subject of late payment: undoubtedly enough to provide insurance lawyers with a great deal to do in the coming years.

82 Report, para. 28.98.

83 *HIH Casualty & General Insurance Ltd v Chase Manhattan Bank* [2003] UKHL 6, [2003] 2 Lloyd's Rep 61 at [76] (Lord Hoffmann).

CHAPTER 7

Contracting out of the Insurance Act 2015 in commercial insurance contracts

*Dr George Leloudas**

7.1 Introduction

Lord Davidson argued during the Parliamentary debate on the Insurance Bill that the British Government should "monitor and test the efficacy of Clause 16".[1] The reason for making this suggestion was to "avoid relentless contracting out simply by way of forms [because it] . . . would undermine much of the benefit of this reform".[2]

This hostility towards the contracting out provisions of the Insurance Act 2015 ("2015 Act") should not come as a surprise. Even the Law Commission viewed them as a necessary evil in the context of non-consumer insurance, treating the relevant sections as the result of a balancing act. They were included in order to persuade the insurance industry to support the most comprehensive insurance law development since the enactment of the Marine Insurance Act (MIA) 1906. This overarching goal also explains the absence of any distinction among the different classes of non-consumer insurance that the 2015 Act covers.

However, the Law Commission recommended that this "one-size-fits-all" drafting philosophy should not be reflected in the interpretation of the contracting out provisions. Instead, it suggested that courts should make a distinction between small to medium-sized enterprises (SMEs) that buy insurance online or via non-specialised brokers, and sophisticated commercial entities which opt for tailor-made policies, instructing as a matter of practice specialised brokers and lawyers to influence and advise on the wordings.

With respect to the first category ("SMEs insurance") the Commission argued against "boilerplate clauses which opt out of the default regime as a matter of routine".[3] These buyers of insurance should be treated as "quasi-consumers". As such, they will be given the option to "make an informed decision . . . about whether to agree to the alternative position, to negotiate for the default position or to seek an alternative insurance provider".[4]

* Associate Professor, Institute of International Shipping and Trade Law, Swansea University.

1 HL Deb 29 July 2014, col GC627.

2 Ibid.

3 *Insurance Contract Law: Business Disclosure; Warranties; Insurers' Remedies for Fraudulent Claims; and Late Payment*, Joint Consultation Paper, (2014), Law Com No 353/Scot Law Com No 238, at [29.24] ("Law Commission Report").

4 Ibid. at [29.29].

With respect to the second category ("sophisticated insurance"), the Law Commission acknowledged that the insurers' contractual freedom is one of the (worth preserving) advantages of the UK insurance market: "[t]he enormous value of the UK insurance market depends on the existence of a flexible legal regime . . . Given the range of risks which may be covered by the non-consumer regime, parties may need freedom to agree bespoke arrangements in their contracts."[5] As a result, the Commission predicted that this flexibility would result in widespread contracting out of the 2015 Act. The British Government during the Parliamentary debate made a different prediction arguing that there was no "pent-up demand for widespread contracting out".[6] Still, the Government committed that a review will be undertaken within five years from the enactment of the 2015 Act.

Fast forward to March 2016 and the London insurance market has already drafted clauses to fit into the 2015 Act.[7] Prominent among them are the ones on contracting out. Five out of the eighteen clauses published by the Lloyd's Market Association (LMA) provide for ways of bypassing the 2015 Act. Whether they will actually be used is an issue that remains to be seen. The dominant view among marine insurers is that they will be popular. At the same time, aviation insurers are not convinced yet: "[t]he prevailing view of AICG members seemed to be to apply the Act correctly within existing contractual provisions rather than provide opt-out options".[8]

Having said that, the general feeling is that the contracting out provisions will be among the first sections of the 2015 Act to attract judicial attention.[9] Judicial intervention was actually encouraged by the Law Commission in 2014. The contracting out provisions are intentionally drafted in a broad manner to enable courts "to differentiate between different scenarios, from well-advised, commercially aware insurance buyers to smaller insureds buying 'off the shelf' and, increasingly, online".[10]

The aim of this chapter is to provide an analysis of the contracting out sections of the 2015 Act as applicable to non-consumer insurance contracts. As part of the analysis an attempt to predict the attitude of English courts will be made, fully cognisant of the fact that predicting the future is a fool's game.

7.2 The philosophy behind the contracting out provisions of the 2015 Act

Considering the draconian effect of contracting out, it might come as a surprise that the 2015 Act contains only two relevant sections, namely ss. 16 and 17. This "light" approach reflects the aim of the Law Commission to avoid the creation of

5 Ibid. at [29.25].
6 HL Deb 29 July 2014, col GC629.
7 See http://www.lmalloyds.com/actclauses (last accessed 8 April 2016).
8 See http://www.aicg.co.uk/AICG_Web/Minutes/Minutes28January2016.aspx, at [3.2] (last accessed 8 April 2016).
9 B. Soyer, "Risk control clauses in insurance law: law reform and the future" [2016] CLJ 109, at p. 124 ("Soyer risk control clauses").
10 Law Commission Report, at [29.29].

a complicated test. In that respect, litigation-sensitive concepts, such as fairness and reasonableness, were intentionally ignored. Their inclusion would have opened the door to further qualitative considerations, such as good faith and inducement, that would inevitably attract protracted litigation. Such a development would most probably jeopardise one of the stated aims of the 2015 Act, i.e. "[t]o ensure that the contracting out provisions are not so onerous as to interfere with the smooth running of the insurance market".[11] In that respect, the Law Commission did want courts to have flexibility in applying them, yet it did not want to give insurers great leeway to judicially redraft them.

To safeguard the smooth running of the insurance market, the 2015 Act imposes very few restrictions "on the *extent* to which the regime can be altered (or excluded) in a non-consumer insurance contract".[12] In essence, insurers are at liberty to opt out of individual Parts of the 2015 Act (with the exception of s. 9 on "basis of contract" clauses)[13] provided they satisfy the transparency requirements of s. 17.

The counterargument is that this wide liberty threatens the overarching aim of the 2015 Act, namely to ensure "a better balance of interests between policyholders and insurers".[14] A cynic would say that this liberty actually works against the reform as it permits insurers to retain the legal regime that the 2015 Act purports to change. The prohibition of "basis of contract" clauses, the argument continues, is mostly aesthetic as they were not very popular in sophisticated insurance markets even before the 2015 Act. In that respect, the contracting out provisions are predominantly a political compromise to water down the opposition to the reform of sophisticated insurance markets. A compromise that comes in the face of evidence that "even large businesses find the disclosure duty difficult to comply with and that the issue is a common source of dispute".[15]

The Law Commission took a pragmatic approach by sacrificing the uniform application of the 2015 Act to ensure its enactment. It addressed the concerns of a segment of the insurance market that had the political power to prevent the implementation of the 2015 Act; with the end result being that no insured would be able to get its benefits. For the Commission, the extent that the contracting out provisions threaten the overarching aim of the Act would depend on the way this liberty is exercised. In that respect, the aim of ss. 16 and 17 should be to manage the way insurers opt out of the 2015 Act, fully aware that some of them might opt out as a matter of practice.

Inevitably, the following question is raised: to what extent do ss. 16 and 17 reflect this philosophy of the Law Commission? To answer it an overview of the relevant sections is required.

11 Ibid.
12 Ibid. at [29.30].
13 See s. 16(1) of the Insurance Act 2015.
14 Law Commission Report, at [1.6].
15 Ibid. at [5.58].

7.3 The contracting out provisions of the 2015 Act

The default position is found in s. 16(2): a term in a non-consumer insurance contract that puts the insured "in a worse position" regarding the duty of fair presentation (Part 2), warranties and other "risk reduction" terms (Part 3) and fraudulent claims (Part 4) than the 2015 Act ("disadvantageous term") is of no effect. For the disadvantageous term to be valid, the 2015 Act requires insurers to satisfy both of the following transparency requirements of s. 17:

1. They "must take sufficient steps to draw the disadvantageous term to the insured's attention before the contract is entered into or the variation agreed";[16]
2. They must make sure that the effect of the "disadvantageous term [is] clear and unambiguous".[17]

Reflecting the spirit of compromise, s. 17(4) provides some guidance on how to interpret these two requirements: "the characteristics of insured persons of the kind in question, and the circumstances of the transaction, are to be taken into account". This is not the end of the story as the 2015 Act gives insurers a second bite at the cherry. If they are unable to satisfy these two transparency requirements, insurers will still be able to use a disadvantageous term provided they prove that "the insured (or its agent) had actual knowledge of the disadvantageous term when the contract was entered into or the variation agreed".[18]

7.4 A critical analysis of the contracting out provisions of the 2015 Act

7.4.1 An analysis of s. 16(2)

The 2015 Act steers clear of legal terminology in s. 16(2). The test of putting the insured "in a worse position" is copied from the Consumer Insurance (Disclosure and Representations) Act 2012,[19] yet it does not have judicial history. Its perceived simplicity in application was the main reason behind its acceptance. It was considered that it would be relatively straightforward to decide on a term-by-term basis whether they are detrimental to the interests of the insured. That will be the case in the majority of situations, especially when dealing with warranties and other "risk reduction" terms. The drafters worked on the assumption that, despite the criticism of s. 11, the Act provides a regime friendlier to the insured.

However, this is not always a correct assumption as s. 16 does not consider the interrelation among the various terms used in the policy. The following is a (rather extreme) example of how ss. 16 and 17 can be manipulated. An insurer retains the effect of MIA 1906 on warranties in a policy by fulfilling the transparency requirements of s. 17. At the same time, it retains the effect of s. 11 of the 2015

16 Section 17(2) of the Insurance Act 2015.
17 Section 17(3) of the Insurance Act 2015.
18 Section 17(5) of the Insurance Act 2015.
19 Section 10 of the Consumer Insurance (Disclosure and Representations) Act 2012.

Act with respect to exclusion clauses. In that respect, there is no requirement to inform the insured about the effects of s. 11 on exclusion clauses as there is a presumption that it improves its position.

However, it is likely that this is a wrong presumption. If exclusion clauses fall into the scope of s. 11 (as the Law Commission suggests),[20] the effect is to reverse the burden of proof: "the insured would have the burden of proving that non-compliance with the term could not have increased the risk of the loss that actually occurred, in the circumstances in which it occurred".[21] In this case, the insurer has done nothing wrong. It complied with s. 17 regarding warranties in the policy and applied the 2015 Act to exclusions without explaining the effect of its application. Yet, the insured is put in an overall "worse position" as the insurers picked the best (for them) of both worlds. His/her position is worse than it would have been if MIA 1906 applied to the entirety of the policy. There is nothing in the 2015 Act to prevent such "cherry-picking" as soon as the insurer complies with the transparency requirements. Still, it is unlikely that this end result is what the Law Commission had in mind when agreeing to the contracting out compromise. It dents the overarching aim of the 2015 Act and leaves it open to manipulation. In sophisticated insurance markets the burden is on the broker to protect the insured from such manipulative application of the 2015 Act, raising the question whether the broker would expose itself to liability if it fails to identify the pitfall. Yet, in SMEs insurance markets, where brokers are frequently not retained, it is unlikely that the insured would be forewarned. It is to be hoped that judicial intervention will close this loophole.

7.4.2 An analysis of s. 17(2)

The transparency requirements of s. 17 are a combination of old and new. Section 17(2) adapts the test on contractual incorporation of terms, while s. 17(3) adds the requirement that the disadvantageous term must be "clear and unambiguous as to its effect". To ensure that SMEs are treated differently to sophisticated insurance buyers, s. 17(4) provides that the interpretation of the said sections shall consider the characteristics of the insured and the insurance market in which it operates. The requirement in s. 17(2) essentially reflects existing law on incorporation, i.e. that "adequate steps have been taken to bring [the incorporated terms] reasonably to the attention of the [buyer] before or at the time he enters into the contract".[22]

In that respect s. 17(2) requires the insurer to:

a) "take sufficient steps" to;
b) "draw the disadvantageous term to the insured's attention";
c) "before the contract is entered into or the variation agreed".

20 Law Commission Report, at [A.82].

21 H. Wright, "The Insurance Act 2015: a practical guide to changes in UK Insurance Law, prepared for members of the Lloyd's Market Association and the International Underwriting Association" (2016), at [71] (available at http://www.7kbw.co.uk/media/uploaded_files/Guide_to_the_Insurance_Act.pdf, last accessed 8 April 2016) ("Insurers' report on the 2015 Act").

22 J. Wilson, *Carriage of Goods by Sea*, (2010, Pearson Education), at p. 248.

It is important that the disadvantageous term be identified before the insurer signs the slip or accepts the insurance proposal online. When the insured uses a broker to buy insurance it is likely that the insurer will bring the term to the attention of the broker during the placement (or renewal) discussions, with relevant notes to that effect to be made. The Law Commission has suggested that placing an asterisk next to the disadvantageous term(s) is the bare minimum to satisfy s. 17(2).[23] This is the case even if a number of other (irrelevant for the application of the 2015 Act) terms are similarly highlighted. In that respect, the onus is on the broker to review the relevant clauses and question the insurer or negotiate their amendment. This approach of the Law Commission is not surprising and reflects the overall attitude of English courts towards the responsibilities of brokers to insureds. They are required to take an active role in advising their clients regarding the cover, including the consequences of the 2015 Act. The Law Commission also (rightly) suggests that such highlighting would not be sufficient to satisfy s. 17(2) when the insured deals directly with the insurer either in person or online.[24] In such situations highlighting is required to alert the insured that the term is not necessarily in his/her best interests and direct him/her to the relevant sections for understanding the reasons and the consequences; whereas, in the case of the broker, the highlighting is only required to alert him/her that the term requires further attention.

With respect to sophisticated insurance markets, the Commission raises the following two examples. In the first one a broker negotiates a tailor-made marine policy with an insurer. The insurer persuades the broker following extensive discussions to include the codes of two standard contracting out clauses in the slip (assuming that their wordings comply with s. 17(3)). The Commission rightly concludes that s. 17(2) is satisfied but for reasons that are subject to criticism.[25] In the second example the broker and the insurer agree to use a standard marine policy that recently incorporated these two standard clauses excluding the application of the 2015 Act on warranties. The Commission comes to the (arguably mistaken) conclusion that s. 17(2) is not satisfied because the insurer "does not mention [the standard clauses], or its desire to exclude certain portions of the [2015] Act".[26]

In these two examples the decisive point for the Law Commission seems to be whether the preference to have the standard contracting out clauses incorporated into the slip was ever raised by the insurers. If this is the case, the disadvantageous clauses were drawn to the broker's attention in accordance with s. 17(2). The Commission argues that it is important for the contracting out clauses to "have been discussed with [the broker]", which they did in the first situation.[27] However, s. 17(2) does not require a detailed discussion on the effect of the clauses or the reasons behind their inclusion as the Commission suggests (this discussion might

23 Law Commission Report, at [29.64]–[29.65].
24 Ibid. at [29.62], [29.63] and [29.65].
25 Ibid. at [29.66].
26 Ibid. at [29.67].
27 Ibid. at [29.66].

come into play under s. 17(3)). If the view of the Commission is correct, the insurer who deals with a broker in a sophisticated insurance market is in a worse position than an insurer operating in an SMEs insurance market. Such a distinction would reverse the philosophy behind s. 17(4): the more sophisticated the insurance market, the more steps the insurer is required to take to draw the term to the broker's attention. This surely cannot be the case.

In the second example the Commission argues that the failure of the insurer to raise the issue of contracting out during the negotiations with the broker means that (s)he did not take sufficient steps to bring the clauses to the broker's attention. This is a conclusion that is subject to criticism and even the Commission expressed doubts whether it can be used as a principle of general application. It is true that a literal interpretation of s. 17(2) would require the insurer to take a positive step to inform the broker. Silence would not satisfy this requirement. Yet, it is open to debate whether reference to a standard policy which contains standard contracting out provisions would qualify as a positive step. The Commission's default answer is negative, but it (rightly) leaves the door open: "it would depend on the exact circumstances of the case: for example, the extent to which the detail of [the standard policy], as recently modified, was known by brokers generally; the availability of [the standard policy] for inspection; and the extent to which other standard sets of voyage conditions would be known by brokers to include such exclusions".[28]

It is submitted that a broker placing risks in a sophisticated insurance market is likely to know the content of standard policies together with their (recent) modifications, if any. One of the reasons is that a number of sophisticated insurance markets have moved towards greater transparency. First, standard policies and clauses are often published online (in free to use websites) as soon as they are approved by the market.[29] Second, long gone are the days when the drafting of standard clauses and policies was covered in secrecy. In the aviation market, for example, the Aviation Insurance Clauses Group (AICG) was set up in 2005 by LMA and International Underwriting Association (IUA) following an investigation of the European Commission on the transparency of the London aviation insurance market.[30] Part of the investigation was triggered by complaints submitted by buyers of aviation insurance that London aviation insurers were offering little explanation for drafting (and using) new standard policies and clauses. The end result of this investigation was the creation of AICG, which not only publishes standard terms, but, most importantly, publishes the minutes of the meetings of LMA and IUA aviation insurers that lead to the adoption of new clauses and policies. At the same time, the terms of reference of AICG provide for a mechanism for brokers (via the British Insurers' Association (LMBC)) or buyers of aviation

28 Ibid. at [29.67].

29 See www.iua.co.uk for marine, aviation, as well as property and casualty standard clauses and policies (last accessed 8 April 2016).

30 See K. Posner, T. Marland and P. Crystal, *Margo on Aviation Insurance*, (2014, Lexis Nexis), at [4.64] ("*Margo*"); see also www.aicg.co.uk (last accessed 8 April 2016).

insurance (via the International Air Transport Association (IATA)) to recommend clauses and participate in the discussion.[31]

In such a market there is little doubt that reference to a contracting out clause, even without further discussion, constitutes a "sufficient step to draw the disadvantageous term" to the broker's attention. We believe that there is little difference (at least in a sophisticated insurance market) between highlighting a term and suggesting the inclusion in the policy of a standard contracting out clause by reference to its code. Section 17(2) requires the insurer to take steps to bring the term to the broker's attention. By referring to the code the insurer takes such steps as the clause in question only contains the disadvantageous term. Any other conclusion would fly in the face of standard placement practices in sophisticated markets. The wording of standard clauses is not reproduced in slips (Lloyd's Market Reform Contract (MRC) slips or any others) but a reference to their codes is deemed sufficient with only the amending wording included.

Whether the placement of a risk in a sophisticated market by reference to the code of a standard policy that incorporates standard contracting out clauses will satisfy s. 17(2) is doubtful. In such a situation, it is expected that insurers will face strong arguments that the disadvantageous term was not brought to the attention of the broker as the standard contracting out clause was one of the many in the policy. It remains to be seen whether courts will adopt a test for sophisticated markets that is less strict than the one likely to be used in the SMEs market. If not, the behaviour of the insurer in the second example produced by the Law Commission will not satisfy s. 17(2).

7.4.3 An analysis of s. 17(5)

The 2015 Act provides that an insurer who fails to comply with s. 17(2) may remedy this failure by taking advantage of s. 17(5) and proving that "the insured (or its agent) had actual knowledge of the disadvantageous term when the contract was entered into or the variation agreed". Insurers operating in sophisticated insurance markets have already argued that they can take advantage of this section when the broker prepares the wording of the policy: "[i]n 'open market' business, it is common for wordings to be prepared by a broker. In those circumstances, it is likely that the broker will have 'actual knowledge' of any disadvantageous term in the policy, since it will have drafted the term itself. It would therefore be surprising if it did not have actual awareness of the term."[32]

This statement, correct as it is in principle, requires the following qualifications. The policy wording that brokers prepare must be in place when the contract is entered into. Section 17(5) does not require prior-to-the-agreement knowledge (as in the case of s. 17(2)), yet it is not an open-ended provision. Evidence of "actual knowledge" is required at the time of the agreement with any knowledge acquired afterwards not being taken into consideration. This is important because there are

31 See cl. 5.6 of the Terms of Reference of the AICG.
32 Insurers' report on the 2015 Act, at [78].

insurance markets where policy wordings are prepared long after the terms in the slip are agreed or policies are never issued with the slip being the operative document.[33] In these markets, the argument of the insurers is difficult to apply as the broker would prepare the wording long after "the contract was entered into", if ever.

Can s. 17(5) be used when the placement is taking place on the basis of standard clauses and policies? To answer this question a number of alternative situations can be identified:

a) when the broker includes the code of the standard contracting out clause in the slip, there is little doubt that (s)he had actual knowledge of the disadvantageous term;
b) when the request to use a standard policy that contains the standard contracting out clauses comes from the broker, there is again little doubt that (s)he had actual knowledge. This is so, even if the standard policy was recently amended to incorporate the clauses;
c) when the insurer requests the inclusion of the code of the standard clause/policy without any discussion over their content, whether the broker acquires "actual knowledge" for the purposes of s. 17(5) will depend on the following factors:
    - if the broker has already used the relevant standard clause in a placement, it can be argued that (s)he acquired "actual knowledge" of the disadvantageous term at that moment. The code is unique to the contracting out clause and the broker is aware of its content in all subsequent placements. The same applies to standard policies that incorporate the standard contracting out clauses. It can also be argued that attending professional training on the application of the standard clauses/policies (as is common in the market) is evidence of "actual knowledge". This is so even if the broker in question has never used these clauses/policies in a placement;
    - can it be argued that the broker deliberately refrained from knowing the content of the clauses ("blind eye knowledge")? Considering the publicity that the 2015 Act and the relevant contracting out clauses have attracted, it would be relatively straightforward to establish that a sophisticated broker must have "realised their implication" for the risk it places.[34] Whether insurers would be able to satisfy the second limb of the test, namely, that the broker deliberately refrained from investigating the standard clause is doubtful. It is not sufficient that the broker negligently ignored the contents of the clause, but that "he made a deliberate decision not to check in order to avoid gaining direct knowledge of what he had reason to believe was" the consequence of the clause.[35] This is a high threshold to pass;

33 See *Margo*, at [6.47].

34 *Compania Maritima San Basilio SA v Oceanus Mutual Underwriting Association (Bermuda) Ltd* (*The Eurysthenes*) [1976] 2 Lloyd's Rep. 171, at p. 184.

35 J. Gilman et al., *Arnould: Law Marine Insurance and Average*, (2013, Sweet & Maxwell), at [951].

- the constructive knowledge of the broker (whether he ought to be aware that the codes refer to the standard contracting out clauses/policy) is not a relevant factor. This is so even after consideration of the publicity that the said clauses and the enactment of the 2015 Act have attracted in the market. Section 17(5) refers to "actual" knowledge, which does not include "constructive" knowledge – the wording would have suggested otherwise if that was the intention.[36]

7.4.4 An analysis of s. 17(3)

Assuming that the insurer brings the disadvantageous term to the attention of the insured or its broker, the next requirement is for the term to be "clear and unambiguous as to its effect" (s. 17(3)). Of essence in this provision is that the consequences of the disadvantageous terms are spelled out clearly: "it is not enough merely that the term is drafted in a way that is clear and unambiguous".[37] In other words, the clause is required to describe how the term in question will disadvantage the insured. The Law Commission (rightly) argued that a clause which provides that "section 14 of the Insurance . . . Act . . . does not apply to this contract" does not satisfy s. 17(3) although it is clear and unambiguous.[38] The mistake is that it does not identify the term's effect. Insurers were quick to capitulate on this suggestion of the Commission and prepared five standard contracting out clauses.[39]

The following three clauses provide for a blanket contracting out from three different parts of the 2015 Act:

- LMA 5257 contracts out of the remedies in the Act for breach of the duty of fair presentation (s. 8(2) and Schedule 1 of the 2015 Act);
- LMA 5258 contracts out of s. 10 that regulates the effect of the breach of a warranty;
- LMA 5260 contracts out of s. 11 that regulates the effect of terms that reduce the risk of loss of a particular kind or at a particular location or time.

At the suggestion of the Commission their design is similar. In the first sentence they state the Part of the 2015 Act that is contracted out. This is welcome because it clearly states the *raison d'être* of the clause in question. Yet, it is not essential as it does not describe the effect of the clause. This comes in the second sentence (onwards) of the three clauses. For example, in LMA 5258 it is stated that "[i]f any such warranty is breached, the Insurer's liability shall be discharged from the time of the breach of warranty, regardless of whether the breach is subsequently remedied".

36 See s. 4(1) of the Insurance Act 2015.
37 Insurers' report on the 2015 Act, at [79].
38 Law Commission Report, at [A.140].
39 See http://www.lmalloyds.com/actclauses (last accessed 8 April 2016).

The benefit of using these blanket contracting out clauses is that the insurer is required to highlight this one clause to the insured or its broker rather than each individual term of the policy that falls into ss. 10 or 11. They are the terms that "put the insured in a worse position" and will be checked in respect of the transparency requirements of s. 17. Such an arrangement satisfies the text of the 2015 Act and it is in line with the way that sophisticated insurance markets operate.

Whether such an arrangement would be satisfactory with respect to SMEs that buy insurance without instructing a broker is open to question. The Commission suggests that the description of the consequences of the disadvantageous term to these buyers may be required to be more detailed. Laborious as this might be for the insurers it is not surprising considering the philosophy behind ss. 16 and 17.

In these markets it is likely for disputes to arise over whether insurers should describe the effect of each and every term in the policy that has been contracted out of the application of ss. 10 or 11. The argument is that one of the aims of the contracting out provisions is to warn the insured about the consequences of his/her conduct. In a sophisticated market the insured will most probably seek clarification from the broker by expecting an answer to the following question: to which terms of this policy does the contracting out provision apply? Yet, the average owner of a high-street shop does not have such a luxury and it is likely that courts will require insurers to be more detailed by identifying the relevant terms in the policy and describing the consequences of their breach. The counterargument is that the 2015 Act imposes no requirement to classify the terms of an insurance contract and "does not redefine whether a term is or is not a warranty (which is, and remains a question of contractual construction)".[40] Still, this is not a classification of the terms of the contract but rather a classification of their effect. It is plausible (and permitted on literal reading of ss. 16(2) and 17(3)) that the disadvantageous term is not only the blanket contracting out provision but also the actual terms to which it refers. It is true that a warranty that is subject to MIA 1906 damages the position of the insured only because of the existence of a contracting out clause in the policy. Yet, it is likely that a court will not make such fine distinctions when dealing with SMEs, but instead will examine whether the insured was actually informed about the consequences of breaching specific clauses in the policy.

To cater for such situations, the LMA has prepared clauses 5259 and 5261 that provide for term-specific contracting out: "[s]ection 10 of the Insurance Act 2015 shall not apply to {this warranty/these warranties/refer to specific warranties}. If {this warranty/these warranties/refer to specific warranties} is breached, the Insurer's liability shall be discharged from the time of the breach of warranty, regardless of whether the breach is subsequently remedied."[41] In that respect, the insured is informed about both the legal nature of the clauses in question and the consequences of breaching them. It is submitted that such wording would pass even the strictest test of application of s. 17(3). The risk that the insurer runs under these two clauses is to wrongly classify a clause as a warranty when actually it is

40 Insurers' report on the 2015 Act, at [57].
41 LMA 5259.

a condition precedent to liability or a suspensory condition. In such a situation, it is arguable that s. 17(2) is not satisfied and the term is of no effect. If it qualifies as a "risk-reduction" term, s. 11 of the Act would apply to it; otherwise, MIA 1906 will apply.

7.5 Concluding thoughts

Coming back to the question of whether the contracting out provisions of the 2015 Act reflect the philosophy of the Law Commission, we believe that the answer is affirmative. Sections 16 and 17 reach the compromise that the Commission had in mind with minimum disruption to the overarching aim of the 2015 Act. Insurers have enough flexibility to bypass the 2015 Act, if they so desire, by following a test that is relatively straightforward in its application: pragmatism has prevailed over legalism. It is inevitable that the application of the contracting out provisions will be tested before the courts once the Act comes into force, yet we agree with the prediction of a commentator that these disputes will be short-lived: "in all probability, such disputes will settle rather quickly once a judicial view on the matter is expressed".[42]

It is highly likely that the centrepiece of this line of litigation will be s. 17(4) and the issue will be to decide how to apply the transparency requirement to different types of insurance markets. We agree with the Commission that s. 17(4) is drafted in a broad manner to give enough flexibility to courts to take into consideration developments in the way insurance is being placed and the characteristics of the individual insured – not every owner of a high street shop or a shipowner/airline has the same level of insurance expertise. Certainty dictates that the 2015 Act should have provided a clear distinction line between sophisticated and SMEs insurance markets. Yet, such identification was a "hot potato" threatening to jeopardise the entire Act and, rightly, the decision was left to judicial discretion.

Once the 2015 Act comes into force it would be interesting to check the approach that sophisticated insurance markets will adopt regarding its contracting out provisions. It is likely that insurers will take different positions based on the size of their accounts, as well as the size and the ethos of the industries they insure. These factors arguably explain the division already expressed between marine and aviation insurers, with the latter preparing amendments to their standard policies and clauses to accommodate rather than contract out of the 2015 Act. This might be surprising for an insurance bystander, yet it makes sense if one looks carefully into the aviation insurance sector. The aviation industry is heavily regulated and insurance policies reflect that, traditionally, by avoiding the use of warranties.[43] They opt instead for conditions precedent, suspensory conditions and more extensive use of exclusions. At the same time, the majority of aviation insurers deal with airline risks by insuring their hull, passengers and third party liabilities in the same

42 Soyer risk control clauses, at p. 124.
43 See *Margo*, at [10.10] ff.

policy. Considering that passenger and third party liability insurance is compulsory, the use of warranties has been problematic.

All things considered, the contracting out provisions of the 2015 Act are a necessary evil with the operative word being necessary. In the words of a commentator the "ability to alter default rules and respond to needs of the assured and changes that occur in law and practice have enabled the market, in particular in the fields of marine energy and transport, to flourish and establish itself as a leading insurance centre over the course of the last decade".[44] The ball is now firmly in the insurers' court with them deciding what better supports their interests. Aviation insurance suggests that the 2015 Act might be of better service than originally thought.

44 Soyer risk control clauses, at p. 124.

CHAPTER 8

Conclusion

General reflections on the law reform

*Sir Bernard Rix**

The Insurance Act 2015 (the "Act"), together with its earlier sibling, the Consumer Insurance (Disclosure and Representations) Act 2012 (CIDRA), is the most significant reform of the nation's insurance law since Lord Mansfield in the eighteenth century, some 250 years ago, started to lay down the elements of what would hitherto have been described as the current law. The Marine Insurance Act 1906 (the "1906 Act"), designed for marine insurance but with huge impact on our insurance law generally, was not itself a reform but in essence a codification of the then existing common law.

As in the eighteenth century when Lord Mansfield was at work, and his knowledge of the civil law influenced him in his development of the concept of good faith, so in this second reform of the twenty-first century the influence of Europe (but also of the modern statutes in Australia and New Zealand) can be traced in the ideas for proportionate remedies contained in Schedule 1 to the Act.

In recent years, the jurisprudence of the courts could be seen struggling against the limitations imposed by the ossification of the law imposed by the 1906 Act. In particular, the single remedy of retrospective avoidance for breach of the duty of good faith was criticised as both inadequate and draconian; and the automatic discharge of an insurance contract engendered by breach of warranty, however remote that breach was from the cause of loss, however slight the breach, and even if the breach had been remedied before loss, has been deplored as unjust. Nevertheless, both these remedies were demanded by the 1906 Act. Section 17 stated that "if the utmost good faith be not observed by either party, the contract may be avoided by the other party"; section 18(1) said that "[i]f the assured fails to make such disclosure, the insurer may avoid the contract"; section 20(1) stated that if any material pre-contractual representation was untrue "the insurer may avoid the contract"; and section 33(3) said that if a warranty was not complied with, then, subject to contrary agreement "the insurer is discharged from liability as from the date of the breach". All those provisions have now gone.

It would take a work of legal history to trace how and why these provisions took root as they did. Lord Mansfield might have been surprised to discover that his introduction of the doctrine of good faith in *Carter v Boehm*[1] had ended in the

* Professor of International Commercial Law at QMUL, Arbitrator and Mediator (20 Essex Street), former Lord Justice of Appeal.

1 (1766) 3 Burr 1905.

demanding jurisprudence of later centuries on the subject of non-disclosure. He was concerned with the danger of dishonest concealment: *aliud est celare, aliud tacere*.[2] As he said, in rejecting the underwriter's defence in that case:

> If the defendant's objection prevails, the rule against concealment would be an instrument of fraud. He took the premium without asking questions, knowing that if such concealment vacates the policy, it was thereby void, and drew the governor in to suppose himself insured when he was not so. He waived the objection then, and shall not take it up now. We may say of this rule, as has been said of the Statute of Frauds: "It shall not itself be turned into an instrument of Fraud."[3]

On the other hand, in *De Hahn v Hartley*[4] a ship was insured on the warranty that she had sailed with "50 hands or upwards"; she sailed with 46, but six hours later picked up an additional six, making 52; and was afterwards lost by capture. The underwriter paid, but afterwards learned of the fact that the vessel had sailed with only 46 hands and sued for the return of his payment, and succeeded. Lord Mansfield compared representations and warranties:

> There is a material distinction between a warranty and a representation. A representation may be equitably and substantially answered; but a warranty must be strictly complied with . . . A warranty in a policy of insurance is a condition or a contingency, and unless that be performed, there is no contract. It is perfectly immaterial for what purpose a warranty is introduced; but, being inserted, the contract does not exist unless it be literally complied with.

So, in Lord Mansfield's opinion, the real vice of non-disclosure was a true lack of good faith, and otherwise a representation could be viewed equitably, meaning I suppose that if in *De Hahn v Hartley* there had only been a misrepresentation concerning the number of hands with which the vessel "sailed" or was to sail, then it might have been open to say that the representation had been substantially complied with when the full complement had been taken on board within a few hours and before the ocean voyage proper had been commenced. As it was, however, the warranty had been written on the policy and had to be strictly construed and strictly complied with. It was not possible even to consider whether the breach should be regarded as remedied by asking to what extent, if at all, it had affected the risk insured. If that had been possible, it might have been said that the breach sounded in only nominal damages.

In more modern times, however, there has been a tendency to define a warranty and to distinguish it from other terms of an insurance contract by asking whether it defined the risk. This may be a difficult enough exercise in contractual interpretation, but it avoids Lord Mansfield's rather conclusory view that the contract failed because the term was a condition precedent. Of course, it was only a condition precedent if the contract failed by its breach. It is, nevertheless, understandable as a matter of doctrine (even if it is unsatisfactory in a pragmatic sense) that if a term is an essential part of the definition of a risk then an insurer should not be

2 *Carter v Boehm* (1766) 1 Blackstone Wm 593 at 594.
3 *Carter v Boehm* (1766) 1 Blackstone Wm 593 at 596, 96 ER 342 at 344.
4 (1786) 1 Term Reports 343, 99 ER 1130.

bound if the risk actually undertaken is different from the risk contracted for: irrespective of any connection with the loss and irrespective of the breach being remedied before loss. But Lord Mansfield's view was that "[i]t is perfectly immaterial for what purpose a warranty is introduced". The courts of his day obviously did not want to enter into any consideration of the relationships between risk undertaken, non-compliance, and loss as experienced.

How do the reforms of the Act impinge on these historic concerns, and what problems might be anticipated in the future as the courts get to grips with the new provisions? Those provisions have been described and analysed elsewhere in this book. The purpose of this closing chapter is to look at the reforms more broadly and with the potential for future disputes in mind.

Two preliminary points can, however, be made.

First, the Act is in certain respects unlike anything previously to be found in the context of the law of contract. It not only provides tests, but repeatedly goes on in some considerable detail to define how those tests are to operate, as well as how remedies for breach are to operate. For instance, section 3(1) lays down the duty of fair presentation; sections 3(3), 3(4) and 3(5) immediately proceed to define what that duty requires or does not require. In particular, section 3(4)(a) requires disclosure of every material circumstance which "the insured knows or ought to know". That in its essentials is a familiar enough test: see section 18(1) of the 1906 Act. However, section 4 goes on to answer further questions about such knowledge, such as *whose* knowledge counts as the knowledge of the assured, or *how* and *what* knowledge is to be attributed to the assured ("ought to know"). Section 5 deals similarly with the issue of the knowledge of the insurer for the purposes of section 3(5) which speaks of what the insurer knows or ought to know or is presumed to know, where the insured's disclosure, in the absence of enquiry by the insurer, is unnecessary. Section 6 deals with other more general issues of knowledge. Section 8 by reference to Schedule 1 deals with remedies for breach of the duty of fair presentation in not only novel but detailed ways. Then, on the subject of warranties and other terms (sections 9, 10 and 11), further detailed provisions are made not only in abolition of the old law (section 10(1)) but in the creation of an entirely new regime, of some complexity. The same may be said for sections 12 and 13 on the subject of fraudulent claims, where section 13 in particular enters into really detailed draftsmanship on the extent to which an insured is insulated from the fraud of a fraudulent beneficiary of a group insurance contract.

Another new idiosyncrasy of the Act shows it partaking almost of the style of a restatement, as where it provides non-exhaustive examples of "any other person" (section 4(7)) or of a "relevant event" (section 12(4)). Questions might arise as to whether the examples, although plainly non-exhaustive, somehow define or limit the broader expression.

The second preliminary point is to raise the question as to the broad principles of the Act. What are the principles which lie behind the Act, to assist in the interpretation of its detailed provisions? Can such principles be extracted, or is it merely a matter of giving attention to its detailed and sometimes difficult language? A number of sub-issues arise here. One raises the question as to the extent to which previous jurisprudence will remain relevant. Another is to what extent attention is paid to the Law Commission's considerable explanations in its report of July 2014;[5] and to the Explanatory Notes which accompanied the Act's enactment. Both may be expected to have a considerable influence. Even though certain aspects of the old law have been abolished and that will have to be respected, nevertheless in general, and in particular on the subject of the duty of fair presentation, the stated ambition of the Law Commission is to build on the past. As to the principles in play, they seem to encompass a desire for fairness, for holding in balance the interests of both parties to the insurance contract, insurer and insured, for making remedies proportionate to the nature of the breach or non-compliance with a duty or a term, and for recognising modern developments in the world of business, such as the vast growth of consumer insurance, and the equally vast growth of enormous companies and information technology.

A consideration of the Act's more difficult or controversial provisions can properly start with the doctrine of good faith itself, even though the Act relegates this to Part 5. As a result of section 14 of the Act, section 17 of the 1906 Act simply reads: "A contract of marine insurance is a contract based upon the utmost good faith", with the reference to the remedy of avoidance deleted. Moreover, section 14 of the Act also modifies any rule of law based on that surviving doctrine, applicable of course to insurance contracts generally, save to the extent that it survives the provisions of both the Act and CIDRA. What then is the surviving role of the doctrine, shorn of the sanction of avoidance? The Law Commission surmises that it will play three roles: to assist in the interpretation of the duty of fair presentation, to inform the need for implication of terms, and to leave room for judicial flexibility. It is not contemplated, however, that it would give rise to a claim in damages, even in the post-contractual context. And authority has already determined that the duty of good faith ceases where litigation begins.[6]

Nevertheless, the survival of the doctrine is consistent with the Act's purpose of bringing a greater balance into the role of pre-contractual disclosure through the need for insurers to be alive to the role of asking questions: see below. It is possible, moreover, that it may affect an insurer's right to cancel under the policy, a matter briefly discussed in prior jurisprudence[7] albeit under the shadow of the old law. We could, therefore, see a development of the civil law concept of abuse of rights. The common law shares with the civil law a concern about the misuse of rights of cancellation, but in narrow circumstances which probably depend on the implication of terms.[8] It is possible that we will now see a more

5 Law Commission, *Insurance Contract Law: Business Disclosure; Warranties; Insurers' Remedies for Fraudulent Claims; and Late Payment* (Law Com No 353, July 2014)

6 *Manifest Shipping Co Ltd v Uni-Polaris Insurance Co Ltd (The Star Sea)* [2001] UKHL 1, [2003] 1 AC 469 at [77].

7 For instance in *Drake Insurance plc v Provident Insurance plc* [2003] EWCA Civ 1834, [2004] QB 601 at [79]-[93], [143]-[145], cf. [165]-[178].

8 See *Rede v Farr* (1817) 6 M&S 121, 124–125, *New Zealand Shipping Co v Société des Ateliers et Chantiers de France* [1919] 1 AC 1 (HL) at 8, 9, *Cheall v Association of Professional Executive Clerical and Computer Staff* [1983] AC 180 (HL) at 188–189, *Alghussein Establishment v Eton College* [1988] 1 WLR 587 (HL), *Kensland Realty Limited v Whale View Investment Limited* [2001] HKFCA 17 at [96]-[97].

nuanced use of the doctrine of good faith to achieve a just result or avoid an unjust one.

In this context, the case of *WISE (Underwriting Agency) Ltd v Grupo National Provincial SA*[9] may be illuminating. There a reinsurance contract was avoided when a jewellery shop in a Mexican resort reinsured its imports under an all risks policy. The shop's business had been presented in considerable detail, but with an error in the translation from the Spanish as a result of which *relojes*, which can mean watches or clocks, was translated as clocks. Of course, the shop's business was in watches rather than clocks, as the financial details of monthly shipments implicitly made clear, and which in any event ought to have been a matter of common knowledge of jewellery shops. The defendant underwriters' evidence was to the effect that so much was their distaste for insuring the shipment of expensive watches that they invariably stipulated for a warranty against watches. There was, however, no such warranty in the reinsurance contract in question. The case was argued along different lines, but it might now perhaps be said that good faith on the part of the reinsurer should have led it to disclose its insistence on the absence of insuring watches, e.g. "We would normally insist on a warranty against watches, but as we note that you do not sell watches (only clocks), we do not require one here." That would have immediately exposed the error, and the parties could have proceeded more suitably from there. This point, which arises from the reinsurer's own evidence about its use of warranties, is separate from the different issue of whether in any event the error should have been exposed by the need for the reinsurer to ask questions, on the basis that it had been given sufficient information to put it on notice of the need to make further enquiries (see section 3(4)(b) of the Act). In the overall scheme of things, however, it might well be said that the doctrine of good faith, either standing alone, or in any event in the context of the new more balanced provisions concerning the duty of fair presentation, makes the error in translation less serious than the failure of the reinsurer to make it clear that it was not in the business of insuring a jewellery importer against the loss of watches under an all risks policy.

It will be interesting to see where the doctrine of good faith, shorn of its sole remedy of avoidance, leads. In the past, the doctrine, although mutual, has been of little or no use to insureds, since they are rarely or ever in a situation where they wish to avoid their policy. In reality, however, it is the doctrine of good faith which has created the duty of disclosure. Normally, in commercial affairs, the rule is *caveat emptor*. Even a seller of things has no obligation save that which the law imposes on him or which he undertakes voluntarily, or which a misrepresentation engages him in. He has, however, no obligation to speak. A buyer certainly has no obligation to speak. In the insurance context, however, the seller is the insurer, and the insured, as proposer, is the buyer. Of course, he is a special kind of buyer who brings his own particular needs to the formation of a contract which is all about risk. And so, as things have turned out, it is the insured who is the party with the primary obligation to speak, to disclose, which the duty of good faith has

9 [2004] EWCA Civ 962, [2004] 2 All ER 613.

imposed on him. However, the reciprocal duty of the insurer, who is similarly under a mutual obligation to observe the utmost good faith, has generally been lost to sight, because, unlike most sellers, it is not he who makes the proposal, but his buyer.[10] Now, however, that the duty of good faith is not merely a door to avoidance and the duty of fair presentation has become a more balanced affair, there may be cases where doctrines of fairness and good faith merge to produce a different answer from yesteryear.

This leads into the duty of fair presentation generally, the subject of Part 2 of the Act. It is to be observed that the duty covers both non-disclosure and misrepresentation on an equal footing (section 3(3)). Two possibly controversial aspects of this duty are the alternative ways of fulfilling that duty set out in section 3(4)(b), and the reference to a "reasonable search" in section 3(6).

As to the former,[11] the availability of two alternative means of complying with the duty runs the risk that it is the lesser duty which is the true duty, even though it is introduced by the words "failing that", a reference to the primary duty, so that the greater (and traditional) duty (to disclose "every material circumstance which the insured knows or ought to know") will come to be regarded as unnecessary gold-plating. Even so, the virtue of the formulation is that it emphasises that although the duty of fair presentation starts with and rests upon the proposer, nevertheless, a sensible and fair result requires the co-operation of both parties to the prospective contract, and that the insurer cannot just sit back and, as the expression has come to be used, do its "underwriting at the claims stage". I think that Clarke J put it well, and the Law Commission acknowledges this,[12] when he said:

> A minute disclosure of every material circumstance is not required. The assured complies with the duty if he discloses sufficient to call the attention of the underwriter to the relevant facts and matters in such a way that, if the latter desires further information, he can ask for it. A fair and accurate presentation of a summary of the material facts is sufficient if it would enable a prudent underwriter to form a proper judgment, either on the presentation alone, or by asking questions if he was sufficiently put upon enquiry and wanted to know further details, whether to accept the proposal and, if so, on what terms.[13]

The Act's section 3(4)(b) formulation may, nevertheless, be said to emphasise that the aim is to achieve the greater disclosure, and that evidence that the proposer has not in good faith attempted to meet that primary duty will be likely to result in a finding that a fair presentation has not been made. So, if an insured

10 In consumer contracts, however, the insurer is much more like the traditional seller, and the insured is not doing much more than providing personal details and choosing between the options which the insurer makes available to him. This has effectively been recognised by the changes adopted by CIDRA, which place the burden on the insurer to ask questions, and on the insured to respond.

11 Section 3(4): "The disclosure required is . . . (a) disclosure of every material circumstance which the insured knows or ought to know, or (b) failing that, disclosure which gives the insurer sufficient information to put a prudent insurer on notice that it needs to make further enquiries for the purpose of revealing those material circumstances."

12 Para 7.35 of the July 2014 report.

13 *Garnat Trading & Shipping (Singapore) Pte Ltd v Baominh Insurance Corporation* [2010] EWHC 2578 (Comm), [2011] 1 Lloyd's Rep 589 at [135].

deliberately pulls its punches on disclosure, it is likely to be in difficulties; but a careless slip, such as occurred in translation in *WISE*, against the background of the details provided as to the monthly value of shipments of "clocks", would leave the insurer with the choice of asking questions or else having to accept that he had been provided with sufficient information. This is an aspect of the doctrine of waiver which has always existed, since the 1906 Act had itself said that its section 19 disclosure duty was "subject to" the provisions of section 18 as to matters which need not be disclosed, and those matters included matters as to which the insurer waived disclosure (section 19(3)(c)). Jurisprudence had developed the doctrine that an insurer's failure to enquire when sufficiently put on notice was a waiver. The exception of waiver is still contained in the Act at section 3(5)(e). Thus, the new formulation of section 3(4)(b) is in essence a drawing forth into express language of what had developed, or was in process of being developed, under the old dispensation. Its virtue is that by bringing the language of such jurisprudence into the express words of the statute, the Act emphasises the bilateral and mutual aspects of achieving a presentation of the risk which is sufficient for the purposes of good underwriting.

In this context, the Law Commission gives the example[14] of a valve manufacturer seeking product liability insurance which merely describes itself as a maker of valves and does not disclose that its valves are used in the petrochemical industry, where a defect may cause huge losses. A presentation for such purposes which was so jejune as effectively to fail to describe the nature of the insured's business and its customer base may well be seen to be inadequate. But it must all depend: some businesses are well known as suppliers of services and goods to certain industries.

Also in this context, it is relevant to point out the correlative provisions relating to the knowledge of the insurer, since sections 3(5)(b), (c) and (d) retain the provision that in the absence of enquiry the duty of fair presentation does not require the disclosure of what the insurer knows, ought to know or is presumed to know. In particular, sections 5(1) and (2) *limit* the insurer's knowledge or "ought to know" knowledge, by various tests, to the knowledge of particular individuals and to information "held" by the insurer and "readily available" to such individuals. Section 5(3) retains the essence of the 1906 Act's section 18(3)(b) concerning presumed knowledge, but the Law Commission has helpfully rephrased this in terms of what insurers "offering insurance of the *class in question* to insurers *in the field of activity in question* would reasonably be expected to know in the ordinary course of business" (emphasis added). It may be expected that insurers and brokers in the relevant classes and fields will draw up protocols to assist in the definition of such presumed knowledge.

Similarly, in terms of the knowledge of the insured, section 4 deals variously with limitations on whose knowledge counts as the knowledge of an insured. The driving theory in all of this is to bring accountability home to individuals, but at the same time to *limit* such accountability to the individuals concerned: whether

14 Para 7.38 of the July 2014 report.

they are individual insureds, in which case accountability stops with the individual insureds and the individuals "responsible for the insured's insurance", a new phrase to describe agents, brokers and other intermediaries and the like; or whether they are business organisations ("not an individual"), in which case accountability is again limited, to either their "senior management" (which may well go beyond the board of directors), or again those responsible for their insurance.

In general, one sees in such provisions of the Act a new willingness to be more prescriptive, more definitional and more limiting about what counts as the requisite knowledge. Many of the Act's new phrases may give rise to some disputes in the courts, but there is unlikely to be much difficulty with them, with the exception perhaps of the tests which attempt to define the body of knowledge which lies in the background as the source for arguments that insureds or insurers "ought to know" the information in question: such as the concepts of information which "should *reasonably have been revealed* by a *reasonable search* of information *available to the insured*" (section 4(6)) or information *held* by the insurer and *reasonably available* to the insurer (section 5(2)(b)).

The Law Commission is to be congratulated on bringing these issues of the modern world of information technology and retrieval into the statutory arena. Such, however, is the speed of change in this field that one could be concerned that such expressions will have become dated long before the Act is half as old as the 1906 Act. This is a general problem of statutory obsolescence. In the meantime, it is to be hoped that the courts do not become too pedantic as to what is a *reasonable search* or is *held* or *available*. These are essentially matters of fact, and none the worse for that. Those critics of the new legislation who have deplored the factual questions which arise on the provisions of the Act ignore the plain truth that matters of knowledge inevitably raise multiple issues of fact, and that what one needs is some simple guidance, now provided by the relevant provisions, as to the tests to be applied: whose knowledge, what kind of knowledge, how acquired and so on. The Law Commission recognises that the issues thrown up by individual cases will depend on their own facts. The tests are objective, but objective as they are, because they are liberally sprinkled with the concept of reasonableness in its adjectival or adverbial form, it may be expected that much will depend on the size and organisation of particular insureds; and that protocols will develop to assist on such matters as the reasonable search.

It may be noted that whereas the insured is bound to make a reasonable search or to be stuck with the consequences of what it would reasonably have revealed, the insurer has a more limited accountability, in that nothing is said about a reasonable search but instead the concept is of information held and readily (*not* reasonably) available to it. This is consistent with the primary obligation of disclosure of material information being on the insured, not on the insurer. Although one is familiar with a computer search (which has indeed become commonplace in the world of litigation or arbitration disclosure), section 4(6) makes it clear that the underlying concept is that of making enquiries ("whether the search is conducted by making enquiries or by any other means"). Therefore, the insured may be required to make enquiries of employees or departments within the insured's organisation (and possibly even outside its own corporate status) or of outside advisors. The combination of "reasonably . . . revealed by a reasonable search" may also be noted. One question is how widely the search has reasonably to be conducted; another question is what the search reveals, where again the test is that of objective reasonableness. It might be suggested that the insured does not have to be a detective, whether of the Poirot or even the Clouseau variety, as long as he acts as a reasonable man of business in the relevant context.

The insurer, however, is only taken to what is *held* by him. That would seem to exclude the outside advisors; and the question has been raised whether it would also exclude matters which could be researched on the internet but are beyond its own internal records. The context, and the contrast of the language of reasonable search in the case of the insured, suggest that the limitation to information held by the insurer is deliberately narrow and is not to be expanded.[15] Similarly, the language of "readily available" suggests that information may be held by the insurer but not be readily available. However, if the information is held by the insurer and is readily available to him, there appears to be no additional test of what is "reasonably revealed", save to the extent that it must be readily available. The point is discussed by the Law Commission in terms of what might be withheld through negligence or fraud,[16] but the point equally or perhaps more commonly arises where the question is what would be revealed by the information in question: if it is a matter of having to put together two plus two to make four, or even five, is that within the test? Perhaps the test should really be one of "reasonably revealed" rather than "readily available"?

Before leaving the subject of the duty of fair presentation for that of warranties, it is important to address the Schedule 1 remedies for breach of duty. In an important sense, this is the heart of the Act (as the CIDRA remedies were in that statute). The small adjustments and glosses on the previous law regarding the duty to disclose, although they may be fairly numerous, are evolutionary rather than revolutionary. The duty of good faith remains. The duty of disclosure has been reformulated as a duty of fair presentation, but probably without much essential change in its content, beyond an important degree of rebalancing of the roles of insured and insurer. Warranties remain. The problem of fraudulent claims remains. But in all these respects what has fundamentally changed is that, when something has gone wrong, when a presentation has been less than fair, when there has been non-disclosure, and when there has been a breach of warranty or a fraudulent claim, *remedies* have become infinitely more flexible. It is an interesting question whether the common law could have proceeded to or towards a similar change of landscape. In one sense, remedies ought to be the meat and drink of common law evolution. However, the manacles of the statutory code and the doctrine of precedent have held the law back.

In one sense the key to the new Schedule 1 remedies lies in a concept which the common law did, albeit belatedly, develop, and that is the concept of inducement. In *Pan Atlantic*[17] the House of Lords discovered for the first time, buried

15 This is supported by the Law Commission's own view: see para 10.54 of the July 2014 report.
16 Para 8. 87/87 of the July 2014 report.
17 *Pan Atlantic Insurance Co Ltd v Pine Top Insurance Co Ltd* [1995] 1 AC 1.

implicitly in the 1906 Act, the concept of inducement. The test of a remedy for non-disclosure did not depend entirely on the objective question of what a prudent insurer would have regarded as material to underwriting the risk, but also on the subjective question of whether the particular insurer concerned was actually induced to contract, on the terms on which he contracted, by the material non-disclosure concerned. The practical importance of this development was significantly increased when jurisprudence went on to clarify that inducement was not simply to be presumed.[18] This was a revolution engendered by common law jurisprudence, although said to be discovered in the ruling statute, and it has aided the move under the Act for remedies which depend upon a more refined assessment of both the cause and the effect of the breach of the duty of fair insurer presentation. It is reduplicated now expressly in statute, in section 8 of the Act, by the provision that an insurer has a remedy for breach of the duty of fair presentation "only if the insurer shows that, but for the breach" the insurer would either not have entered into the contract at all or would have done so only on different terms. So, the burden of proving inducement rests squarely on the insurer.

Thus, also the new proportionate remedies in Schedule 1 are made to depend in part on the nature of the breach and in part on the effect of the breach. If the breach is dishonest (my gloss, the statute says "deliberate or reckless" but both of those are difficult words), then the insurer may avoid the contract (and refuse all claims) and keep the premium; but, although Schedule 1 does not say so, the critical condition remains that expressed in section 8, that there still has to be the necessary inducement. If, on the other hand, the breach is not dishonest, then the remedy depends entirely on the effect that the breach had on the insurer. If he would not have entered into the contract at all, he may avoid the contract (and refuse all claims) but must return the premium. If he would have entered into the contract, but on different terms, those terms get written into the contract, for better or worse: they may mean that a claim fails or is limited in some way. If, either alternatively or in addition, the insurer would have charged a higher premium, then the insured's recovery on any claim will be reduced proportionately.

These provisions do not raise any particular issues of law, but the factual scenarios are likely to prove interesting. Since the insurer bears the burden of proof, he will need to keep good records of his underwriting practice, both as to terms and conditions required in different situations and as to premium rates. It can be imagined that the insured challenged by an allegation that would destroy his claim will press for discovery of relevant documents. There may well be some important decisions at the interlocutory stage as to how widely that discovery may go. Expert witnesses as to underwriting practice may be sought to be produced. To some extent, such expert evidence as to underwriting practice generally may miss the mark, since the critical question is as to the particular insured's practice: it is only if market practice generally can fairly be said to be relevant to the insurer's position that such evidence is likely to be helpful or even admissible.

18 *Assicurazioni Generali SpA v Arab Insurance Group (BSC)* [2002] EWCA 1642, [2003] 1 WLR 577.

In general, this is a new world, and it will be interesting to observe how matters are dealt with.

Warranties "and other terms" being "[t]erms not relevant to the actual loss" are the subject of Part 3 of the Act. The abolition of basis of contract clauses and their like (section 9) may be noted, the effect of which is to ensure that any promissory warranty of the insurance contract has to stand on its own feet and cannot arise out of a mere pre-contractual representation. Thus, the duty of fair presentation and the working of the insurance contract itself are sought to be insulated from one another.

As for warranties themselves, the Act does not seek to change their recognition. Thus, although the second sentence of section 33(3) and the whole of section 34 of the 1906 Act are abolished,[19] that leaves untouched the 1906 Act's definition of a warranty in its entirety: as a "warranty by which the assured undertakes that some particular thing shall or shall not be done, or that some condition shall be fulfilled, or whereby he affirms or negatives the existence of a particular state of facts" and which "is a condition which must be exactly complied with".

Nevertheless, the distinction between a warranty and other terms of an insurance contract remains elusive. It is a matter of construction, and jurisprudence veers between defining a warranty as a condition precedent to the insurer's liability,[20] which recognises it by its effect, which may be said to be the issue in the first place, and a special term which contains a material definition of the risk.[21] The Law Commission prefers the latter approach, for it states:[22] "Our analysis of warranties regards them primarily as tools which allow the insurer to define precisely the risk it is willing to underwrite."[23] To some considerable degree, however, the changes wrought by the Act render the importance of the distinction between a warranty and other terms of the insurance contract less important. This is because the Act renders two radical changes in the previous law: first, it abolishes the rule that a breach of warranty automatically discharges the contract from the moment of breach; and second, it provides that if a breach of warranty occurs and the actual loss cannot be attributed to the breach as long as it lasted, then the breach has no effect.[24] In other words, a breach of warranty can be remedied and pending remedy its effect on liability is suspensory only. One consequence is to reverse the decision in *De Hahn v Hartley*.[25]

What counts as a breach being remedied? There are at least three situations. First, some breaches are not capable of being remedied at all. The Act does not deal expressly with them (other than the acknowledgment contained in section

19 By section 10(7) of the Act.

20 *The Good Luck* [1992] 1 AC 233 at 263 *per* Lord Goff of Chieveley. See also Professor Malcolm Clarke, "Insurance Warranties: The Absolute End?" [2007] LMCLQ 474, 475.

21 *HIH Casualty & General Insurance Ltd v New Hampshire Insurance Co* [2001] EWCA Civ 735, [2001] 2 All ER 39 at [101]. In *Bean v Stupart* (1778) 1 Doug 11, 14 Lord Mansfield described a warranty as "a condition on which the contract is founded".

22 Para 17.37 of the July 2014 report.

23 *Sed quaere* that "precisely".

24 See sections 10(2), 10(4) and 10(5).

25 (1786) 1 Term Reports 343, 99 ER 1130.

10(4)(b): "if the breach can be remedied"), but the consequence is that liability will be permanently suspended, although the contract will not have been discharged. Questions might arise as to how a permanently suspended but living contract operates. What about the payment of quarterly premiums and the like? Second, there are warranties which in one sense are not capable of being remedied and in another sense are, such as warranties that something be done by a certain time. The Law Commission, but not the statute, calls these "time-specific warranties",[26] and they are dealt with in sections 10(5)(a) and (6), where the test is introduced of the situation where "the risk to which the warranty relates becomes essentially the same as that originally contemplated by the parties". This is not an easy test. However, it is designed to deal with the time-specific warranty where, although history cannot be rewritten, nevertheless, the position is restored to what it should always have been. Thus, in *De Hahn v Hartley* itself, it made no essential difference to the risk that the full complement of crew was not on board on departure but only six hours later. The third situation is everything else, where the test, contained in section 10(5)(b), is "if the insured ceases to be in breach of the warranty".

However, it is not clear whether the distinction between time-specific warranties and other warranties is entirely valid. What of a warranty against a vessel sailing within certain zones, such as a war zone? Once the vessel has sailed into a forbidden zone, in one sense the breach can never be remedied; but, of course, when once the vessel is again outside the forbidden zone, the risk reverts to what it had originally been. The same question might be asked of a warranty against business use of a car, which has occurred but has not continued. Why are such cases dealt with by the section 10(5)(b) test rather than by the section 10(5)(a) test? In one sense the breach has ceased, but in another sense it cannot be written out of the history books, and that is particularly so in the case of the car which is used intermittently for private and business use. And what if the warranty is against all business use or "only for private use"? There is a potential overlap here which might prove troublesome: but if the insured can meet either test, then the problem is simplified.

What, however, of the problem where, before the breach is remedied, the situation is affected in some way which has consequences for the insured even after the breach has been remedied, on whatever is the applicable test? The case has been put of the improperly stored wine, or of the vessel in a war zone: in either case the loss on which the claim is based occurred after the breach of warranty had been remedied, but there is some connection between what occurred while the insured was in breach and the actual later loss. Such situations are under the Act intended to be dealt with by the test of a "loss . . . attributable to something happening . . . before the breach is remedied": see the language of section 10(2) and section 10(4). Thus, an insurer has no liability for a loss attributable to something happening after breach and before remedy (section 10(2)), but his liability is not affected by a loss attributable to something happening before breach or after a breach has been remedied (section 10(4)). Section 10(4) goes as far as to say

26 Paras 17.40 ff. of the July 2014 report.

that sub-section (2) "does not affect the liability" in a case within sub-section (2). However, there are two problems. The first is that the cases put in those two sub-sections are not binary: a loss might be attributable to *both* something happening during breach *and* something else happening after the breach has been remedied. Is liability affected or not? One would think it should be, unless the subsequent event so altered matters as to make the earlier event irrelevant and thus not something to which the loss was attributable.

The second is that the Law Commission is generally unwilling to allow that its solutions to the problems of warranties (or other terms dealt with in Part 3) depend upon any doctrine of causation.[27] However, it seems clear that the test of "attributable to" is a causation test. As the Explanatory Notes say:[28]

> The "attributable to something happening" wording is intended to cater for the situation in which loss arises as a result of an event which occurred during the period of suspension, but is not actually suffered until after the breach has been "remedied".

There are of course cases where actual loss is entirely caused by something which occurs at an earlier time but is not suffered until a later date; and other cases where the actual loss is caused by a combination of events. The language of "attributable to" seems designed to cover both cases. It may be that the Law Commission's aversion to the concept of causation is not directed to the section 10 situation so much as to the section 11 situation, to which attention is now turned.

Section 11 has given the Law Commission trouble. Consultees disapproved of an earlier version on the ground that it involved the concept of causation; but in the end a new version was approved in the course of the bill getting Parliamentary approval.[29] Section 11 is designed to deal with the situation where a loss occurs while the insured is still in breach of a term of the insurance contract – so that section 10 cannot help the insured – but the loss is unrelated to the breach. The classic example is that of the warranty concerning a burglar alarm and a loss by fire (or *vice versa*). Such problems can arise whether or not the term is a warranty. Thus, section 11 is written broadly in relation to "[t]erms not relevant to the loss". In particular, three types of such terms are identified: those compliance with which would tend to reduce the risk of loss (a) of a particular kind, (b) at a particular place, and (c) at a particular time.[30] However, "a term defining the risk as a whole" is excluded from the operation of the section.

Section 11 is designed, as indicated, to deal with loss unrelated to the insured's breach. So, non-compliance by the insured does not excuse the insurer if the insured shows, the burden thus being on the insured, that such non-compliance "could not have increased the risk of the loss which actually occurred in the circumstances in which it occurred".

27 See, e.g. paras 14.23 ff. of the July 2014 report.

28 Explanatory Notes at para 89.

29 The story is told by R. Merkin and O. Gürses, "The Insurance Act 2015: Rebalancing the Interests of Insurer and Assured," (2015) 78(6) MLR 1004, 1019–1022.

30 The drafting has been influenced by the New York code (2013 New York Consolidated Laws ISC – Insurance): see para 18.15 of the July 2014 report.

However, two major problems remain. How does one tell if a term defines the risk as a whole? And second, how can it be true, as the Law Commission would seem to wish, that the reformulated clause avoids a causation test?[31]

As for the first, it would seem that a term defining the risk as a whole is a form of super-warranty. If it was a warranty, the Act would say so, and then the application of section 11 would be much reduced. So it appears that section 11 has created a new category of term, which is probably intended to be something rather special. The Explanatory Notes merely say[32] that the phrase is expected to include, e.g. a requirement that a property or vehicle is not to be used commercially. The Law Commission did not have this concept of a term which defines the risk as a whole in mind in its draft bill current with its July 2014 report.[33] Nevertheless, that report appears to suggest[34] that terms excluding commercial use of a vehicle or relating to a vessel's class are different in kind from the terms which clause 11, even in its earlier draft form, had in mind. However, it is one thing to say that terms such as those just mentioned are not terms within the meaning of clause 11: it is understandable to say that a warranty against commercial use or that a vessel is in a class is something entirely different from a term compliance with which would tend to reduce the risk of particular kinds of losses or losses at particular locations or times. It is another to say that even terms within the meaning of clause 11 are excluded from its operation if they define the risk as a whole.

It may be anticipated, therefore, that the courts will be exercised as to the true scope of clause 11(1). The answer will need to be addressed with the help of a proper understanding of the function of clause 11(1) as a definitional description of the terms which clause 11 addresses in the context of the solution provided by sub-clauses (2) and (3). As stated, the solution is that the insurer cannot avoid liability for non-compliance with a relevant term if such non-compliance could not have increased the risk of the loss which actually occurred. Putting aside for the moment the second problem which has been anticipated, namely whether clause 11(3) is concerned with a causation test or not, the courts might find inspiration in the thought that even a loss totally unrelated to the risk function of the term which has been breached should not result in a recovery from the insurer when the insured has broken a term of such a kind that recovery would mean that the insured had obtained the benefit of an insurance of an entirely different category from that which the parties had in fact entered into.

An example might be a fire policy which contained a clause forbidding the storing of inflammable or explosive material on the premises, or the carrying out of hot work on the premises. The insured is in breach of those terms, and the premises suffer fire damage, but not from anything to do with the storing of the forbidden materials or the carrying out of hot work. Should the insured be able to recover,

31 See the Explanatory Notes at para 96: "A direct causal link between the breach and the ultimate loss is not required. That is, the relevant test is not whether the non-compliance caused or contributed to the loss which has been suffered." That, however, causation aside, is putting the problem the wrong way round.

32 Explanatory Notes at para 94.

33 See clause 11 at p. 356 of the July 2014 report.

34 Paras 18.23/24 of the July 2014 report.

when he would thereby have obtained the benefit of an insurance which was essentially different in kind, and would no doubt have demanded a significantly different premium, from that which was the subject of the parties' contract? The example of damage caused to a vehicle insured for private use and not commercial use is similar, in that everyone would recognise that the insurance of private cars and cars used for commercial purposes are essentially different categories of insurance, for which very different premiums are charged. Even so, it is difficult to think that such a term would otherwise fall within the clause 11(1) definition of a term which is designed to reduce the risk of losses of particular kinds or at particular times or places, which would suggest that such a term was not in the mind of the draftsman. The courts are likely to struggle with these difficulties.

The second problem is that it is suggested that the clause 11(3) solution has nothing to do with causation. It can be accepted that the phrase "the non-compliance . . . could not have increased the risk" raises a theoretical risk evaluation rather than a pragmatic assessment of cause and effect. However, when one comes to the words "the risk of the loss of which actually occurred in the circumstances in which it occurred", it might seem to the courts that it is impossible to avoid an exercise in causative enquiry. Moreover, even a theoretical risk evaluation is essentially based in matters of causation. It has been suggested that an enquiry into causation is too uncertain to be palatable. It is hard to understand the objection. Causation is endemic to legal problems and their solutions. It is central to issues of responsibility throughout the law. The doctrine of proximate cause is central to insurance. It may not be all simple "common sense",[35] but the law nevertheless seems to manage.

It is to be noted, however, that clause 11(3) places a burden of proof upon the insured ("The insured satisfies this subsection if it shows"). It appears that the insured is faced with the difficult burden of excluding any possible increase of risk of the loss which actually occurred. That is, it seems, a causation test but one which involves a heavy burden in which even somewhat speculative possibilities of risk aggravation have to be excluded.

Part 4 deals with fraudulent claims. Some of the issues which have exercised the courts in the past are dealt with. The Act does not favour forfeiture of the policy, but only of the claim concerned. A valid claim in respect of an earlier loss remains valid, even if the insurer exercises his right to treat the contract as having been terminated upon the occasion of the fraudulent claim; and if that right is not exercised, a subsequent valid loss will be able to give rise to a further valid claim.

One issue which still hangs in the balance is whether a fraudulent device in support of a valid claim is to be treated as a "fraudulent claim". The issue is currently being debated in *Versloot Dredging BV v HDI Gerling Industrie Versicherung AG*.[36] So far the decision has gone against the insured. The answer will be known soon enough.

35 Cf. *Galoo v Bright Grahame Murray* [1994] 1 WLR 1360, 1374–1375 (CA).

36 [2013] EWHC 1666 (Comm), [2013] 2 All ER (Comm) 465 (Popplewell J), [2014] EWCA Civ 1349, [2015] QB 609. The case is currently before the Supreme Court.

In sum, whereas CIDRA has brought about a much-needed revolution, bringing consumer insurance back within the fold of the rule of law,[37] in commercial and non-consumer insurance the Insurance Act 2015 has rendered a revolutionary non-revolution.

The Act is non-revolutionary in that the duty of fair presentation remains much as it was in its pre-Act form: the test, as before, is objective in that what is fair and material depends upon an objective viewpoint, and subjective in that any remedy depends on the subjective inducement of the insurer in question. The Act is non-revolutionary in that it allows widespread, almost total, contracting out. But it is revolutionary in the remedies which are provided in case of breach of duty or non-compliance with warranties and other terms excluding or limiting risk. The new remedies are much more flexible, proportionate, refined, nuanced, and for those reasons fairer than the old law.

What are the potential or likely consequences of this revolution in remedies? It may be thought that it will be to the great benefit of insurance, and thus to the benefit of both parties to the insurance contract. Its effects will be greater transparency, greater proportionality, the growth of agreed guidelines which will themselves promote greater transparency and proportionality, and the product of all this will be greater fairness and the promotion of insurance as better answering to the needs of industry and commerce. Insurance cover will no longer be so much in the discretion of the insurer, but will be available on a principled but also flexible and fair basis. The minority of fraudsters and deceitful seekers of insurance will not be any better off, but the great majority of lawful and honest users of insurance will be better served by a great and important industry. In the short run, there will be litigation about some of the new language in the Act. In the short run, the lawyers will benefit and the judges will have to elucidate the principles of the Act. In the long run, however, these new remedies will work their own solutions; and one of their benefits will be that judges and arbitrators will be able, for the first time in a long while, to stop looking for ways in which they can protect insureds against the over-rigid provisions of an out of date law. Everyone will benefit from that.

37 See *Regina (Heather Moor & Edgecomb Ltd) v Financial Ombudsman Service* [2008] EWCA Civ 642, [2008] Bus LR 1486 at [87]-[90].

APPENDIX 1

Marine Insurance Act 1906
1906 (6 Edw. 7 C. 41)

An Act to codify the Law relating to Marine Insurance.

[21st December 1906]

MARINE INSURANCE

1. Marine insurance defined.

A contract of marine insurance is a contract whereby the insurer undertakes to indemnify the assured, in manner and to the extent thereby agreed, against marine losses, that is to say, the losses incident to marine adventure.

2.—Mixed sea and land risks.

(1) A contract of marine insurance may, by its express terms, or by usage of trade, be extended so as to protect the assured against losses on inland waters or on any land risk which may be incidental to any sea voyage.

(2) Where a ship in course of building, or the launch of a ship, or any adventure analogous to a marine adventure, is covered by a policy in the form of a marine policy, the provisions of this Act, in so far as applicable, shall apply thereto; but, except as by this section provided, nothing in this Act shall alter or affect any rule of law applicable to any contract of insurance other than a contract of marine insurance as by this Act defined.

3.—Marine adventure and maritime perils defined.

(1) Subject to the provisions of this Act, every lawful marine adventure may be the subject of a contract of marine insurance.

(2) In particular there is a marine adventure where –

  (a) Any ship goods or other moveables are exposed to maritime perils. Such property is in this Act referred to as "insurable property";

  (b) The earning or acquisition of any freight, passage money, commission, profit, or other pecuniary benefit, or the security for any advances, loan, or disbursements, is endangered by the exposure of insurable property to maritime perils;

  (c) Any liability to a third party may be incurred by the owner of, or other person interested in or responsible for, insurable property, by reason of maritime perils.

"Maritime perils" means the perils consequent on, or incidental to, the navigation of the sea, that is to say, perils of the seas, fire, war perils, pirates, rovers, thieves, captures, seisures, restraints, and detainments of princes and peoples, jettisons, barratry, and any other perils, either of the like kind or which may be designated by the policy.

INSURABLE INTEREST

4.—Avoidance of wagering or gaming contracts.

(1) Every contract of marine insurance by way of gaming or wagering is void.

(2) A contract of marine insurance is deemed to be a gaming or wagering contract –

(a) Where the assured has not an insurable interest as defined by this Act, and the contract is entered into with no expectation of acquiring such an interest; or

(b) Where the policy is made "interest or no interest," or "without further proof of interest than the policy itself," or "without benefit of salvage to the insurer," or subject to any other like term:

Provided that, where there is no possibility of salvage, a policy may be effected without benefit of salvage to the insurer.

5.—Insurable interest defined.

(1) Subject to the provisions of this Act, every person has an insurable interest who is interested in a marine adventure.

(2) In particular a person is interested in a marine adventure where he stands in any legal or equitable relation to the adventure or to any insurable property at risk therein, in consequence of which he may benefit by the safety or due arrival of insurable property, or may be prejudiced by its loss, or by damage thereto, or by the detention thereof, or may incur liability in respect thereof.

6.—When interest must attach.

(1) The assured must be interested in the subject-matter insured at the time of the loss though he need not be interested when the insurance is effected:

Provided that where the subject-matter is insured "lost or not lost," the assured may recover although he may not have acquired his interest until after the loss, unless at the time of effecting the contract of insurance the assured was aware of the loss, and the insurer was not.

(2) Where the assured has no interest at the time of the loss, he cannot acquire interest by any act or election after he is aware of the loss.

7.—Defeasible or contingent interest.

(1) A defeasible interest is insurable, as also is a contingent interest.

(2) In particular, where the buyer of goods has insured them, he has an insurable interest, notwithstanding that he might, at his election, have rejected the goods, or have treated them as at the seller's risk, by reason of the latter's delay in making delivery or otherwise.

8. Partial interest.

A partial interest of any nature is insurable.

9.—Re-insurance.

(1) The insurer under a contract of marine insurance has an insurable interest in his risk, and may re-insure in respect of it.
(2) Unless the policy otherwise provides, the original assured has no right or interest in respect of such re-insurance.

10. Bottomry.

The lender of money on bottomry or respondentia has an insurable interest in respect of the loan.

11. Master's and seamen's wages.

The master or any member of the crew of a ship has an insurable interest in respect of his wages.

12. Advance freight.

In the case of advance freight, the person advancing the freight has an insurable interest, in so far as such freight is not repayable in case of loss.

13. Charges of insurance.

The assured has an insurable interest in the charges of any insurance which he may effect.

14.—Quantum of interest.

(1) Where the subject-matter insured is mortgaged, the mortgagor has an insurable interest in the full value thereof, and the mortgagee has an insurable interest in respect of any sum due or to become due under the mortgage.
(2) A mortgagee, consignee, or other person having an interest in the subject-matter insured may insure on behalf and for the benefit of other persons interested as well as for his own benefit.
(3) The owner of insurable property has an insurable interest in respect of the full value thereof, notwithstanding that some third person may have agreed, or be liable, to indemnify him in case of loss.

15. Assignment of interest.

Where the assured assigns or otherwise parts with his interest in the subject-matter insured, he does not thereby transfer to the assignee his rights under the contract of insurance, unless there be an express or implied agreement with the assignee to that effect.

But the provisions of this section do not affect a transmission of interest by operation of law.

INSURABLE VALUE

16. Measure of insurable value.

Subject to any express provision or valuation in the policy, the insurable value of the subject-matter insured must be ascertained as follows:—

(1) In insurance on ship, the insurable value is the value, at the commencement of the risk, of the ship, including her outfit, provisions and stores for the officers and crew, money advanced for seamen's wages, and other disbursements (if any) incurred to make the ship fit for the voyage or adventure contemplated by the policy, plus the charges of insurance upon the whole:

The insurable value, in the case of a steamship, includes also the machinery, boilers, and coals and engine stores if owned by the assured, and, in the case of a ship engaged in a special trade, the ordinary fittings requisite for that trade:

(2) In insurance on freight, whether paid in advance or otherwise, the insurable value is the gross amount of the freight at the risk of the assured, plus the charges of insurance:

(3) In insurance on goods or merchandise, the insurable value is the prime cost of the property insured, plus the expenses of and incidental to shipping and the charges of insurance upon the whole:

(4) In insurance on any other subject-matter, the insurable value is the amount at the risk of the assured when the policy attaches, plus the charges of insurance.

DISCLOSURE AND REPRESENTATIONS

17. Insurance is uberrimae fidei.

A contract of marine insurance is a contract based upon the utmost good faith, and, if the utmost good faith be not observed by either party, the contract may be avoided by the other party.

18.—Disclosure by assured.

(1) Subject to the provisions of this section, the assured must disclose to the insurer, before the contract is concluded, every material circumstance which is known to the assured, and the assured is deemed to know every circumstance which, in the ordinary course of business, ought to be known by him. If the assured fails to make such disclosure, the insurer may avoid the contract.

(2) Every circumstance is material which would influence the judgment of a prudent insurer in fixing the premium, or determining whether he will take the risk.

(3) In the absence of inquiry the following circumstances need not be disclosed, namely:—

   (a) Any circumstance which diminishes the risk;

   (b) Any circumstance which is known or presumed to be known to the insurer. The insurer is presumed to know matters of common notoriety or knowledge, and matters which an insurer in the ordinary course of his business, as such, ought to know;

   (c) Any circumstance as to which information is waived by the insurer;

   (d) Any circumstance which it is superfluous to disclose by reason of any express or implied warranty.

(4) Whether any particular circumstance, which is not disclosed, be material or not is, in each case, a question of fact.

(5) The term "circumstance" includes any communication made to, or information received by, the assured.

19. Disclosure by agent effecting insurance.

(1) Subject to the provisions of the preceding section as to circumstances which need not be disclosed, where an insurance is effected for the assured by an agent, the agent must disclose to the insurer—

(a) Every material circumstance which is known to himself, and an agent to insure is deemed to know every circumstance which in the ordinary course of business ought to be known by, or to have been communicated to, him; and

(b) Every material circumstance which the assured is bound to disclose, unless it come to his knowledge too late to communicate it to the agent.

(2) This section does not apply in relation to a contract of marine insurance if it is a consumer insurance contract within the meaning of the Consumer Insurance (Disclosure and Representations) Act 2012.

20.—Representations pending negotiation of contract.

(1) Every material representation made by the assured or his agent to the insurer during the negotiations for the contract, and before the contract is concluded, must be true. If it be untrue the insurer may avoid the contract.

(2) A representation is material which would influence the judgment of a prudent insurer in fixing the premium, or determining whether he will take the risk.

(3) A representation may be either a representation as to a matter of fact, or as to a matter of expectation or belief.

(4) A representation as to a matter of fact is true, if it be substantially correct, that is to say, if the difference between what is represented and what is actually correct would not be considered material by a prudent insurer.

(5) A representation as to a matter of expectation or belief is true if it be made in good faith.

(6) A representation may be withdrawn or corrected before the contract is concluded.

(7) Whether a particular representation be material or not is, in each case, a question of fact.

21. When contract is deemed to be concluded.

A contract of marine insurance is deemed to be concluded when the proposal of the assured is accepted by the insurer, whether the policy be then issued or not; and, for the purpose of showing when the proposal was accepted, reference may be made to the slip or covering note or other customary memorandum of the contract [. . .][1]

---

1 Words repealed by Finance Act 1959 (c. 58), Sch. 8 Pt. II.

THE POLICY

22. Contract must be embodied in policy.

Subject to the provisions of any statute, a contract of marine insurance is inadmissible in evidence unless it is embodied in a marine policy in accordance with this Act. The policy may be executed and issued either at the time when the contract is concluded, or afterwards.

23. What policy must specify.

A marine policy must specify –

(1) The name of the assured, or of some person who effects the insurance on his behalf:
(2) [. . .][2]
(3) [. . .][3]
(4) [. . .][4]
(5) [. . .][5]

24.—Signature of insurer.

(1) A marine policy must be signed by or on behalf of the insurer, provided that in the case of a corporation the corporate seal may be sufficient, but nothing in this section shall be construed as requiring the subscription of a corporation to be under seal.
(2) Where a policy is subscribed by or on behalf of two or more insurers, each subscription, unless the contrary be expressed, constitutes a distinct contract with the assured.

25.—Voyage and time policies.

(1) Where the contract is to insure the subject-matter "at and from," or from one place to another or others, the policy is called a "voyage policy," and where the contract is to insure the subject-matter for a definite period of time the policy is called a "time policy." A contract for both voyage and time may be included in the same policy.
(2) [. . .][6]

26.—Designation of subject-matter.

(1) The subject-matter insured must be designated in a marine policy with reasonable certainty.
(2) The nature and extent of the interest of the assured in the subject-matter insured need not be specified in the policy.

---

2 S. 23(2) repealed as to instruments made or executed after 1.8.1959 by Finance Act 1959 (c. 58), Sch. 8 Pt. II.

3 S. 23(3) repealed as to instruments made or executed after 1.8.1959 by Finance Act 1959 (c. 58), Sch. 8 Pt. II.

4 S. 23(4) repealed as to instruments made or executed after 1.8.1959 by Finance Act 1959 (c. 58), Sch. 8 Pt. II.

5 S. 23(5) repealed as to instruments made or executed after 1.8.1959 by Finance Act 1959 (c. 58), Sch. 8 Pt. II.

6 Repealed by Finance Act 1959 (c. 58), Sch. 8 Pt. II.

(3) Where the policy designates the subject-matter insured in general terms, it shall be construed to apply to the interest intended by the assured to be covered.
(4) In the application of this section regard shall be had to any usage regulating the designation of the subject-matter insured.

27.—Valued policy.

(1) A policy may be either valued or unvalued.
(2) A valued policy is a policy which specifies the agreed value of the subject-matter insured.
(3) Subject to the provisions of this Act, and in the absence of fraud, the value fixed by the policy is, as between the insurer and assured, conclusive of the insurable value of the subject intended to be insured, whether the loss be total or partial.
(4) Unless the policy otherwise provides, the value fixed by the policy is not conclusive for the purpose of determining whether there has been a constructive total loss.

28. Unvalued policy.

An unvalued policy is a policy which does not specify the value of the subject-matter insured, but, subject to the limit of the sum insured, leaves the insurable value to be subsequently ascertained, in the manner herein-before specified.

29.—Floating policy by ship or ships.

(1) A floating policy is a policy which describes the insurance in general terms, and leaves the name of the ship or ships and other particulars to be defined by subsequent declaration.
(2) The subsequent declaration or declarations may be made by indorsement on the policy, or in other customary manner.
(3) Unless the policy otherwise provides, the declarations must be made in the order of dispatch or shipment. They must, in the case of goods, comprise all consignments within the terms of the policy, and the value of the goods or other property must be honestly stated, but an omission or erroneous declaration may be rectified even after loss or arrival, provided the omission or declaration was made in good faith.
(4) Unless the policy otherwise provides, where a declaration of value is not made until after notice of loss or arrival, the policy must be treated as an unvalued policy as regards the subject-matter of that declaration.

30.—Construction of terms in policy.

(1) A policy may be in the form in the First Schedule to this Act.
(2) Subject to the provisions of this Act, and unless the context of the policy otherwise requires, the terms and expressions mentioned in the First Schedule to this Act shall be construed as having the scope and meaning in that schedule assigned to them.

31.—Premium to be arranged.

(1) Where an insurance is effected at a premium to be arranged, and no arrangement is made, a reasonable premium is payable.
(2) Where an insurance is effected on the terms that an additional premium is to be arranged in a given event, and that event happens but no arrangement is made, then a reasonable additional premium is payable.

DOUBLE INSURANCE

32.—Double insurance.

(1) Where two or more policies are effected by or on behalf of the assured on the same adventure and interest or any part thereof, and the sums insured exceed the indemnity allowed by this Act, the assured is said to be over-insured by double insurance.
(2) Where the assured is over-insured by double insurance –

  (a) The assured, unless the policy otherwise provides, may claim payment from the insurers in such order as he may think fit, provided that he is not entitled to receive any sum in excess of the indemnity allowed by this Act;
  (b) Where the policy under which the assured claims is a valued policy, the assured must give credit as against the valuation for any sum received by him under any other policy without regard to the actual value of the subject-matter insured;
  (c) Where the policy under which the assured claims is an unvalued policy he must give credit, as against the full insurable value, for any sum received by him under any other policy:
  (d) Where the assured receives any sum in excess of the indemnity allowed by this Act, he is deemed to hold such sum in trust for the insurers, according to their right of contribution among themselves.

WARRANTIES, &C.

33.—Nature of warranty.

(1) A warranty, in the following sections relating to warranties, means a promissory warranty, that is to say, a warranty by which the assured undertakes that some particular thing shall or shall not be done, or that some condition shall be fulfilled, or whereby he affirms or negatives the existence of a particular state of facts.
(2) A warranty may be express or implied.
(3) A warranty, as above defined, is a condition which must be exactly complied with, whether it be material to the risk or not. If it be not so complied with, then, subject to any express provision in the policy, the insurer is discharged from liability as from the date of the breach of warranty, but without prejudice to any liability incurred by him before that date.

34.—When breach of warranty excused.

(1) Non-compliance with a warranty is excused when, by reason of a change of circumstances, the warranty ceases to be applicable to the circumstances of the contract, or when compliance with the warranty is rendered unlawful by any subsequent law.
(2) Where a warranty is broken, the assured cannot avail himself of the defence that the breach has been remedied, and the warranty complied with, before loss.
(3) A breach of warranty may be waived by the insurer.

35.—Express warranties.

(1) An express warranty may be in any form of words from which the intention to warrant is to be inferred.
(2) An express warranty must be included in, or written upon, the policy, or must be contained in some document incorporated by reference into the policy.
(3) An express warranty does not exclude an implied warranty, unless it be inconsistent therewith.

36.—Warranty of neutrality.

(1) Where insurable property, whether ship or goods, is expressly warranted neutral, there is an implied condition that the property shall have a neutral character at the commencement of the risk, and that, so far as the assured can control the matter, its neutral character shall be preserved during the risk.
(2) Where a ship is expressly warranted "neutral" there is also an implied condition that, so far as the assured can control the matter, she shall be properly documented, that is to say, that she shall carry the necessary papers to establish her neutrality, and that she shall not falsify or suppress her papers, or use simulated papers. If any loss occurs through breach of this condition, the insurer may avoid the contract.

37. No implied warranty of nationality.

There is no implied warranty as to the nationality of a ship, or that her nationality shall not be changed during the risk.

38. Warranty of good safety.

Where the subject-matter insured is warranted "well" or "in good safety" on a particular day, it is sufficient if it be safe at any time during that day.

39.—Warranty of seaworthiness of ship.

(1) In a voyage policy there is an implied warranty that at the commencement of the voyage the ship shall be seaworthy for the purpose of the particular adventure insured.

(2) Where the policy attaches while the ship is in port, there is also an implied warranty that she shall, at the commencement of the risk, be reasonably fit to encounter the ordinary perils of the port.
(3) Where the policy relates to a voyage which is performed in different stages, during which the ship requires different kinds of or further preparation or equipment, there is an implied warranty that at the commencement of each stage the ship is seaworthy in respect of such preparation or equipment for the purposes of that stage.
(4) A ship is deemed to be seaworthy when she is reasonably fit in all respects to encounter the ordinary perils of the seas of the adventure insured.
(5) In a time policy there is no implied warranty that the ship shall be seaworthy at any stage of the adventure, but where, with the privity of the assured, the ship is sent to sea in an unseaworthy state, the insurer is not liable for any loss attributable to unseaworthiness.

40.—No implied warranty that goods are seaworthy.

(1) In a policy on goods or other moveables there is no implied warranty that the goods or moveables are seaworthy.
(2) In a voyage policy on goods or other moveables there is an implied warranty that at the commencement of the voyage the ship is not only seaworthy as a ship, but also that she is reasonably fit to carry the goods or other moveables to the destination contemplated by the policy.

41. Warranty of legality.

There is an implied warranty that the adventure insured is a lawful one, and that, so far as the assured can control the matter, the adventure shall be carried out in a lawful manner.

THE VOYAGE

42.—Implied condition as to commencement of risk.

(1) Where the subject-matter is insured by a voyage policy "at and from" or "from" a particular place, it is not necessary that the ship should be at that place when the contract is concluded, but there is an implied condition that the adventure shall be commenced within a reasonable time, and that if the adventure be not so commenced the insurer may avoid the contract.
(2) The implied condition may be negatived by showing that the delay was caused by circumstances known to the insurer before the contract was concluded, or by showing that he waived the condition.

43. Alteration of port of departure.

Where the place of departure is specified by the policy, and the ship instead of sailing from that place sails from any other place, the risk does not attach.

44. Sailing for different destination.

Where the destination is specified in the policy, and the ship, instead of sailing for that destination, sails for any other destination, the risk does not attach.

45.—Change of voyage.

(1) Where, after the commencement of the risk, the destination of the ship is voluntarily changed from the destination contemplated by the policy, there is said to be a change of voyage.

(2) Unless the policy otherwise provides, where there is a change of voyage, the insurer is discharged from liability as from the time of change, that is to say, as from the time when the determination to change it is manifested; and it is immaterial that the ship may not in fact have left the course of voyage contemplated by the policy when the loss occurs.

46.—Deviation.

(1) Where a ship, without lawful excuse, deviates from the voyage contemplated by the policy, the insurer is discharged from liability as from the time of deviation, and it is immaterial that the ship may have regained her route before any loss occurs.

(2) There is a deviation from the voyage contemplated by the policy –

(a) Where the course of the voyage is specifically designated by the policy, and that course is departed from; or

(b) Where the course of the voyage is not specifically designated by the policy, but the usual and customary course is departed from.

(3) The intention to deviate is immaterial; there must be a deviation in fact to discharge the insurer from his liability under the contract.

47.—Several ports of discharge.

(1) Where several ports of discharge are specified by the policy, the ship may proceed to all or any of them, but, in the absence of any usage or sufficient cause to the contrary, she must proceed to them, or such of them as she goes to, in the order designated by the policy. If she does not there is a deviation.

(2) Where the policy is to "ports of discharge," within a given area, which are not named, the ship must, in the absence of any usage or sufficient cause to the contrary, proceed to them, or such of them as she goes to, in their geographical order. If she does not there is a deviation.

48. Delay in voyage.

In the case of a voyage policy, the adventure insured must be prosecuted throughout its course with reasonable dispatch, and, if without lawful excuse it is not so prosecuted, the insurer is discharged from liability as from the time when the delay became unreasonable.

49.—Excuses for deviation or delay.

(1) Deviation or delay in prosecuting the voyage contemplated by the policy is excused
  (a) Where authorised by any special term in the policy; or
  (b) Where caused by circumstances beyond the control of the master and his employer; or
  (c) Where reasonably necessary in order to comply with an express or implied warranty; or
  (d) Where reasonably necessary for the safety of the ship or subject-matter insured; or
  (e) For the purpose of saving human life, or aiding a ship in distress where human life may be in danger; or
  (f) Where reasonably necessary for the purpose of obtaining medical or surgical aid for any person on board the ship; or
  (g) Where caused by the barratrous conduct of the master or crew, if barratry be one of the perils insured against.

(2) When the cause excusing the deviation or delay ceases to operate, the ship must resume her course, and prosecute her voyage, with reasonable dispatch.

ASSIGNMENT OF POLICY

50.—When and how policy is assignable.

(1) A marine policy is assignable unless it contains terms expressly prohibiting assignment. It may be assigned either before or after loss.

(2) Where a marine policy has been assigned so as to pass the beneficial interest in such policy, the assignee of the policy is entitled to sue thereon in his own name; and the defendant is entitled to make any defence arising out of the contract which he would have been entitled to make if the action had been brought in the name of the person by or on behalf of whom the policy was effected.

(3) A marine policy may be assigned by indorsement thereon or in other customary manner.

51. Assured who has no interest cannot assign.

Where the assured has parted with or lost his interest in the subject-matter insured, and has not, before or at the time of so doing, expressly or impliedly agreed to assign the policy, any subsequent assignment of the policy is inoperative:
Provided that nothing in this section affects the assignment of a policy after loss.

THE PREMIUM

52. When premium payable.

Unless otherwise agreed, the duty of the assured or his agent to pay the premium, and the duty of the insurer to issue the policy to the assured or his agent, are concurrent conditions, and the insurer is not bound to issue the policy until payment or tender of the premium.

53.—Policy effected through broker.

(1) Unless otherwise agreed, where a marine policy is effected on behalf of the assured by a broker, the broker is directly responsible to the insurer for the premium, and the insurer is directly responsible to the assured for the amount which may be payable in respect of losses, or in respect of returnable premium.

(2) Unless otherwise agreed, the broker has, as against the assured, a lien upon the policy for the amount of the premium and his charges in respect of effecting the policy; and, where he has dealt with the person who employs him as a principal, he has also a lien on the policy in respect of any balance on any insurance account which may be due to him from such person, unless when the debt was incurred he had reason to believe that such person was only an agent.

54. Effect of receipt on policy.

Where a marine policy effected on behalf of the assured by a broker acknowledges the receipt of the premium, such acknowledgement is, in the absence of fraud, conclusive as between the insurer and the assured, but not as between the insurer and broker.

LOSS AND ABANDONMENT

55.—Included and excluded losses.

(1) Subject to the provisions of this Act, and unless the policy otherwise provides, the insurer is liable for any loss proximately caused by a peril insured against, but, subject as aforesaid, he is not liable for any loss which is not proximately caused by a peril insured against.

(2) In particular –

(a) The insurer is not liable for any loss attributable to the wilful misconduct of the assured, but, unless the policy otherwise provides, he is liable for any loss proximately caused by a peril insured against, even though the loss would not have happened but for the misconduct or negligence of the master or crew;

(b) Unless the policy otherwise provides, the insurer on ship or goods is not liable for any loss proximately caused by delay, although the delay be caused by a peril insured against;

(c) Unless the policy otherwise provides, the insurer is not liable for ordinary wear and tear, ordinary leakage and breakage, inherent vice or nature of the subject-matter insured, or for any loss proximately caused by rats or vermin, or for any injury to machinery not proximately caused by maritime perils.

56.—Partial and total loss.

(1) A loss may be either total or partial. Any loss other than a total loss, as hereinafter defined, is a partial loss.

(2) A total loss may be either an actual total loss, or a constructive total loss.

(3) Unless a different intention appears from the terms of the policy, an insurance against total loss includes a constructive, as well as an actual, total loss.

(4) Where the assured brings an action for a total loss and the evidence proves only a partial loss, he may, unless the policy otherwise provides, recover for a partial loss.

(5) Where goods reach their destination in specie, but by reason of obliteration of marks, or otherwise, they are incapable of identification, the loss, if any, is partial, and not total.

57.—Actual total loss.

(1) Where the subject-matter insured is destroyed, or so damaged as to cease to be a thing of the kind insured, or where the assured is irretrievably deprived thereof, there is an actual total loss.

(2) In the case of an actual total loss no notice of abandonment need be given.

58. Missing ship.

Where the ship concerned in the adventure is missing, and after the lapse of a reasonable time no news of her has been received, an actual total loss may be presumed.

59. Effect of transhipment, &c.

Where, by a peril insured against, the voyage is interrupted at an intermediate port or place, under such circumstances as, apart from any special stipulation in the contract of affreightment, to justify the master in landing and reshipping the goods or other moveables, or in transhipping them, and sending them on to their destination, the liability of the insurer continues, notwithstanding the landing or transhipment.

60.—Constructive total loss defined.

(1) Subject to any express provision in the policy, there is a constructive total loss where the subject-matter insured is reasonably abandoned on account of its actual total loss appearing to be unavoidable, or because it could not be preserved from actual total loss without an expenditure which would exceed its value when the expenditure had been incurred.

(2) In particular, there is a constructive total loss –

(i) Where the assured is deprived of the possession of his ship or goods by a peril insured against, and *(a)* it is unlikely that he can recover the ship or goods, as the case may be, or *(b)* the cost of recovering the ship or goods, as the case may be, would exceed their value when recovered; or

(ii) In the case of damage to a ship, where she is so damaged by a peril insured against that the cost of repairing the damage would exceed the value of the ship when repaired. In estimating the cost of repairs, no deduction is to be made in respect of general average contributions to those repairs payable by other interests, but account is to be taken of the expense of future salvage operations and of any future general average contributions to which the ship would be liable if repaired; or

(iii) In the case of damage to goods, where the cost of repairing the damage and forwarding the goods to their destination would exceed their value on arrival.

61. Effect of constructive total loss.

Where there is a constructive total loss the assured may either treat the loss as a partial loss, or abandon the subject-matter insured to the insurer and treat the loss as if it were an actual total loss.

62.—Notice of abandonment.

(1) Subject to the provisions of this section, where the assured elects to abandon the subject-matter insured to the insurer, he must give notice of abandonment. If he fails to do so the loss can only be treated as a partial loss.
(2) Notice of abandonment may be given in writing, or by word of mouth, or partly in writing and partly by word of mouth, and may be given in any terms which indicate the intention of the assured to abandon his insured interest in the subject-matter insured unconditionally to the insurer.
(3) Notice of abandonment must be given with reasonable diligence after the receipt of reliable information of the loss, but where the information is of a doubtful character the assured is entitled to a reasonable time to make inquiry.
(4) Where notice of abandonment is properly given, the rights of the assured are not prejudiced by the fact that the insurer refuses to accept the abandonment.
(5) The acceptance of an abandonment may be either express or implied from the conduct of the insurer. The mere silence of the insurer after notice is not an acceptance.
(6) Where notice of abandonment is accepted the abandonment is irrevocable. The acceptance of the notice conclusively admits liability for the loss and the sufficiency of the notice.
(7) Notice of abandonment is unnecessary where, at the time when the assured receives information of the loss, there would be no possibility of benefit to the insurer if notice were given to him.
(8) Notice of abandonment may be waived by the insurer.
(9) Where an insurer has re-insured his risk, no notice of abandonment need be given by him.

63.—Effect of abandonment.

(1) Where there is a valid abandonment the insurer is entitled to take over the interest of the assured in whatever may remain of the subject-matter insured, and all proprietary rights incidental thereto.
(2) Upon the abandonment of a ship, the insurer thereof is entitled to any freight in course of being earned, and which is earned by her subsequent to the casualty causing the loss, less the expenses of earning it incurred after the casualty; and, where the ship is carrying the owner's goods, the insurer is entitled to a reasonable remuneration for the carriage of them subsequent to the casualty causing the loss.

PARTIAL LOSSES (INCLUDING SALVAGE AND GENERAL AVERAGE AND PARTICULAR CHARGES)

64.—Particular average loss.

(1) A particular average loss is a partial loss of the subject-matter insured, caused by a peril insured against, and which is not a general average loss.

(2) Expenses incurred by or on behalf of the assured for the safety or preservation of the subject-matter insured, other than general average and salvage charges, are called particular charges. Particular charges are not included in particular average.

65.—Salvage charges.

(1) Subject to any express provision in the policy, salvage charges incurred in preventing a loss by perils insured against may be recovered as a loss by those perils.

(2) "Salvage charges" means the charges recoverable under maritime law by a salvor independently of contract. They do not include the expenses of services in the nature of salvage rendered by the assured or his agents, or any person employed for hire by them, for the purpose of averting a peril insured against. Such expenses, where properly incurred, may be recovered as particular charges or as a general average loss, according to the circumstances under which they were incurred.

66.—General average loss.

(1) A general average loss is a loss caused by or directly consequential on a general average act. It includes a general average expenditure as well as a general average sacrifice.

(2) There is a general average act where any extraordinary sacrifice or expenditure is voluntarily and reasonably made or incurred in time of peril for the purpose of preserving the property imperilled in the common adventure.

(3) Where there is a general average loss, the party on whom it falls is entitled, subject to the conditions imposed by maritime law, to a rateable contribution from the other parties interested, and such contribution is called a general average contribution.

(4) Subject to any express provision in the policy, where the assured has incurred a general average expenditure, he may recover from the insurer in respect of the proportion of the loss which falls upon him; and, in the case of a general average sacrifice, he may recover from the insurer in respect of the whole loss without having enforced his right of contribution from the other parties liable to contribute.

(5) Subject to any express provision in the policy, where the assured has paid, or is liable to pay, a general average contribution in respect of the subject insured, he may recover therefor from the insurer.

(6) In the absence of express stipulation, the insurer is not liable for any general average loss or contribution where the loss was not incurred for the purpose of avoiding, or in connexion with the avoidance of, a peril insured against.

(7) Where ship, freight, and cargo, or any two of those interests, are owned by the same assured, the liability of the insurer in respect of general average losses or contributions is to be determined as if those subjects were owned by different persons.

MEASURE OF INDEMNITY

67.—Extent of liability of insurer for loss.

(1) The sum which the assured can recover in respect of a loss on a policy by which he is insured, in the case of an unvalued policy to the full extent of the insurable value, or, in the case of a valued policy to the full extent of the value fixed by the policy is called the measure of indemnity.

(2) Where there is a loss recoverable under the policy, the insurer, or each insurer if there be more than one, is liable for such proportion of the measure of indemnity as the amount of his subscription bears to the value fixed by the policy in the case of a valued policy, or to the insurable value in the case of an unvalued policy.

68. Total loss.

Subject to the provisions of this Act and to any express provision in the policy, where there is a total loss of the subject-matter insured,—

(1) If the policy be a valued policy, the measure of indemnity is the sum fixed by the policy:

(2) If the policy be an unvalued policy, the measure of indemnity is the insurable value of the subject-matter insured.

69. Partial loss of ship.

Where a ship is damaged, but is not totally lost, the measure of indemnity, subject to any express provision in the policy, is as follows:

(1) Where the ship has been repaired, the assured is entitled to the reasonable cost of the repairs, less the customary deductions, but not exceeding the sum insured in respect of any one casualty:

(2) Where the ship has been only partially repaired, the assured is entitled to the reasonable cost of such repairs, computed as above, and also to be indemnified for the reasonable depreciation, if any, arising from the unrepaired damage, provided that the aggregate amount shall not exceed the cost of repairing the whole damage, computed as above:

(3) Where the ship has not been repaired, and has not been sold in her damaged state during the risk, the assured is entitled to be indemnified for the reasonable depreciation arising from the unrepaired damage, but not exceeding the reasonable cost of repairing such damage, computed as above.

70. Partial loss of freight.

Subject to any express provision in the policy, where there is a partial loss of freight, the measure of indemnity is such proportion of the sum fixed by the policy in the case of a valued policy, or of the insurable value in the case of an unvalued policy, as the proportion of freight lost by the assured bears to the whole freight at the risk of the assured under the policy.

71. Partial loss of goods, merchandise, &c.

Where there is a partial loss of goods, merchandise, or other moveables, the measure of indemnity, subject to any express provision in the policy, is as follows:—

(1) Where part of the goods, merchandise or other moveables insured by a valued policy is totally lost, the measure of indemnity is such proportion of the sum fixed by the policy as the insurable value of the part lost bears to the insurable value of the whole, ascertained as in the case of an unvalued policy:

(2) Where part of the goods, merchandise, or other moveables insured by an unvalued policy is totally lost, the measure of indemnity is the insurable value of the part lost, ascertained as in case of total loss:

(3) Where the whole or any part of the goods or merchandise insured has been delivered damaged at its destination, the measure of indemnity is such proportion of the sum fixed by the policy in the case of a valued policy, or of the insurable value in the case of an unvalued policy, as the difference between the gross sound and damaged values at the place of arrival bears to the gross sound value:

(4) "Gross value" means the wholesale price, or, if there be no such price, the estimated value, with, in either case, freight, landing charges, and duty paid beforehand; provided that, in the case of goods or merchandise customarily sold in bond, the bonded price is deemed to be the gross value. "Gross proceeds" means the actual price obtained at a sale where all charges on sale are paid by the sellers.

72.—Apportionment of valuation.

(1) Where different species of property are insured under a single valuation, the valuation must be apportioned over the different species in proportion to their respective insurable values, as in the case of an unvalued policy. The insured value of any part of a species is such proportion of the total insured value of the same as the insurable value of the part bears to the insurable value of the whole, ascertained in both cases as provided by this Act.

(2) Where a valuation has to be apportioned, and particulars of the prime cost of each separate species, quality, or description of goods cannot be ascertained, the division of the valuation may be made over the net arrived sound values of the different species, qualities, or descriptions of goods.

73.—General average contributions and salvage charges.

(1) Subject to any express provision in the policy, where the assured has paid, or is liable for, any general average contribution, the measure of indemnity is the full amount of such contribution, if the subject-matter liable to contribution is insured for its full contributory value; but, if such subject-matter be not insured for its full contributory value, or if only part of it be insured, the indemnity payable by the insurer must be reduced in proportion to the under insurance, and where there has been a particular average loss which constitutes a deduction from the contributory value, and for which the insurer is liable, that amount must be deducted from the insured value in order to ascertain what the insurer is liable to contribute.

(2) Where the insurer is liable for salvage charges the extent of his liability must be determined on the like principle.

74. Liabilities to third parties.

Where the assured has effected an insurance in express terms against any liability to a third party, the measure of indemnity, subject to any express provision in the policy, is the amount paid or payable by him to such third party in respect of such liability.

75.—General provisions as to measure of indemnity.

(1) Where there has been a loss in respect of any subject-matter not expressly provided for in the foregoing provisions of this Act, the measure of indemnity shall be ascertained, as nearly as may be, in accordance with those provisions, in so far as applicable to the particular case.

(2) Nothing in the provisions of this Act relating to the measure of indemnity shall affect the rules relating to double insurance, or prohibit the insurer from disproving interest wholly or in part, or from showing that at the time of the loss the whole or any part of the subject-matter insured was not at risk under the policy.

76.—Particular average warranties.

(1) Where the subject-matter insured is warranted free from particular average, the assured cannot recover for a loss of part, other than a loss incurred by a general average sacrifice, unless the contract contained in the policy be apportionable; but, if the contract be apportionable, the assured may recover for a total loss of any apportionable part.

(2) Where the subject-matter insured is warranted free from particular average, either wholly or under a certain percentage, the insurer is nevertheless liable for salvage charges, and for particular charges and other expenses properly incurred pursuant to the provisions of the suing and labouring clause in order to avert a loss insured against.

(3) Unless the policy otherwise provides, where the subject-matter insured is warranted free from particular average under a specified percentage, a general average loss cannot be added to a particular average loss to make up the specified percentage.

(4) For the purpose of ascertaining whether the specified percentage has been reached, regard shall be had only to the actual loss suffered by the subject-matter insured. Particular charges and the expenses of and incidental to ascertaining and proving the loss must be excluded.

77.—Successive losses.

(1) Unless the policy otherwise provides, and subject to the provisions of this Act, the insurer is liable for successive losses, even though the total amount of such losses may exceed the sum insured.

(2) Where, under the same policy, a partial loss, which has not been repaired or otherwise made good, is followed by a total loss, the assured can only recover in respect of the total loss:

Provided that nothing in this section shall affect the liability of the insurer under the suing and labouring clause.

78.—Suing and labouring clause.

(1) Where the policy contains a suing and labouring clause, the engagement thereby entered into is deemed to be supplementary to the contract of insurance, and the assured may recover from the insurer any expenses properly incurred pursuant to the clause, notwithstanding that the insurer may have paid for a total loss, or that the subject-matter may have been warranted free from particular average, either wholly or under a certain percentage.
(2) General average losses and contributions and salvage charges, as defined by this Act, are not recoverable under the suing and labouring clause.
(3) Expenses incurred for the purpose of averting or diminishing any loss not covered by the policy are not recoverable under the suing and labouring clause.
(4) It is the duty of the assured and his agents, in all cases, to take such measures as may be reasonable for the purpose of averting or minimising a loss.

RIGHTS OF INSURER ON PAYMENT

79.—Right of subrogation.

(1) Where the insurer pays for a total loss, either of the whole, or in the case of goods of any apportionable part, of the subject-matter insured, he thereupon becomes entitled to take over the interest of the assured in whatever may remain of the subject-matter so paid for, and he is thereby subrogated to all the rights and remedies of the assured in and in respect of that subject-matter as from the time of the casualty causing the loss.
(2) Subject to the foregoing provisions, where the insurer pays for a partial loss, he acquires no title to the subject-matter insured, or such part of it as may remain, but he is thereupon subrogated to all rights and remedies of the assured in and in respect of the subject-matter insured as from the time of the casualty causing the loss, in so far as the assured has been indemnified, according to this Act, by such payment for the loss.

80.—Right of contribution.

(1) Where the assured is over-insured by double insurance, each insurer is bound, as between himself and the other insurers, to contribute rateably to the loss in proportion to the amount for which he is liable under his contract.
(2) If any insurer pays more than his proportion of the loss, he is entitled to maintain an action for contribution against the other insurers, and is entitled to the like remedies as a surety who has paid more than his proportion of the debt.

81. Effect of under insurance.

Where the assured is insured for an amount less than the insurable value or, in the case of a valued policy, for an amount less than the policy valuation, he is deemed to be his own insurer in respect of the uninsured balance.

RETURN OF PREMIUM

82. Enforcement of return.

Where the premium or a proportionate part thereof is, by this Act, declared to be returnable,—

(a) If already paid, it may be recovered by the assured from the insurer; and
(b) If unpaid, it may be retained by the assured or his agent.

83. Return by agreement.

Where the policy contains a stipulation for the return of the premium, or a proportionate part thereof, on the happening of a certain event, and that event happens, the premium, or, as the case may be, the proportionate part thereof, is thereupon returnable to the assured.

84.—Return for failure of consideration.

(1) Where the consideration for the payment of the premium totally fails, and there has been no fraud or illegality on the part of the assured or his agents, the premium is thereupon returnable to the assured.
(2) Where the consideration for the payment of the premium is apportionable and there is a total failure of any apportionable part of the consideration, a proportionate part of the premium is, under the like conditions, thereupon returnable to the assured.
(3) In particular –
  (a) Where the policy is void, or is avoided by the insurer as from the commencement of the risk, the premium is returnable, provided that there has been no fraud or illegality on the part of the assured; but if the risk is not apportionable, and has once attached, the premium is not returnable:
  (b) Where the subject-matter insured, or part thereof, has never been imperilled, the premium, or, as the case may be, a proportionate part thereof, is returnable:

  Provided that where the subject-matter has been insured "lost or not lost" and has arrived in safety at the time when the contract is concluded, the premium is not returnable unless, at such time, the insurer knew of the safe arrival.
  (c) Where the assured has no insurable interest throughout the currency of the risk, the premium is returnable, provided that this rule does not apply to a policy effected by way of gaming or wagering;
  (d) Where the assured has a defeasible interest which is terminated during the currency of the risk, the premium is not returnable;
  (e) Where the assured has over-insured under an unvalued policy, a proportionate part of the premium is returnable;
  (f) Subject to the foregoing provisions, where the assured has over-insured by double insurance, a proportionate part of the several premiums is returnable:

  Provided that, if the policies are effected at different times, and any earlier policy has at any time borne the entire risk, or if a claim has been paid on the policy in respect of the full sum insured thereby, no premium is returnable in respect of that policy, and when the double insurance is effected knowingly by the assured no premium is returnable.

MUTUAL INSURANCE

85.—Modification of Act in case of mutual insurance.

(1) Where two or more persons mutually agree to insure each other against marine losses there is said to be a mutual insurance.

(2) The provisions of this Act relating to the premium do not apply to mutual insurance, but a guarantee, or such other arrangement as may be agreed upon, may be substituted for the premium.

(3) The provisions of this Act, in so far as they may be modified by the agreement of the parties, may in the case of mutual insurance be modified by the terms of the policies issued by the association, or by the rules and regulations of the association.

(4) Subject to the exceptions mentioned in this section, the provisions of this Act apply to a mutual insurance.

SUPPLEMENTAL

86. Ratification by assured.

Where a contract of marine insurance is in good faith effected by one person on behalf of another, the person on whose behalf it is effected may ratify the contract even after he is aware of a loss.

87.—Implied obligations varied by agreement or usage.

(1) Where any right, duty, or liability would arise under a contract of marine insurance by implication of law, it may be negatived or varied by express agreement, or by usage, if the usage be such as to bind both parties to the contract.

(2) The provisions of this section extend to any right, duty, or liability declared by this Act which may be lawfully modified by agreement.

88. Reasonable time, &c. a question of fact.

Where by this Act any reference is made to reasonable time, reasonable premium, or reasonable diligence, the question what is reasonable is a question of fact.

89. Slip as evidence.

Where there is a duly stamped policy, reference may be made, as heretofore, to the slip or covering note, in any legal proceeding.

90. Interpretation of terms.

In this Act, unless the context or subject-matter otherwise requires,—

"Action" includes counter-claim and set off:

"Freight" includes the profit derivable by a shipowner from the employment of his ship to carry his own goods or moveables, as well as freight payable by a third party, but does not include passage money:

"Moveables" means any moveable tangible property, other than the ship, and includes money, valuable securities, and other documents:

"Policy" means a marine policy.

91.—Savings.

(1) Nothing in this Act, or in any repeal effected thereby, shall affect –
  (a) The provisions of the Stamp Act 1891, or any enactment for the time being in force relating to the revenue;
  (b) The provisions of the Companies Act 1862, or any enactment amending or substituted for the same;
  (c) The provisions of any statute not expressly repealed by this Act.

(2) The rules of the common law including the law merchant, save in so far as they are inconsistent with the express provisions of this Act, shall continue to apply to contracts of marine insurance.

92. [. . .][7]

93. [. . .][8]

94. Short title.

This Act may be cited as the Marine Insurance Act 1906.

FIRST SCHEDULE

Section 30

FORM OF POLICY

[Form not available in online format. Please see original printed copy.]

RULES FOR CONSTRUCTION OF POLICY

The following are the rules referred to by this Act for the construction of a policy in the above or other like form, where the context does not otherwise require:—

1. Lost or not lost.

Where the subject-matter is insured "lost or not lost," and the loss has occurred before the contract is concluded, the risk attaches unless, at such time the assured was aware of the loss, and the insurer was not.

---

7 Repealed by Statute Law Revision Act 1927 (c. 42).
8 Repealed by Statute Law Revision Act 1927 (c. 42).

2. From.

Where the subject-matter is insured "from" a particular place, the risk does not attach until the ship starts on the voyage insured.

3.—At and from [Ship].

(a) Where a ship is insured "at and from" a particular place, and she is at that place in good safety when the contract is concluded, the risk attaches immediately.
(b) If she be not at that place when the contract is concluded, the risk attaches as soon as she arrives there in good safety, and, unless the policy otherwise provides, it is immaterial that she is covered by another policy for a specified time after arrival.
(c) Where chartered freight is insured "at and from" a particular place, and the ship is at that place in good safety when the contract is concluded the risk attaches immediately. If she be not there when the contract is concluded, the risk attaches as soon as she arrives there in good safety.
(d) Where freight, other than chartered freight, is payable without special conditions and is insured "at and from" a particular place, the risk attaches pro rata as the goods or merchandise are shipped; provided that if there be cargo in readiness which belongs to the shipowner, or which some other person has contracted with him to ship, the risk attaches as soon as the ship is ready to receive such cargo.

4. From the loading thereof.

Where goods or other moveables are insured "from the loading thereof," the risk does not attach until such goods or moveables are actually on board, and the insurer is not liable for them while in transit from the shore to the ship.

5. Safely landed.

Where the risk on goods or other moveables continues until they are "safely landed," they must be landed in the customary manner and within a reasonable time after arrival at the port of discharge, and if they are not so landed the risk ceases.

6. Touch and stay.

In the absence of any further licence or usage, the liberty to touch and stay "at any port or place whatsoever" does not authorise the ship to depart from the course of her voyage from the port of departure to the port of destination.

7. Perils of the seas.

The term "perils of the seas" refers only to fortuitous accidents or casualties of the seas. It does not include the ordinary action of the winds and waves.

8. Pirates.

The term "pirates" includes passengers who mutiny and rioters who attack the ship from the shore.

9. Thieves.

The term "thieves" does not cover clandestine theft or a theft committed by any one of the ship's company, whether crew or passengers.

10. Restraint of princes.

The term "arrests, &c., of kings, princes, and people" refers to political or executive acts, and does not include a loss caused by riot or by ordinary judicial process.

11. Barratry.

The term "barratry" includes every wrongful act wilfully committed by the master or crew to the prejudice of the owner, or, as the case may be, the charterer.

12. All other perils.

The term "all other perils" includes only perils similar in kind to the perils specifically mentioned in the policy.

13. Average unless general.

The term "average unless general" means a partial loss of the subject-matter insured other than a general average loss, and does not include "particular charges."

14. Stranded.

Where the ship has stranded, the insurer is liable for the excepted losses, although the loss is not attributable to the stranding, provided that when the stranding takes place the risk has attached and, if the policy be on goods, that the damaged goods are on board.

15. Ship.

The term "ship" includes the hull, materials and outfit, stores and provisions for the officers and crew, and, in the case of vessels engaged in a special trade, the ordinary fittings requisite for the trade, and also, in the case of a steamship, the machinery, boilers, and coals and engine stores, if owned by the assured.

16. Freight.

The term "freight" includes the profit derivable by a shipowner from the employment of his ship to carry his own goods or moveables, as well as freight payable by a third party, but does not include passage money.

17. Goods.

The term "goods" means goods in the nature of merchandise, and does not include personal effects or provisions and stores for use on board.

In the absence of any usage to the contrary, deck cargo and living animals must be insured specifically, and not under the general denomination of goods.

SECOND SCHEDULE[. . .][9]

9 Repealed by Statute Law Revision Act 1927 (c. 42).

APPENDIX 2

Insurance Act 2015

CHAPTER 4

CONTENTS

PART 5

GOOD FAITH AND CONTRACTING OUT

Good faith

Contracting out

PART 6

AMENDMENT OF THE THIRD PARTIES (RIGHTS AGAINST INSURERS) ACT 2010

PART 7

GENERAL

ELIZABETH II

Insurance Act 2015

2015 CHAPTER 4

An Act to make new provision about insurance contracts; to amend the Third Parties (Rights against Insurers) Act 2010 in relation to the insured persons to whom that Act applies; and for connected purposes. [12th February 2015]

BE IT ENACTED by the Queen's most Excellent Majesty, by and with the advice and consent of the Lords Spiritual and Temporal, and Commons, in this present Parliament assembled, and by the authority of the same, as follows: —

PART 1

INSURANCE CONTRACTS: MAIN DEFINITIONS

1 Insurance contracts: main definitions

In this Act (apart from Part 6) —

"consumer insurance contract" has the same meaning as in the Consumer Insurance (Disclosure and Representations) Act 2012;

"non-consumer insurance contract" means a contract of insurance that is not a consumer insurance contract;

"insured" means the party to a contract of insurance who is the insured under the contract, or would be if the contract were entered into;

"insurer" means the party to a contract of insurance who is the insurer under the contract, or would be if the contract were entered into;

"the duty of fair presentation" means the duty imposed by section 3(1).

PART 2

THE DUTY OF FAIR PRESENTATION

2 Application and interpretation

(1) This Part applies to non-consumer insurance contracts only.

(2) This Part applies in relation to variations of non-consumer insurance contracts as it applies to contracts, but—

(a) references to the risk are to be read as references to changes in the risk relevant to the proposed variation, and

(b) references to the contract of insurance are to the variation.

3 The duty of fair presentation

(1) Before a contract of insurance is entered into, the insured must make to the insurer a fair presentation of the risk.

(2) The duty imposed by subsection (1) is referred to in this Act as "the duty of fair presentation".

(3) A fair presentation of the risk is one—

(a) which makes the disclosure required by subsection (4),

(b) which makes that disclosure in a manner which would be reasonably clear and accessible to a prudent insurer, and

(c) in which every material representation as to a matter of fact is substantially correct, and every material representation as to a matter of expectation or belief is made in good faith.

(4) The disclosure required is as follows, except as provided in subsection (5)—

(a) disclosure of every material circumstance which the insured knows or ought to know, or

(b) failing that, disclosure which gives the insurer sufficient information to put a prudent insurer on notice that it needs to make further enquiries for the purpose of revealing those material circumstances.

(5) In the absence of enquiry, subsection (4) does not require the insured to disclose a circumstance if—

(a) it diminishes the risk,

(b) the insurer knows it,

(c) the insurer ought to know it,

(d) the insurer is presumed to know it, or

(e) it is something as to which the insurer waives information.

(6) Sections 4 to 6 make further provision about the knowledge of the insured and of the insurer, and section 7 contains supplementary provision.

4 Knowledge of insured

(1) This section provides for what an insured knows or ought to know for the purposes of section 3(4)(a).

(2) An insured who is an individual knows only—

(a) what is known to the individual, and

(b) what is known to one or more of the individuals who are responsible for the insured's insurance.

(3) An insured who is not an individual knows only what is known to one or more of the individuals who are—

(a) part of the insured's senior management, or

(b) responsible for the insured's insurance.

(4) An insured is not by virtue of subsection (2)(b) or (3)(b) taken to know confidential information known to an individual if—

(a) the individual is, or is an employee of, the insured's agent; and

(b) the information was acquired by the insured's agent (or by an employee of that agent) through a business relationship with a person who is not connected with the contract of insurance.

(5) For the purposes of subsection (4) the persons connected with a contract of insurance are—

(a) the insured and any other persons for whom cover is provided by the contract, and

(b) if the contract re-insures risks covered by another contract, the persons who are (by virtue of this subsection) connected with that other contract.

(6) Whether an individual or not, an insured ought to know what should reasonably have been revealed by a reasonable search of information available to the insured (whether the search is conducted by making enquiries or by any other means).

(7) In subsection (6) "information" includes information held within the insured's organisation or by any other person (such as the insured's agent or a person for whom cover is provided by the contract of insurance).

(8) For the purposes of this section—

(a) "employee", in relation to the insured's agent, includes any individual working for the agent, whatever the capacity in which the individual acts,

(b) an individual is responsible for the insured's insurance if the individual participates on behalf of the insured in the process of procuring the insured's insurance (whether the individual does so as the insured's employee or agent, as an employee of the insured's agent or in any other capacity), and

(c) "senior management" means those individuals who play significant roles in the making of decisions about how the insured's activities are to be managed or organised.

5 Knowledge of insurer

(1) For the purposes of section 3(5)(b), an insurer knows something only if it is known to one or more of the individuals who participate on behalf of the insurer in the decision whether to take the risk, and if so on what terms (whether the individual does so as the insurer's employee or agent, as an employee of the insurer's agent or in any other capacity).

(2) For the purposes of section 3(5)(c), an insurer ought to know something only if—

(a) an employee or agent of the insurer knows it, and ought reasonably to have passed on the relevant information to an individual mentioned in subsection (1), or

(b) the relevant information is held by the insurer and is readily available to an individual mentioned in subsection (1).

(3) For the purposes of section 3(5)(d), an insurer is presumed to know—

(a) things which are common knowledge, and

(b) things which an insurer offering insurance of the class in question to insureds in the field of activity in question would reasonably be expected to know in the ordinary course of business.

6 Knowledge: general

(1) For the purposes of sections 3 to 5, references to an individual's knowledge include not only actual knowledge, but also matters which the individual suspected, and of which the individual would have had knowledge but for deliberately refraining from confirming them or enquiring about them.

(2) Nothing in this Part affects the operation of any rule of law according to which knowledge of a fraud perpetrated by an individual ("F") either on the insured or on the insurer is not to be attributed to the insured or to the insurer (respectively), where—

(a) if the fraud is on the insured, F is any of the individuals mentioned in section 4(2)(b) or (3), or

(b) if the fraud is on the insurer, F is any of the individuals mentioned in section 5(1).

7 Supplementary

(1) A fair presentation need not be contained in only one document or oral presentation.

(2) The term "circumstance" includes any communication made to, or information received by, the insured.

(3) A circumstance or representation is material if it would influence the judgement of a prudent insurer in determining whether to take the risk and, if so, on what terms.

(4) Examples of things which may be material circumstances are—

(a) special or unusual facts relating to the risk,

(b) any particular concerns which led the insured to seek insurance cover for the risk,

(c) anything which those concerned with the class of insurance and field of activity in question would generally understand as being something that should be dealt with in a fair presentation of risks of the type in question.

(5) A material representation is substantially correct if a prudent insurer would not consider the difference between what is represented and what is actually correct to be material.

(6) A representation may be withdrawn or corrected before the contract of insurance is entered into.

8 Remedies for breach

(1) The insurer has a remedy against the insured for a breach of the duty of fair presentation only if the insurer shows that, but for the breach, the insurer—

(a) would not have entered into the contract of insurance at all, or

(b) would have done so only on different terms.

(2) The remedies are set out in Schedule 1.

(3) A breach for which the insurer has a remedy against the insured is referred to in this Act as a "qualifying breach".

(4) A qualifying breach is either—
  (a) deliberate or reckless, or
  (b) neither deliberate nor reckless.

(5) A qualifying breach is deliberate or reckless if the insured —
  (a) knew that it was in breach of the duty of fair presentation, or
  (b) did not care whether or not it was in breach of that duty.

(6) It is for the insurer to show that a qualifying breach was deliberate or reckless.

PART 3

WARRANTIES AND OTHER TERMS

9 Warranties and representations

(1) This section applies to representations made by the insured in connection with—
  (a) a proposed non-consumer insurance contract, or
  (b) a proposed variation to a non-consumer insurance contract.

(2) Such a representation is not capable of being converted into a warranty by means of any provision of the non-consumer insurance contract (or of the terms of the variation), or of any other contract (and whether by declaring the representation to form the basis of the contract or otherwise).

10 Breach of warranty

(1) Any rule of law that breach of a warranty (express or implied) in a contract of insurance results in the discharge of the insurer's liability under the contract is abolished.

(2) An insurer has no liability under a contract of insurance in respect of any loss occurring, or attributable to something happening, after a warranty (express or implied) in the contract has been breached but before the breach has been remedied.

(3) But subsection (2) does not apply if—
  (a) because of a change of circumstances, the warranty ceases to be applicable to the circumstances of the contract,
  (b) compliance with the warranty is rendered unlawful by any subsequent law, or
  (c) the insurer waives the breach of warranty.

(4) Subsection (2) does not affect the liability of the insurer in respect of losses occurring, or attributable to something happening—
  (a) before the breach of warranty, or
  (b) if the breach can be remedied, after it has been remedied.

(5) For the purposes of this section, a breach of warranty is to be taken as remedied—

(a) in a case falling within subsection (6), if the risk to which the warranty relates later becomes essentially the same as that originally contemplated by the parties,

(b) in any other case, if the insured ceases to be in breach of the warranty.

(6) A case falls within this subsection if—

(a) the warranty in question requires that by an ascertainable time something is to be done (or not done), or a condition is to be fulfilled, or something is (or is not) to be the case, and

(b) that requirement is not complied with.

(7) In the Marine Insurance Act 1906—

(a) in section 33 (nature of warranty), in subsection (3), the second sentence is omitted,

(b) section 34 (when breach of warranty excused) is omitted.

11 Terms not relevant to the actual loss

(1) This section applies to a term (express or implied) of a contract of insurance, other than a term defining the risk as a whole, if compliance with it would tend to reduce the risk of one or more of the following—

(a) loss of a particular kind,

(b) loss at a particular location,

(c) loss at a particular time.

(2) If a loss occurs, and the term has not been complied with, the insurer may not rely on the non-compliance to exclude, limit or discharge its liability under the contract for the loss if the insured satisfies subsection (3).

(3) The insured satisfies this subsection if it shows that the non-compliance with the term could not have increased the risk of the loss which actually occurred in the circumstances in which it occurred.

(4) This section may apply in addition to section 10.

PART 4

FRAUDULENT CLAIMS

12 Remedies for fraudulent claims

(1) If the insured makes a fraudulent claim under a contract of insurance—

(a) the insurer is not liable to pay the claim,

(b) the insurer may recover from the insured any sums paid by the insurer to the insured in respect of the claim, and

(c) in addition, the insurer may by notice to the insured treat the contract as having been terminated with effect from the time of the fraudulent act.

(2) If the insurer does treat the contract as having been terminated—

(a) it may refuse all liability to the insured under the contract in respect of a relevant event occurring after the time of the fraudulent act, and

(b) it need not return any of the premiums paid under the contract.

(3) Treating a contract as having been terminated under this section does not affect the rights and obligations of the parties to the contract with respect to a relevant event occurring before the time of the fraudulent act.

(4) In subsections (2)(a) and (3), "relevant event" refers to whatever gives rise to the insurer's liability under the contract (and includes, for example, the occurrence of a loss, the making of a claim, or the notification of a potential claim, depending on how the contract is written).

13 Remedies for fraudulent claims: group insurance

(1) This section applies where—
- (a) a contract of insurance is entered into with an insurer by a person ("A"),
- (b) the contract provides cover for one or more other persons who are not parties to the contract ("the Cs"), whether or not it also provides cover of any kind for A or another insured party, and
- (c) a fraudulent claim is made under the contract by or on behalf of one of the Cs ("CF").

(2) Section 12 applies in relation to the claim as if the cover provided for CF were provided under an individual insurance contract between the insurer and CF as the insured; and, accordingly—
- (a) the insurer's rights under section 12 are exercisable only in relation to the cover provided for CF, and
- (b) the exercise of any of those rights does not affect the cover provided under the contract for anyone else.

(3) In its application by virtue of subsection (2), section 12 is subject to the following particular modifications—
- (a) the first reference to "the insured" in subsection (1)(b) of that section, in respect of any particular sum paid by the insurer, is to whichever of A and CF the insurer paid the sum to; but if a sum was paid to A and passed on by A to CF, the reference is to CF,
- (b) the second reference to "the insured" in subsection (1)(b) is to A or CF,
- (c) the reference to "the insured" in subsection (1)(c) is to both CF and A,
- (d) the reference in subsection (2)(b) to the premiums paid under the contract is to premiums paid in respect of the cover for CF.

PART 5

GOOD FAITH AND CONTRACTING OUT

Good faith

14 Good faith

(1) Any rule of law permitting a party to a contract of insurance to avoid the contract on the ground that the utmost good faith has not been observed by the other party is abolished.

(2) Any rule of law to the effect that a contract of insurance is a contract based on the utmost good faith is modified to the extent required by the provisions of this Act and the Consumer Insurance (Disclosure and Representations) Act 2012.

(3) Accordingly—

(a) in section 17 of the Marine Insurance Act 1906 (marine insurance contracts are contracts of the utmost good faith), the words from ", and" to the end are omitted, and

(b) the application of that section (as so amended) is subject to the provisions of this Act and the Consumer Insurance (Disclosure and Representations) Act 2012.

(4) In section 2 of the Consumer Insurance (Disclosure and Representations) Act 2012 (disclosure and representations before contract or variation), subsection (5) is omitted.

Contracting out

15 Contracting out: consumer insurance contracts

(1) A term of a consumer insurance contract, or of any other contract, which would put the consumer in a worse position as respects any of the matters provided for in Part 3 or 4 of this Act than the consumer would be in by virtue of the provisions of those Parts (so far as relating to consumer insurance contracts) is to that extent of no effect.

(2) In subsection (1) references to a contract include a variation.

(3) This section does not apply in relation to a contract for the settlement of a claim arising under a consumer insurance contract.

16 Contracting out: non-consumer insurance contracts

(1) A term of a non-consumer insurance contract, or of any other contract, which would put the insured in a worse position as respects representations to which section 9 applies than the insured would be in by virtue of that section is to that extent of no effect.

(2) A term of a non-consumer insurance contract, or of any other contract, which would put the insured in a worse position as respects any of the other matters provided for in Part 2, 3 or 4 of this Act than the insured would be in by virtue of the provisions of those Parts (so far as relating to non-consumer insurance contracts) is to that extent of no effect, unless the requirements of section 17 have been satisfied in relation to the term.

(3) In this section references to a contract include a variation.

(4) This section does not apply in relation to a contract for the settlement of a claim arising under a non-consumer insurance contract.

17 The transparency requirements

(1) In this section, "the disadvantageous term" means such a term as is mentioned in section 16(2).

(2) The insurer must take sufficient steps to draw the disadvantageous term to the insured's attention before the contract is entered into or the variation agreed.

(3) The disadvantageous term must be clear and unambiguous as to its effect.

(4) In determining whether the requirements of subsections (2) and (3) have been met, the characteristics of insured persons of the kind in question, and the circumstances of the transaction, are to be taken into account.

(5) The insured may not rely on any failure on the part of the insurer to meet the requirements of subsection (2) if the insured (or its agent) had actual knowledge of the disadvantageous term when the contract was entered into or the variation agreed.

18 Contracting out: group insurance contracts

(1) This section applies to a contract of insurance referred to in section 13(1)(a); and in this section—

"A" and "the Cs" have the same meaning as in section 13,

"consumer C" means an individual who is one of the Cs, where the cover provided by the contract for that individual would have been a consumer insurance contract if entered into by that person rather than by A, and

"non-consumer C" means any of the Cs who is not a consumer C.

(2) A term of the contract of insurance, or any other contract, which puts a consumer C in a worse position as respects any matter dealt with in section 13 than that individual would be in by virtue of that section is to that extent of no effect.

(3) A term of the contract of insurance, or any other contract, which puts a non-consumer C in a worse position as respects any matter dealt with in section 13 than that person would be in by virtue of that section is to that extent of no effect, unless the requirements of section 17 have been met in relation to the term.

(4) Section 17 applies in relation to such a term as it applies to a term mentioned in section 16(2), with references to the insured being read as references to A rather than the non-consumer C.

(5) In this section references to a contract include a variation.

(6) This section does not apply in relation to a contract for the settlement of a claim arising under a contract of insurance to which this section applies.

PART 6

AMENDMENT OF THE THIRD PARTIES (RIGHTS AGAINST INSURERS) ACT 2010

19 Power to change meaning of "relevant person" for purposes of 2010 Act

For section 19 of the Third Parties (Rights against Insurers) Act 2010 (power to amend sections 4 to 6 of the Act) substitute—

"19 Power to change the meaning of "relevant person"

(1) The Secretary of State may by regulations make provision adding or removing circumstances in which a person is a "relevant person" for the purposes of this Act, subject to subsection (2).

(2) Regulations under this section may add circumstances only if, in the Secretary of State's opinion, the additional circumstances—

(a) involve actual or anticipated dissolution of a body corporate or an unincorporated body,

(b) involve actual or anticipated insolvency or other financial difficulties for an individual, a body corporate or an unincorporated body, or

(c) are similar to circumstances for the time being described in sections 4 to 7.

(3) Regulations under this section may make provision about—

(a) the persons to whom, and the extent to which, rights are transferred under section 1 in the circumstances added or removed by the regulations (the "affected circumstances"),

(b) the re-transfer of rights transferred under section 1 where the affected circumstances change, and

(c) the effect of a transfer of rights under section 1 on the liability of the insured in the affected circumstances.

(4) Regulations under this section which add or remove circumstances involving actual or anticipated dissolution of a body corporate or unincorporated body may change the cases in which the following provisions apply so that they include or exclude cases involving that type of dissolution or any other type of dissolution of a body—

(a) section 9(3) (cases in which transferred rights are not subject to a condition requiring the insured to provide information or assistance to the insurer), and

(b) paragraph 3 of Schedule 1 (notices requiring disclosure).

(5) Regulations under this section which add circumstances may provide that section 1 of this Act applies in cases involving those circumstances in which either or both of the following occurred in relation to a person before the day on which the regulations come into force—

(a) the circumstances arose in relation to the person;

(b) a liability against which the person was insured under an insurance contract was incurred.

(6) Regulations under this section which—

(a) add circumstances, and

(b) provide that section 1 of this Act applies in a case involving those circumstances in which both of the events mentioned in subsection (5)(a) and (b) occurred in relation to a person before the day on which the regulations come into force,

must provide that, in such a case, the person is to be treated for the purposes of this Act as not having become a relevant person until that day or a later day specified in the regulations.

(7) Regulations under this section which remove circumstances may provide that section 1 of this Act does not apply in cases involving those circumstances in which one of the events mentioned in subsection (5)(a) and (b) (but not both) occurred in relation to a person before the day on which the regulations come into force.

(8) Regulations under this section may—

(a) include consequential, incidental, supplementary, transitional, transitory or saving provision,

(b) make different provision for different purposes, and

(c) make provision by reference to an enactment as amended, extended or applied from time to time,

(and subsections (3) to (7) are without prejudice to the generality of this subsection).

(9) Regulations under this section may amend an enactment, whenever passed or made, including this Act.

(10) Regulations under this section are to be made by statutory instrument.

(11) Regulations under this section may not be made unless a draft of the statutory instrument containing the regulations has been laid before, and approved by a resolution of, each House of Parliament."

20 Other amendments

Schedule 2 amends the Third Parties (Rights against Insurers) Act 2010 in relation to the insured persons to whom the Act applies.

PART 7

GENERAL

21 Provision consequential on Part 2

(1) The provision made by this section is consequential on Part 2 of this Act.

(2) In the Marine Insurance Act 1906, sections 18 (disclosure by assured), 19 (disclosure by agent effecting insurance) and 20 (representations pending negotiation of contract) are omitted.

(3) Any rule of law to the same effect as any of those provisions is abolished.

(4) In section 152 of the Road Traffic Act 1988 (exceptions to duty of insurers to satisfy judgment against persons insured against third-party risks)—

(a) in subsection (2)—

(i) in paragraph (a), for "it either under the Consumer Insurance (Disclosure and Representations) Act 2012 or, if that Act does not apply," substitute "the policy under either of the relevant insurance enactments, or the security",

(ii) in paragraph (b), for "or security under that Act or" substitute "under either of the relevant insurance enactments, or the security";

(b) in subsection (3), after "specifying" insert "the relevant insurance enactment or, in the case of a security,";

(c) after subsection (4) add—

"(5) In this section, "relevant insurance enactment" means the Consumer Insurance (Disclosure and Representations) Act 2012 or Part 2 of the Insurance Act 2015."

(5) In Article 98A of the Road Traffic (Northern Ireland) Order 1981 (S.I. 1981/154 (N.I.)) (exceptions to duty of insurers to satisfy judgement against persons insured against third party risks)—

(a) in paragraph (2)—

(i) in paragraph (a), for "it either under the Consumer Insurance Act (Disclosure and Representations) Act 2012 or, if that Act does not apply," substitute "the policy under either of the relevant insurance enactments, or the security";

(ii) in paragraph (b), for "or security under that Act or" substitute "under either of the relevant insurance enactments, or the security";

(b) in paragraph (3), after "specifying" insert "the relevant insurance enactment or, in the case of a security,";

(c) after paragraph (4) add—

"(5) In this Article, "relevant insurance enactment" means the Consumer Insurance (Disclosure and Representations) Act 2012 or Part 2 of the Insurance Act 2015."

(6) In section 11 of the Consumer Insurance (Disclosure and Representations) Act 2012 (consequential provision), subsections (1) and (2) are omitted.

22 Application etc of Parts 2 to 5

(1) Part 2 (and section 21) and section 14 apply only in relation to—

(a) contracts of insurance entered into after the end of the relevant period, and

(b) variations, agreed after the end of the relevant period, to contracts of insurance entered into at any time.

(2) Parts 3 and 4 of this Act apply only in relation to contracts of insurance entered into after the end of the relevant period, and variations to such contracts.

(3) In subsections (1) and (2) "the relevant period" means the period of 18 months beginning with the day on which this Act is passed.

(4) Unless the contrary intention appears, references in Parts 2 to 5 to something being done by or in relation to the insurer or the insured include its being done by or in relation to that person's agent.

23 Extent, commencement and short title

(1) This Act extends to England and Wales, Scotland and Northern Ireland, except for—

(a) section 21(4), which does not extend to Northern Ireland; and

(b) section 21(5), which extends to Northern Ireland only.

(2) This Act (apart from Part 6 and this section) comes into force at the end of the period of 18 months beginning with the day on which it is passed.

(3) In Part 6—

(a) section 19 comes into force at the end of the period of two months beginning with the day on which this Act is passed; and

(b) section 20 and Schedule 2 come into force on the day appointed under section 21(2) of the Third Parties (Rights against Insurers) Act 2010 for the coming into force of that Act.

(4) This section comes into force on the day on which this Act is passed.

(5) This Act may be cited as the Insurance Act 2015.

SCHEDULES

SCHEDULE 1

Section 8(2).

INSURERS' REMEDIES FOR QUALIFYING BREACHES

PART 1

CONTRACTS

General

1 This Part of this Schedule applies to qualifying breaches of the duty of fair presentation in relation to non-consumer insurance contracts (for variations to them, see Part 2).

Deliberate or reckless breaches

2 If a qualifying breach was deliberate or reckless, the insurer—
(a) may avoid the contract and refuse all claims, and
(b) need not return any of the premiums paid.

Other breaches

3 Paragraphs 4 to 6 apply if a qualifying breach was neither deliberate nor reckless.

4 If, in the absence of the qualifying breach, the insurer would not have entered into the contract on any terms, the insurer may avoid the contract and refuse all claims, but must in that event return the premiums paid.

5 If the insurer would have entered into the contract, but on different terms (other than terms relating to the premium), the contract is to be treated as if it had been entered into on those different terms if the insurer so requires.

6 (1) In addition, if the insurer would have entered into the contract (whether the terms relating to matters other than the premium would have been the same or different), but would have charged a higher premium, the insurer may reduce proportionately the amount to be paid on a claim.

(2) In sub-paragraph (1), "reduce proportionately" means that the insurer need pay on the claim only X% of what it would otherwise have been under an obligation to pay under the terms of the contract (or, if applicable, under the different terms provided for by virtue of paragraph 5), where—

$$X = \frac{\text{Premium actually charged}}{\text{Higher premium}} \times 100$$

PART 2

VARIATIONS

General

7 This Part of this Schedule applies to qualifying breaches of the duty of fair presentation in relation to variations to non-consumer insurance contracts.

Deliberate or reckless breaches

8 If a qualifying breach was deliberate or reckless, the insurer—
(a) may by notice to the insured treat the contract as having been terminated with effect from the time when the variation was made, and
(b) need not return any of the premiums paid.

Other breaches

9 (1) This paragraph applies if—
(a) a qualifying breach was neither deliberate nor reckless, and
(b) the total premium was increased or not changed as a result of the variation.

(2) If, in the absence of the qualifying breach, the insurer would not have agreed to the variation on any terms, the insurer may treat the contract as if the variation was never made, but must in that event return any extra premium paid.

(3) If sub-paragraph (2) does not apply—
(a) if the insurer would have agreed to the variation on different terms (other than terms relating to the premium), the variation is to be treated as if it had been entered into on those different terms if the insurer so requires, and
(b) paragraph 11 also applies if (in the case of an increased premium) the insurer would have increased the premium by more than it did, or (in the case of an unchanged premium) the insurer would have increased the premium.

10 (1) This paragraph applies if—
(a) a qualifying breach was neither deliberate nor reckless, and
(b) the total premium was reduced as a result of the variation.

(2) If, in the absence of the qualifying breach, the insurer would not have agreed to the variation on any terms, the insurer may treat the contract as if the variation was never made, and paragraph 11 also applies.

(3) If sub-paragraph (2) does not apply—
(a) if the insurer would have agreed to the variation on different terms (other than terms relating to the premium), the variation is to be treated as if it had been entered into on those different terms if the insurer so requires, and
(b) paragraph 11 also applies if the insurer would have increased the premium, would not have reduced the premium, or would have reduced it by less than it did.

Proportionate reduction

11 (1) If this paragraph applies, the insurer may reduce proportionately the amount to be paid on a claim arising out of events after the variation.

(2) In sub-paragraph (1), "reduce proportionately" means that the insurer need pay on the claim only Y% of what it would otherwise have been under an obligation to pay under the terms of the contract (whether on the original terms, or as varied, or under the different terms provided for by virtue of paragraph 9(3)(a) or 10(3)(a), as the case may be), where—

$$Y = \frac{\text{Total premium actually charged}}{P} \times 100$$

(3) In the formula in sub-paragraph (2), "P"—

(a) in a paragraph 9(3)(b) case, is the total premium the insurer would have charged,

(b) in a paragraph 10(2) case, is the original premium,

(c) in a paragraph 10(3)(b) case, is the original premium if the insurer would not have changed it, and otherwise the increased or (as the case may be) reduced total premium the insurer would have charged.

PART 3

SUPPLEMENTARY

Relationship with section 84 of the Marine Insurance Act 1906

12 Section 84 of the Marine Insurance Act 1906 (return of premium for failure of consideration) is to be read subject to the provisions of this Schedule in relation to contracts of marine insurance which are non-consumer insurance contracts.

SCHEDULE 2

Section 20

RIGHTS OF THIRD PARTIES AGAINST INSURERS: RELEVANT INSURED PERSONS

1 The Third Parties (Rights against Insurers) Act 2010 is amended as follows.

Individuals subject to debt relief orders in Northern Ireland

2 (1) Section 4 (relevant persons: individuals) is amended as follows.

(2) In subsection (3), after paragraph (b) (deed of arrangements registered under the Insolvency (Northern Ireland) Order 1989) insert—

"(ba) subject to subsection (4), a debt relief order made under Part 7A of that Order,".

(3) In subsection (4) (individuals who are relevant persons for the purposes of section 1(1)(b) only), after "(1)(d)" insert "or (3)(ba)".

Corporate bodies etc in administration

3 (1) Section 6 (corporate bodies etc) is amended as follows.

(2) In subsection (2) (events under the Insolvency Act 1986), for paragraph (b) substitute—

"(b) the body is in administration under Schedule B1 to that Act,".

(3) In subsection (4) (events under the Insolvency (Northern Ireland) Order 1989), for paragraph (b) substitute—

"(b) the body is in administration under Schedule B1 to that Order,".

Transitional cases

4 In section 1(5)(b) (definition of "relevant person"), at the end insert "(and see also paragraph 1A of Schedule 3)".

5 (1) Schedule 3 (transitory, transitional and saving provision) is amended as follows.

(2) At the beginning insert—

"Application of this Act".

(3) After paragraph 1 insert—

"Relevant persons

1A (1) An individual, company or limited liability partnership not within sections 4 to 7 is to be treated as a relevant person for the purposes of this Act in the following cases.

(2) The first case is where an individual—

(a) became bankrupt before commencement day, and

(b) has not been discharged from that bankruptcy.

(3) The second case is where—

(a) an individual made a composition or arrangement with his or her creditors before commencement day, and

(b) the composition or arrangement remains in force.

(4) The third case is where—

(a) a winding-up order was made, or a resolution for a voluntary winding-up was passed, with respect to a company or limited liability partnership before commencement day, and

(b) the company or partnership is still wound up.

(5) The fourth case is where a company or limited liability partnership—

(a) entered administration before commencement day, and

(b) is still in administration.

(6) The fifth case is where—

(a) a receiver or manager of the business or undertaking of a company or limited liability partnership was appointed before commencement day, and

(b) the appointment remains in force.

(7) In those cases, the person is a relevant person only in relation to liabilities under a contract of insurance under which the person was insured at the time of the event mentioned in sub-paragraph (2)(a), (3)(a), (4)(a), (5)(a) or (6)(a) (as appropriate)."

(4) Before paragraph 2 insert—

"Bankruptcy and Diligence etc (Scotland) Act 2007".

(5) Before paragraph 3 insert—

"Application of 1930 Acts".

(6) Before paragraph 5 insert—

"Interpretation".

Interpretation

6 After section 19 insert—

"19A Interpretation

(1) The references to enactments in sections 4 to 7, 9(7) and 14(4) and paragraph 3(2)(b), (4) and (5) of Schedule 1 are to be treated as including references to those enactments as amended, extended or applied by another enactment, whenever passed or made, unless the contrary intention appears.

(2) In this Act, "enactment" means an enactment contained in, or in an instrument made under, any of the following—

(a) an Act;

(b) an Act or Measure of the National Assembly for Wales;

(c) an Act of the Scottish Parliament;

(d) Northern Ireland legislation."

INDEX

For Product Safety Concerns and Information please contact our EU representative GPSR@taylorandfrancis.com Taylor & Francis Verlag GmbH, Kaufingerstraße 24, 80331 München, Germany

Batch number: 10726294

Printed by Printforce, the Netherlands